Theatre and Ideology

Theatre and Ideology

Ben B. Halm

Selinsgrove: Susquehanna University Press
London: Associated University Presses

Associated University Presses
440 Forsgate Drive
Cranbury, NJ 08512

Associated University Presses
25 Sicilian Avenue
London WC1A 2QH, England

Associated University Presses
P.O. Box 338, Port Credit
Mississauga, Ontario
Canada L5G 4L8

The paper used in this publication meets the requirements of the American National Standard for Permanence of Paper for Printed Library Materials Z39.48-1984.

Library of Congress Cataloging-in-Publication Data

Halm, Ben B., 1957–
    Theatre and ideology / Ben B. Halm.
        p.   cm.
    Includes bibliographical references.
    ISBN 0-945636-62-8 (alk. paper)
    1. Drama—History and criticism.   2. Mimesis in literature.
3. Theater—Philosophy.   4. Theater—Political aspects.   I. Title.
PN1631.H27   1994
792'01—dc20   94-10125
                                                                                    CIP

PRINTED IN THE UNITED STATES OF AMERICA

Contents

Acknowledgments

My thanks to Associated University Presses for giving my work a chance and to the following publishers and agents for permission to use extended quotations from copyrighted works. Reprinted with the kind permission of Faber and Faber Ltd. from *Muntu: An Outline of the New African Culture* by Janheinz Jahn, translated by Marjorie Grene. Copyright © 1971 by Faber and Faber Ltd. Excerpts from *Brecht on Theatre,* edited by John Willett. Translation copyright © 1964 and renewed © 1992 by John Willett. Reprinted by permission of Hill and Wang, a division of Farrar, Straus and Giroux, Inc. Reprinted by permission of Georges Borchardt, Inc. from *Antonin Artaud: Selected Writings,* edited by Susan Sontag. Copyright © 1956, 1961, 1964, 1967, 1970, 1971, 1974 Éditions Gallimard. Translation copyright © 1976 by Farrar, Straus and Giroux. Reprinted with the kind permission of Grove/Atlantic, Inc. from *The Theater and Its Double* by Antonin Artaud, translated by Mary Caroline Richards. Copyright © 1958 by Grove Press Inc. Reprinted with the permission of Grove Atlantic, Inc. from *Muntu: An Outline of the New African Culture* by Janheinz Jahn, translated by Marjorie Grene. Copyright © 1971 by Grove Press, Inc. Reprinted from *On the Genealogy of Morals* by Friedrich Nietzsche, translated by Walter Kaufmann and R. J. Hollingdale. Copyright © 1967 by Vintage Press, a division of Random House, Inc. Reprinted by permission of Reed Consumer Books Ltd. from *Brecht on Theatre* edited by John Willett. Copyright © 1976 by Methuen London. Reprinted with the permission of Simon and Schuster from the Macmillan College Text *Politics and the Arts: Letter to M. D'Alembert on the Theatre* by Jean-Jacques Rousseau, translated by Allan D. Bloom. Copyright © 1960 by the Free Press, a division of Macmillan, Inc. Reprinted with the permission of Simon and Schuster from the Macmillan College text *The New Organon and Related Writings* by Francis Bacon, edited by Fulton H. Anderson. Copyright © 1960 by Macmillan College Publishing Company, Inc. "The Antichrist" by Friedrich Nietzsche, edited and translated by Walter Kaufmann, from *The Portable Nietzsche* by Walter Kaufmann, editor, translator. Translation copyright 1954 by The Viking Press, renewed © 1982 by Viking Penguin Inc. Used by permission of Viking Penguin, a division of Penguin Books USA Inc.

Introduction: Theatre and Ideology in the Light of Mimesis, the Most Fundamental Form of Human Desire

As conceived in this work, representation initially coincides with Aristotle's view of mimesis as the most fundamental means by which human being give verbal and/or literary form and substance to their existence. Over and above Aristotle's conception, representation is seen in this work as also underlying the physical-material realizations of human experience. Generally, it is suggested that the basis of mimesis and representation is human desire, the most primary of which is the desire for self-fulfillment and self-completion through action and the manipulation of the environment. This irrepressible desire is born out of a recognition or, at least, an intimation of the quintessential incompleteness or insufficiency of the human self. The very existence of palpable things and others who and which lie outside the range and reach of the desiring human self seems to be the primary source of this awareness.

The other or nonself whose autonomous existence and presence signals the insufficiency of the desiring-affirming self can be either animate or inanimate. The inanimate other is the sum total of the natural and physical-material circumstances of the self; the animate other consists of other human beings and/or cultural groups in contrast to whom and to whose representations the self defines itself. Even other (nonhuman) animals can belong to the set of animate others against whom the human defines itself, its world, and its overriding worldview. Thus, whatever appears, or is perceived, to be palpable and desirable but lies outside the actual and imaginative (cultural) space of that self signifies the nontotality or completeness of this self. In symbolic (and sometimes actual/real) terms, a self that presumes or sees/feels itself incomplete or nontotal attempts to complete and totalize itself primarily through consumption of others or nonselves. Extra-self is perhaps the better word to use to describe what is said or perceived to be lying outside the desiring, affirming, and aggrandizing self.

7

Regarded by both Aristotle and Derrida as the most naive or basic form of representation, if not, indeed, its quintessence, mimesis, is a way of imitating or 'making like' others in order to understand and ultimately comprehend (embrace; consume) them. Obviously, the underlining of mimetic conception and representation with consumption means that these two concepts harbor both a power and a pleasure principle. Indeed, if human desire is the cause of mimesis and representation, the beginning of this cause itself is feeling and seeing. What is desired must first be felt and/or seen in an actual or imaginative sense. Of the two motivations to mimesis and self-aggrandizement, seeing is the most tangible and often appears to be the most powerful as well. The perception (seeing) of something that is or appears infinitely desirable but is not (yet) a part of the ever-hungry and ever-insecure self often leads to an attempt to understand and to consume (comprehend) that thing.

Amorous desire and its alias, alibi, and concomitant, love, are mimetic to the extent that they are means by which a human being of one sex signals his or her attraction to a being of the other (or another) sex. In fact, human lovemaking appears very theatrical and mimetic in the sense that the lovers often present themselves to each other in the most flattering light. Each tends to act a part or role, to impersonate a being who is most likely to win the approval of the beloved other. The very fact of desire implies the incompleteness or insufficiency of the loving self, and each lover, in the process of impersonation, increases any initial sense or feeling of incompleteness even further by losing part of the previous (not real or actual) self or mask. With the consummation of love (which often occurs when the twain conjoin and become or make like one, in whatever form that fiction of oneness takes) the two circularly desiring and desired polar selves-in-love come to believe that they are more complete and more total.

In the light of love, then, mimesis appears to be a naive way of bridging the gap between the self and that to which it is attracted after encountering it with the eyes and/or the mind. Another way of stating this is that representation as a whole is motivated by seeing and thinking. In the human being these two activities are profoundly cultural and acculturated (that is, socialized), as against being merely natural or biological. Seeing is seeing in a particular way, and thinking is thinking within a certain framework; both seeing and thinking are deliberately learned by the human child in a formal way, or he or she acquires them informally through imitation and emulation of others. In either case, the interpretations the human mind makes of what the eye encounters or perceives are influenced by cultural factors. The very fact that human perception precedes and drives representation, and that it is nearly always culturally and ideologically influenced, must put an end to the rather tendentious pretense that some forms of representation are intrinsically objective, disinterested, or independent of human wills and affects.

Representation is part and parcel of an unending process of self-and-world definition and circumscription whose common name is "culture." In all human experience, always, everywhere, a formal order is and needs to be imposed on the inchoate formlessness and irrepressible multiplicity of phenomena. Without this ordering and formalization of phenomena, human experience makes no sense; it cannot be understood and, better yet, it cannot be comprehended (embraced). "Acculturation," V. Y. Mudimbe suggests in *The Invention of Africa,* is "the nature of all histories"; or of philosophies, and of any other term that describes a formal or systematic way of articulating human experience. Acculturation is the process in which human beings make self-and-world defining choices by selecting a few scenarios and options from the plethora of possibilities available in phenomenal-material life and weaving them into a body of representations that can facilitate and legitimize a particular or particular kinds of action and being-in-the-world. The enabling of human action vis-à-vis the animate and inanimate other (total surroundings) is, of course, the prime objective of all human culture. As Hegel notes in his writings on tragedy, "action is rather essentially the manifestation of human life."[1] Human culture and acculturation direct or orient the existence-defining pursuit of action in particular, prefigured ways, ways that are often invested with valorizing metaphysical-transcendental notions of rightness, truth, goodness, and felicity.

Empowered and/or transcendentalized representations of human experience such as "metaphysics, morality, religion, science," Nietzsche submits in *The Will to Power,* "merit consideration as various forms of lies: with their help one can have faith in life."[2] These discursive forms and systems can function as satellites and concomitants of culture and acculturation because they are or can be underwritten by the will to action and self-and-world empowerment. The general name this book gives to the potentially limitless forms and ways in which the human self-and-world can be rationalized and oriented toward implicit or explicit ends is ideology. Needless to say, such a description of the concept-phenomenon of ideology does not coincide with its narrow pejorative definition in Western empirical-scientistic critiques.

In this book, ideologies are simply representations of the self-and-world that are widely accepted enough to be effective and affective. Thus, the legitimacy of ideologies does not lie so much in their scientific or empirical-analytical soundness as in their persuasiveness and/or satisfaction of certain context-historical principles of probability and necessity. The fundamental principles of felicity in ideologies might be underscored by actual sensuous-material conditions and needs, but material efficacy, empirical validity, and logical consistency are not their be-all and end-all. As such, some representations of human experience cannot be demonized simply because they appear or are said to lack actual-material efficacy, scientific-empirical validity, and/or logical-philosophical consistency.

Representations of human experience that were once considered both powerful and pleasurable can appear or be seen as false, distortive, or parochial when they have been outstripped by unpacifiable context-historical circumstances. The common Western term for such disempowered forms of representation is ideology. But if the conditions in the time and place in which they exist are what determine the acceptability or nonacceptability of empowered forms of human self-and-world representation, then investigations of ideology that do not take such context-historical probabilities and necessities into account run the risk of being insignificant or irrelevant. Even generally laudable questions regarding the moral responsibility or justice of certain forms of representation can fall prey to irrelevance if they are posed without regard to text and context of particular ideologies.

More often than not, the very critique or act of contestation that attempts to disempower a body of representations by hanging the narrow pejorative label of ideology on it is itself the harbinger of yet another, no more perfect or universal, body of representations. Implicitly or explicitly, critiques of ideology tend to work on behalf of the ascendancy of some form or system of representation as against another. Taken in a comprehensive agonistic sense, therefore, ideology is a rubric for the proliferative formal and informal ways in which human experience is rationalized and organized. It wears many tags and appears in many different guises among them critique, history, philosophy, mythology, theatre, and so on.

Given the manifoldness of ideology and the necessity of specifying its various manifestations in their particular contexts and historical conditions, the best a general notion of ideology can do is suggest the broad forms and the constitutive mechanisms of most ideologies. In chapter 1 of this book, I attempt such a formal and elemental description. The basic form of ideology is expressed in terms of an ostentatious opposition between two constitutive extremes and yet its real force is said to lie in the putative reconciliations and sublations of these self same opposites. If one accepts the traditional Western conception of the sublime as implicated in the reconciliation of opposites, then ideology is a sublime form of representation whose internal motion is directed toward the sublimation of any opposites it presents. Significantly, the ideal-metaphysical figures around whom some Western ritual-religious systems are formed have been conceived in terms of the sublime and sublimation. The Greek god Zeus and the Biblical-Christian God, for instance, are sublime figures in whom the most extreme of human and superhuman possibilities and probabilities (choices) are juxtaposed. To illustrate even further, there seems to be two Christian Gods; the Old Testament God is xenophobic and tends to display the most implacable wrath toward both his chosen people and their adversaries, while the New Testament one is driven by merciful love for humanity and a desire to create a multiethnic and multiracial world. Taken together, the attributes of the biblical Christian God are paradoxical, but the apparent reconciliation of these polar elements in this God makes 'him' both all-powerful and all-merciful. The seductive sway of this Christian God is anchored in sublimity which, approached in a narrow logical-empirical light, appears paradoxical and illogical.

As a matter of fact, the one thing ancient Greek rationalists found most unappealing about mythology was that Zeus, the lord of the gods and head of the Olympic pantheon, was a figure in whom law-abiding sociability co-existed with the most dastardly criminality. This doubleness of self and actions which applies to most of the Greek gods might simply be due to the fact that the inherent plurality of orality and mythology neither requires nor facilitates strict control over various tellings. Such internal paradoxes make mythological and religious figures sublime, but they were not acceptable to ancient Greek protoempiricists and rationalists who viewed them as symptomatic of "the sinful craving of mouth and ear."

Most successful representations of human experience are sublime in a way similar to that involved in the conception of ritual-religious and/or mythological figures. Such representations contain in themselves many possibilities but their internal contradictions and conflicts are said to have been successfully reconciled, sublated, or pacified. In the wake of allegedly successful sublation of internal opposites, sublime representations of human experience appear or are said to be simple and unitary in both form and (e)motion. However, such (an appearance of) outward simplicity and univocality is belied by a chromatic plurality of forms which enable obvious extremes of choice and action to be shaded into hues that bring them closer and closer together.

Claims that empowered representations of human experience successfully reconcile their diametric and dialectical opposites presumes on the palpable possibility of the shading or coloring of extreme of human desire and choices toward and into their opposites. In the Western Enlightenment context, a successful discourse or body of self-and-world representations is often said to be "objective" (that is, "disinterested" or divested from what it represents). Translated into a pneumatic framework, the question of subjectivity and interest in human experience is illuminated by the issue of color in light. In the light of light, the self-empowering claim of objectivity and disinterest in Western Enlightenment discourse is a suggestion that its representations are natural or colorless.

Clear or natural light results from a uniform, collective motion without refraction by certain particular frequencies and extraneous media. Similarly, human experience is said to be clear (colorless) and all-serving in the putative absence of barriers set up by particular human wills and affects. In both cases what is or appears is said to not have been filtered through any particular perspective or tendency (frequency) and does not reflect any subjective or parochial interests. The common name given to experiential and existential refraction or interference in the simple harmonic motion of representation is, of course, subjectivity. The much-feared consequence of subjectivity, at least in the universalism-desiring context of Western Enlightenment rationality, is relativism. Thus, the Western Enlightenment love-claim of universalism and objectivity is part and parcel of its fear of relativism or even perspectivism. When the circle is closed, this fear of relativism harbors a will to power and single morality that is well served by self-empowering and other-reducing claims of universality and objectivity.

Jürgen Habermas, for instance, betrays the other-repressing aspect of Western Enlightenment ideology and critique when he attaches "a claim to *universality* with [the] *Occidental understanding of the world.*" The "will to single morality" underlying this exclusive endorsement of Western-Occidental rationality is disclosed in Habermas's confession of a profound "irritation" at the "mythical

understanding of the world." In the narrow pejorative framework
of the ideology, the mythical understanding of the world would be
termed 'ideology' while Occidental rationality is given the valorizing label of 'critique.' In point of fact, ideology and critique are
dialectical and/or agonistic opposites; Habermas himself has been
quoted to say that "ideology is the product of the critique of ideologies."[3]

Life is like light, and is neither colored nor colorless (clear),
what makes it one form or another is the media or filters through
which it passes as well as the surfaces against which it is thrown
or projected. The presence or absence of certain frequencies of
energy or vibration give light its color. In the same way, the presence or absence of certain will and affects or horizons and frequencies of desire gives form to human experience and to the most
basic, naive, and sublime forms in which it is manifest or represented. The highest claim that can be made for an ideology is that
it is colorless, the implication being that it represents a wide range
of interests that redeem it of particularity and insularity, of local/
particular color. When such a claim is believed or simply left without question, that system of representation is able to satisfy the
two basic conditions of felicity of all ideologies, those of persuasiveness and authoritativeness. Such a form can act as a powerful
and pleasurable means of organizing human experience, or as an
ideology defined in the comprehensive nonpejorative sense.

In this book, I endeavor to illuminate the complex desires and
wills that underwrite the relationship between one form or body
of self-and-representations and its actual or imagined others. Ideology and critique are forms of representation whose relationship of
ostentatious feudings and concealed cooperations illuminate the
process of ceaseless becomings, unbecomings, and overcomings
that is human experience. I will argue that at the point of emergence of Western Enlightenment (Marxian) idea of ideology an
allegedly new critique attacks the central or core concepts and
strategies of an old body of representations by labeling it ideology.
Critique justifies this deconstructive act on behalf of change and
by claiming to be a superior response to context-historical necessities. The quest to make a new self-and-world through the unmaking
of an allegedly old or worn-out body of representations is the common feature of the critique of ideology. This primary objective of
ideology is central to all the theatrical endeavors investigated in
this book.

A successful ideology is simply a self-and-world representation
that is still regarded as persuasive and authoritative largely be-

cause its putative ability to reconcile the constitutive extremes in its referent world is still believed. Conversely, an unsuccessful ideology is one that never had, or once had but lost, its power of persuasion and authority and cannot warrant belief in its claims. What is labeled ideology in narrow pejorative Western critiques, therefore, is in this book merely an unsuccessful or failed self-and-world representation. In any case, the perception of a failure or absence of persuasion and authority in a form of representation is often prefigured in the prior interests and priorities of the critic and critique making the claim. In *The German Ideology,* Karl Marx calls ruling-class representations false consciousness or 'ideology' and working-class ideas truth ('critique') not because of any demonstrable rightness or wrongness of these opposed bodies of representations, but because of his a priori desires and endorsement of the working class.

The prevalence of Marx's interested definition of ideology in the contemporary world, not to mention its endurance through the ages, lies in the persuasiveness of his argument to intellectuals and activists the world over. This persuasiveness itself appears to be rooted in widespread disillusionment with capitalism. Besides, a world that is materialistic and scientist-technological is likely to provide Marx's claims with the requisite amount of belief and acceptance if only because they wear the tag of scientific or historical materialism.

To turn now to the second major concept in this book, the question of theatre in representations of human experience touches on its ideological and/or acculturative potential. This recrudescent issue seems to be founded in the widely alleged ability of theatre (as form and institution) to support and comprehend within itself a multiplicity of terms and perspectives of representation. The acculturative validity of theatre and the theatrical representation of human experience are applauded by the protheatrical writers discussed in this book. On the other side of the coin, unitarist and purist-minded rationalists such as Socrates/Plato and Bacon view the putative multiplicity of terms in theatre and the corollary possibility of contaminations and reconciliations within it as making it an undesirable form of representation. Such a condemnation of theatre is rehearsed in the antitheatrical works of Rousseau and Nietzsche, among others.

On the whole, theatre is, for theatrical and antitheatrical writers alike, mimesis par excellence, the exemplary form of representation. Naturally, the implications of this common view of theatre are not the same for theatrical and antitheatrical writers. In the antitheatrical school, mimesis is perverse and common, and being considered its exemplar simply makes theatre the most perverse, vulgar, and pandering form of representation. Even a protheatrical writer such as Aristotle, perhaps because he shared Socrates/ Plato's disdain for the common people to whom theatre is said to pander, sees performance as the most vulnerable aspect of theatre. In order to endorse theatre, therefore, he excludes performance from its list of essential elements; at least, he argues that performance is not a crucial part of the theatre's quest for self-fulfillment and completion.

In general, protheatrical writers consider mimesis an inalienable feature of human experience, perhaps as the most fundamental means of giving human-phenomenal existence form and direction. Being considered the exemplar of mimesis in such a framework makes theatre a worthy and powerful way of representing and transforming human experiences. It appears to be a valid means for overcoming the pathological forms in which human life has been organized. In contrast to Aristotle and the antitheatrical school, the protheatrical writers see performance as a crucial element of theatre. With Appia and Artaud, for example, the mise-en-scène or total staging of theatre is its most crucial aspect because it means the realization of the ideal or spiritual aspects of human existence in concrete experience; it makes human existence more complete. Such claims are startling, of course, but their barefaced audacity is aimed at enabling human action and self-fulfillment through an intercourse with the total space of existence.

In the name of allowing the arguments made by the writers and movements discussed in this work the necessary space in which to dance and prove or disprove themselves, I often suspend questions of the validity of claims made for or against theatre. My overriding aim is to allow the human desires, wills, and affects that color these views on theatre to shine forth and stay in the light. In a phenomenological sense, theatre is life that cuts into life, seeing that cuts into all seeing. It is a place of seeing that represents and illuminates the interested and fabricated nature of all views of the self and the world. The etymological origin of theory (the ancient Greek *theoria*) is seeing, watching, or contemplation, and as a place for seeing (*theatron*), theatre second-orders all human perception. Thus, etymologically and phenomenologically speaking, theatre is a place for theorizing or for contemplating the fundamental ideals and realities of human existence. By re-presenting the ideas that form and inform the human self-and-world, theatre plays the role of metatheory—it second-orders these ideas. Theatre, then, is embodied philosophy in a sense made evident in recent deconstructive and 'postmodernist' continental philosophies.

Indeed, 'postmodernist' thought is profoundly theatrical; its poetics and politics of surfaces makes the symbol and metaphor of theatre even more indispensable to the representation of human experience. The precession of simulacra in Baudrillard's conception of postmodernism is not only bodily and spectacular, it is also theatrical, if superficially so. In the postmodern theatre of surfaces, appearances are presumed to hide nothing essential, spiritual, or transcendental. What one sees on the surface is said to be all there is. All is simulacra, and nothing of substance belies them. The naive but empowering vision and envisioning of hope in the variegated forms of modernism, the belief in the possibility of significant transformation and redemption that underwrites the works of Appia, Artaud, and Brecht, are lost in the representations of the postmodern theatre. It is true that much of the solipsism and self-intoxication that is found in postmodern theatre, especially in that ugly duckling baptised and named "performance art," can be found in Artaud. Indeed, Artaud is arguably the most pivotal figure in postmodern theatre; Johannes Birringer more or less sees him as such in his book *Theatre, Theory, and Postmodernism.* Still, the solipsism in his works was balanced by an overriding attempt to reorient and revolutionize the occidental self-and-world. While no example of postmodern theatre is treated in this book, this distinction between its assumptions and that of the modernist theatre that preceded and seeded it is worth remarking.

The elemental character of both theatre and ideology, the two central concepts of the present investigation, is manifest in the fact that both are rubrics for a multiplicity of forms and representations. A conspicuous outcome is that a host of concepts important to Western representations of human experience are brought into the picture-frame of this book. The nature of truth and the specific forms in which it is manifest is central to the question of ideology as a whole and my attitude to this vexed question influences the whole of this book.

Humanity is said to have been made in God's image, but some skeptics believe the reverse to be the case, that humanity makes God in its own image. It is also said that God is truth, which simply means that 'he' (or she, as the case might be) is the initial and ultimate source of all human truths. But human truths are subject to the probabilities and necessities of the body or flesh; they struggle eternally against sensuous-material necessity. So, to amend

Nietzsche's question in *Beyond Good and Evil*, "supposing truth is a body (as well), what then?"

First, to suppose truth is a body does not mean it is not a soul or psyche as well, it does not mean the preclusion of the nonbodily and nontangible elements of human experience. It is clear from the works of Appia and Artaud, especially, that human-phenomenal existence is profoundly gnostic and that in its representations opposites meet, mix, and are symbolically reconciled (sublated). Truth cuts into truth, truth cuts into fiction, body cuts into body, body cuts into soul, and they all join in a bacchanalian whirl or totalizing dance.

A rigorously gnostic approach to the representation of human experience sees through the front of simplified dualities or "high naturalisms" to the multiplicities, chromatic conflicts, and ambiguities beneath them. Over and above its intoxicating returns and self-empowering circularities, the gnostic framework highlights the fact that Spirit/Light (the realm of putative essences and ideals) is endlessly contaminated with Flesh/Dark (the realm of materiality and history). In other words, the elevated notions that underscore human experience are periodically taken down into the world and reconciled with the material conditions over which they are said to stand.

In the gnostic or pluralistic framework, truths are of necessity periodically reinvested with metaphysical veils and comforts that facilitate human action. They are a never-ending Becoming framed within a certain context and history rather than in a stabilized or ahistorical Being. Human truths are palimpsests, texts plated over and over again with human wills and affects, with sweat, blood, tears, and fears. Like the human animal who produces and consumes them, truths are bodies with bodily functions; they work, sweat, excrete, and intermittently renovate their worn-out body-cells. "Literature," "carnival," "ritual," "theatre," and so on are forms or systems of representation that cooperate with the renovations and reinvestitures of truth in human-material experience. Such representations periodically violate, inoculate, and, sometimes restore to fuller health and relevance the reigning semiotic and linguistic conventions in the human lifeworld.

A time comes, however, when these carnivals or festivals of truth become ineffective, irrelevant, or are outstripped by sociohistorical contingencies. At this point, a regnant body of truth appears or is either said to be "false consciousness" or a distortion of "real relations" in the lifeworld—this is the definition of ideology in the Marxian sense. A once-triumphant truth is ostracized in the wake of its perception as falseness, and ostracism, as cultural ethnographers are wont to remind us, is a form of death—namely, voodoo death. This kind of death occurs when someone is excluded from participating in all social and cultural life. Truth as body dies a 'voodoo death' when it is made false and denied its force without the benefit of a trial or a demonstration of its context-historical relevance.

On the other hand, the body of truth can die a biological death, a death that occurs through salient criticism and/or its falsification by unpacified and or unpacifiable contextual-historical circumstances in a given world. In this instance, a vocal member or group recognizes a need to renovate or radically transform its dominant conventions and representations and finds the words and arguments to support this belief. Unlike the more precipitate dismissals of the self-and-world representations of others, these internal criticisms treat their family truths with more care and cunning. In fact, they often mimic what they seek to destroy because it is, after all, a part of themselves. Thus, the death that they bring to bear on the prostrated body of familiar or familial truth takes the form of ritual murder.

Critique, carnivalesque, theatricality, and so on are ritual stones cast periodically at the ever-public body of truth; these stones may cut but cannot destroy any body of truth long as it is still powerful. When truth is outstripped by context-historical empirical factors the ritual stones become fatal but, until this point of no return, it appears inviolable. Once it has been accepted, believed, and affirmed in life and act, truth dies hard. The common human tendency is to overlook ignore, suspend, or, even deny the death of truth. The exegetes and adherents of accepted truth would rather stoop to the absurdity of looking for it with lanterns in the full glare of mid day light than passively accept that it has died a mortal death. I pun on Nietzsche's proclamation of the "Death of God" in *The Gay Science* because in almost all human self-and-world representations God is said to be Truth.

Human beings hold on to the dead or dying body of truth for the understandable reason that they are themselves finite bodies who yet think ceaselessly on death and anticipate their own deaths in like manner. "In the midst of life," the biblical saying goes, "we are in death." But humanity does not take death lying down; it rebels at the thought and eventuality of death. In holding on to the dying bodies of truth, god, loved ones, old selves-and-worlds, and so on, human beings, in fact, hold off their own death. "Ask not for whom the bell tolls," they are warned by their thinkers and priests, "it tolls for thee." Through their artists, human beings attempt to symbolically outwit death, or so Artaud, de Sade, Hölderlin, and other modern Western romantics suppose. These writers suggest that literature, and artistic-intellectual endeavor on the whole, are symbolic or ritualistic means of overcoming the death that await all human-phenomenal beings. Silence and madness are harbingers as well as lesser forms of this death, and in doing battle against them with literature and formal writing human beings resist the more final doom even as they mimick and taunt it.

In "Language to Infinity," for example, Michel Foucault conceives modern romantic literature as a strategic differentiation within language and symbolism by means of which humanity attempts to suspend or evade silence, madness, and death. Literature, for him, is the telling of interminable tales, tales linked into an endless loop or circle of signifiers through the fact of convention, reference, and quotation. The most celebrated of such tellings is, of course, the endless tale told by Schehérazade in *The Arabian Nights*. This famous tale reveals that human truth is most powerful and lasting when it is fictional, and that it is even more so if it is fabricated in the palpable shadow of waiting death. It also suggests that truth is the dance of the finite-mortal body around and toward infinity and immortality; truth is a tale told in order to make the temporary and accidental choices and actions of humanity appear to be eternally right and unchanging. Truth, in this sense, is a motion or movement toward rest, stability, and fixity, but this ultimate fixity must itself be in perpetual motion if it is to find itself as rest. In gnostic terms, truth is Spirit that must be Flesh in order to find and return into itself as Spirit. The motion of truth, therefore, never ends because it is most fleeting and fluid especially when and where it appears to be most fixed.

The greatest foe of putatively timeless and unchanging truth is infallible memory, or the pretence to such. This is because truth is most effective when its consumers suspend their disbelief and take its claims for granted. Human memory is most stable and infallible when it is stabilized or reified into a written text, but this material kind of fixity is not the kind that best serves truth. Initially, it appears as though textuality and archivality are the greatest allies, alibis, and sponsors of truth. However, a time comes when such immaculate texts become violable—the passage of time, the throwing of the floodlights of cartesian reason on canonized truth-texts mark the beginning of their falsification. In the face of textual criticism, the old body of truths becomes trapped in its textual-archival materiality, thus, an easy prey for skeptics. What initially increased the power of truth ultimately destroys it; textual exegesis defends and entrenches accepted truths but as textual criticism it turns out to be the great nemesis of canonical truths and texts.

Textual criticism uproots accepted truths of the written word by their roots; it shows that old truths actually fall short of new ones. If truth has been overcome once, it can be overcome again and again and again and again. Subsequently, textual or posttextual humanity comes to believe that truth lasted longer in the "good old days." And, of course, it did. Truth lasted longer in the good old days because it existed in a world without texts, its delicate claims were not reified or placed in one frail basket, but in many baskets, and as such they could not be destroyed in one fell swoop. In other words, the putative longevity and apparent eternity of truth in the good old days is a conceptual and nostalgic illusion. In a world of "primary orality" (to use Walter Ong's formulation), truth is as Good as Perfect because it is fabricated by human beings in as many forms as possible to please and comfort themselves. To quote one disgusted ancient Greek rationalist, the truths of orality and mythologicality are the manifold products of "sinful cravings of mouth and ear."

Jack Goody suggests in *The Domestication of the Savage Mind* that old time (oral-mythological) truth "is largely unanalysed. It [is even] a form of self-deception. . . . The oral mode makes this kind of self-deception easier to carry out and less easy to detect. The process of (constructive) criticism, whether by the speaker [of truth] or by another, is inhibited, made more difficult. . . . But, more than this, the oral form is intrinsically more persuasive because it is less open to criticism (though not, of course, immune from it)."[4] In a context without a reified text of truth, and, more importantly, without cynical cartesians to fixate on it with a view to either clarifying of falsifying it, what God said, so said the first Ancestors or Founding Fathers. This is to say that what was said by the first eternal/divine Speaker can be said to have been perfectly repeated by the first ephemeral-human Speakers. In the framework of orality, indeed, what God and the Ancestors or Founding Fathers once said they continue to say through present humanity, and they will continue to do so through future humanity till the end of time. Understandably, therefore, old-time, prealphabetical, or preliterate truth appears to be at once mortal and immortal, human and divine, here and there, now and then, now and forever. Amen. Sublime, in a word.

When the almighty ephemeral Word of primary orality becomes fixated in an identifiable Text, its authority and persuasion are initially increased, but his advantage is ultimately lost because fixated truth is more vulnerable to criticism and the ravages of time. Under the impress of restless criticism, the allegedly one truth gives way to an endless procession of parochial truths or "ideologies," in the usage of Karl Marx and Western Enlightenment thinkers. Ironically, in his efforts to deconstruct the old ruling-class texts Marx himself creates a new working-class text and, thereby, his work joins the endless masquerade of parochial texts. Furthermore, his communist state, in which the procession of simulacra is to come to an end, is one in which different social categories either do not exist or the differences between are not crucial. Since differentiation, categorization, and listing are axiomatic to writing and literacy, Marx's communist state is a surreptitious return into an undifferentiating state of orality.

The ascendancy of the written text as the prime locus of truth also means the periodic verifications and carnivalizations of this text, which has become a captive of reading. The threat of falsification becomes a Sword of Damocles eternally suspended above the head of crowned literate-textual truth. Postalphabetical truth often compares present-day reality with a largely imagined or imaginary nostalgic past and ends up dismissing the former as alienated and abstracted from its original totality and (w)holiness. For good reason, therefore, post-alphabetical truth tends to be very cynical, but this is an affectation of false bravado and gallows humor. Such truth affects a skepticism that most damns it; nay, it plans its own obsolescence with great jocularity. With an affected shrug, it says to those who might look too closely at its ravaged body, "hey, go on and audit me, make my day; I doubt myself more than you can ever doubt me." But, behind that ostentatious shrug and histrionic voice lurk implicit or explicit affirmations of one thing or another. Whatever truth might do, the fact of its existence in the light of life makes it affirm one thing or another; there is always a perspective at stake, a position to stake.

Some rational-empirical truth-tellers hide the mutual advocacies of truth and fiction behind the smoke screen of a loudly proclaimed "ancient feud between philosophy [rationalist truth] and poetry [mythopoetic fiction or lies]." In fact, truth gets most slippery and absolutist at the point that it insists that its flights and dances through the hostile space of time can only be appreciated, clarified, or understood in retrospect. Here, truth not only hides in the other world, but it also becomes like Hegel's proverbial grey "owl of Minerva" in that its flight through time and space is invisible against the grey sky. In its grey-on-grey flight, putatively absolute or ideal truth appears to be a *dei absconditus* and its flight through time and history a *danse absconditus*. Thus, it is not absurd if the adherents of such absolutist truth hold aloft lighted lanterns in the middle of the day and run through the center of the market-place looking for the absolute and ideal source of their truth, God.

The presumption on a timeless-universal truth is also a presumption on oneness, sanitariness, sanitation, and sanity. Turned around, it is a desire to obviate the fact of unavoidable multiplicity and incessant change in phenomenal existence. The root of this frenetic quest is the desire to make human endeavor meaningful, or, at least, more than a mere shot in the dark. More often than not, quests for oneness, meaning, sanity are attempts to reach a completed and perfected past usually based on the lasting 'oral' truths told once, and told once only, by God, the Ancestors, and/ or Founding Fathers. "In the beginning was the Word, and the Word was with God, and the Word was God." With the naivety or simple faith allowed by the ephemeral Word, whose unwritten form makes it eternally flexible and amenable to emendations, the human being makes believe his or her choices and actions are total in the sense that they express (in Gramsci's words) "the unity of the human spirit" which is also, "the unity of history and nature."

Necessary as they are, human presumptions on unity and godhead cannot be allowed to hide the fact that the truths of human being-and-knowing are not one but many. The kind of truth that is sensitive to what lies outside its limited time and place is only to be found at the crossroads of many truths and human subjectivities. Here, truth is most liable to run across others, trip on their claims, fall on its face, fall back on the earth, and to be buried there. With time, however, it rises again from the dead, ascends into heaven, and sits at the right hand of God the Father Almighty, there to overlook and look over human experience all over again. This restored truth awaits the moment of yet another descent to earth, this time to end the endless cycle of descent and ascent and create on earth a putatively new kingdom of the Spirit of God the Father Almighty.

This New Eden or New Jerusalem, this state that comes to be in the wake of the second coming, is not open to all humanity, but to only those who have been reawakened because they were good, true, beautiful, and just in the past life. Socrates/Plato's "well-ordered city," St. Augustine's "City of God," and Marx's "Communist state" all promise such an end of history, where history is seen as representing human difference, division, and evil (or fall from the oneness of Grace). But humankind ought to know better, ought to know that any state of perfection is a state of final, irrevocable Silence, Madness, and Death. For the sake of life (which is dynamic, processual, and eternally imperfect, which reaches toward perfection but never quite grasps it) human truths must never be seen or said to be perfect or fixed. The endless quest for self-and-world completion is itself the motion and emotion of human existence, and any state that wants or presumes to be able to end this striving must be resisted for the sake of life. This is the view of truth that underwrites this book.

As a consequence of its concern with such basic concepts as theatre, representation, and ideology, a number of other concepts to terms central to Western representations of human experience come into play in this book. Perhaps the most important or ubiquitous of these concepts is alienation. Conceived as a loss of original totality or oneness (belonging), alienation is generally viewed as the definitive malaise of modern Western capitalist existence. As such, it is not surprising that it surfaces in all the three modern Western arguments of theatre discussed in this book. A nonpathological or positive view of alienation is implicated in Brecht's *Verfremdungseffekt* and its view of theatre, and art as a whole, as the most effective means of overcoming alienation. In fact, theatre (variously conceived) is considered the most powerful means of self-and-world disalienation and revolution in the works of Appia, Artaud, and Brecht, the three main modern Western writers discussed in this book. The connection of theatre with disalienation is most explicit in the work of Brecht, that is all.

The Ghana National Theatre Movement's attempt to overcome colonialism is also a quest for disalienation insofar as colonialism involves the prostration of the colonized self-and-world and its alienation from its essential forms and representations. More specifically, the ubiquitous phenomenon of nationalism and/or national-personalism, first adumbrated in Appia's endorsement of the acculturative force of Wagner's music-dramas, is recaptured in arguments of the Ghana National Theatre Movement. Incidentally, the origin of this book was my attempt to understand the Ghana National Theatre Movement's view of the African National Theatre as the singular means of secondary decolonization in postindependence Ghana. The main objective of this postcolonial movement was self-and-world decolonization and disalienation; secondary decolonization, specifically, was conceived as the stage of mental or cultural-ideological emancipation, as opposed to a merely political or institutional one. This movement also aimed at creating a racial or pan-national-(continental) culture and, as such, it emphasized the need for uniform and unifying forms of representation.

A great many of the issues raised in the Ghana National Theatre Movement debates also obtain in the Western commentaries on theatre in preceding chapters. Apart from the issue of what makes a certain form of representation true or valid, besides the question of alienation, or fall from original oneness, the problem of multiple selves and worlds in a given context of theatre and representation is an important issue in this investigation. The existence of an embarrassment of ethnicities and ethnic languages in the specific context of Ghana (as in the general one of Africa) was the central problem or obstacle facing the Ghana National Theatre Movement. The ideal solution to this problem of plurality of ethnic selves, worlds, and languages (media of representation) was impossible insofar as it could neither consist of the institution of one ethnic language as *lingua franca* nor the retention of the language (English) of the colonizer.

There is always measure of serendipity or fortuitousness in every process of selection, and the choice of the Western writers I discuss in this book is no different. It just so happens that the startling claims made for theatre during the Ghana National Theatre debates were rehearsed in various forms in the works of writers well placed in Western theatre and philosophy. The impassioned arguments and polemics for and against theatre in the works of Socrates/Plato, Aristotle, Bacon, Rousseau, Nietzsche, Appia, Artaud, and Brecht, demonstrate that the Ghana National Theatre Movement project was no aberration. The chronological priority of these Western illuminations of the question of theatre and ideology made me delegate my discussion of the Ghana National Theatre Movement to the very last chapter. There is also some measure of chronology in the order of my discussion of the Western writers.

One fortuitous advantage that attends the somewhat chronological arrangement of the chapters of this book is that it enables me to suspend the possibility of hasty Western rationalist dismissal of the Ghana National Theatre Movement acculturative project until the very last chapter. After all, I am writing in a Western intellectual context whose firm belief in the soundness of its own assumptions and its methods of representation makes it tend other symbolic forms and cultures as irrational and/or primitive. It appeared more than likely to me that because of the palpable naivety of its claims and methods the Ghana National Theatre Movement project would be treated in a similar fashion. By leaving it to the very last chapter, therefore it could be protected by a shield erected by its Western theatrical and philosophical familiars and forebears. In the wake of the placement of this protective shield, this book becomes a general investigation of the ubiquity of theatre and theatricality in the representation of human experience, rather than an account of one particular, naive and unscientific, attempt to use theatre as the means of post-colonial Ghanaian-African self-and-world acculturation.

Theatre and Ideology

1

Toward a Comprehensive Framework on Ideology

The Impossible State of Ideology

The slippery character of ideology calls to mind the descriptions of the elephant by the six men of Indostan in John G. Saxe's "The Blindmen and the Elephant." Though blind, the six men went to see the elephant in the firm or foolish conviction that "each by observation might satisfy his mind" as to its essential nature. Each approached the animal from a unique vantage, touched it in a different place, and pronounced it as something different from what the others had felt and observed. The first, touching the side of the elephant, called it a wall; the second, feeling it's tusk, called it a spear; the third, taking its trunk, called it a snake; the fourth, finding a knee, exclaimed "tree!"; the fifth, chancing upon an ear, pronounced it a fan; and the sixth, seizing the tail, said the elephant was a rope. Touched in six different places by the six blindmen whose insights were limited to that one tactile perspective, the one elephant appeared to be six different things, none of which was an elephant as a person with sight sees it. Disinclined to accept the necessary incompleteness of each description of the elephant, the six blindmen "of Indostan / Disputed loud and long / Each in his own opinion / Exceeding stiff and strong / Though each was partly in the right / And all were in the wrong."[1]

Like the statements of the six blind men, Western critiques of ideology have tended to be loud disputations of limited conclusions. They do not so much demonstrate as perform the truth of their claims by rejecting other ways of representing and rationalizing human experience by labeling them "ideology." The quest for unilateral ascendancy over other ways and forms of representation seems to preclude admission of the self-aggrandizing nature of such critiques. In the last analysis, both ideology and the critique that labels it as such become dead-end streets and/or obstructions to a

29

fuller understanding of the basic processes of human existence, primary among them, culture and/as representation. The present work attempts to point the way towards such a fuller understanding.

In *Ideology and Utopia,* Karl Mannheim submits that "everyday experience with political affairs first made man aware and critical toward the ideological element of his thinking." To him, the deep-seated origin of ideology is the general fear of the other, but it is only when this fear of:

> man toward man, becomes explicit and is methodically recognized, that we may properly speak of an ideological taint in the discourse of others. . . . It is only when we more or less consciously seek to discover their untruthfulness in a social factor, that we are properly making an ideological interpretation. We begin to treat our adversary's views as ideologies only when we no longer consider them as calculated lies and when we sense in his total behaviour an unreliability which we regard as a function of the social situation in which he finds himself.[2]

Mannheim's definition of ideology as necessarily a "function of the social situation" recognizes the fact that human experience is always prefigured and framed in particular ways. Human culture presupposes the creation of particularized or customized conventions of thought and action that guide intervention in the inanimate and animate environment. In this work, ideology is the term or rubric for the ways in which human intervention in the total environment is organized and legitimized. This view of ideology is, of course, contrary to the Western Enlightenment conception of it as a rubric for false and/or parochial (as against true, necessary, and universal) forms of representation. In this work, all representations of human experience, despite what labels they are made to wear, are said to be fabricated, arbitrary, and parochial because they make human life possible and meaningful for a particular self-and-world.

All human statements about experience and/or pursuits of actions in the phenomenal world are underwritten by prior ontological-teleological assumptions. To quote Mannheim, "only those . . . who are prey to the positivistic prejudices of a past generation . . . still believe in the possibility of being completely emancipated in their thinking from ontological, metaphysical, and ethical presuppositions." Even the most scientific or empirical-minded objective is often belied by naive and nonempirical assumptions. Mannheim rightly observes that the "faith in progress . . . and naïve realism" at the center of Western positivism-empiricism (one of whose legacies is the critique of ideology) are themselves "metaphysical and ontological judgements." All told, the:

> unavoidable implicit ontology which is at the basis of our actions, even when we do not want to believe it, is not something which is arrived at by romantic yearning and which we impose upon reality at will. It marks the horizon within which lies our world of reality and which cannot be disposed of by simply labelling it ideology. . . . The exposure of ideological and utopian elements in thought is effective in destroying only those ideas in which we ourselves are not too intimately identified. Thus it may be asked whether under certain circumstances, while we are destroying the validity of certain ideas by means of the ideological analysis, we are not, at the same time, erecting a new construction—whether in the very way we call old beliefs into question is not unconsciously implied the new decision.[3]

The labeling of other or unfamiliar forms and systems of representation as ideologies in the narrow pejorative sense means the dismissal and demonization of ways in which other people think and represent their experiences. This does not only disempower the other self-and-world, but also makes the claimant self-and-world both unwilling and unable to understand other or unfamiliar ways and cultures. Thus is cultural parochialism and prejudice enthroned at the expense of multicultural coexistence, and the whole world is made poorer. Human cultures are ad hoc or context-historical solutions to the problems and challenges of existence, and a multiplicity of cultures means a multiplicity of solutions and/or paradigms of choice and action. A multicultural world is, thus, a potentially rich and vital world.

On the other hand, when and where one particular self-and-world representation is made to triumph over and prostrate its encountered or imagined others the world becomes less vital and less resistant to problems. Other cultures (forms of self-and-world representation) are alternatives, and as such sources of possible solutions to the pitfalls and shortcomings of one triumphant yet entropic culture or ideology. A monocultural world is not only less rich and less diverse than a multicultural or multisubjective one but also in it the appurtenant problems of the one triumphant form/system of representation have no other cultures from which to draw solutions. Like a purebred organism, a monocultural world tends to repeat its genetic defects and pathologies. Hence, unless the trend toward monoculturalism is arrested the existence of viable and vital alternatives to the one dominant culture and ideology will be denied.

The possibility that a monocultural and monoideological world might lose the ability to automatically generate new forms and modes of self-and-world representation that can help it overcome its problems and meet any new challenges is very palpable. As Mannheim suggests, "an ontology handed down through tradition obstructs new developments, especially in the basic modes of thinking," and when allowance is not made for other forms of thinking about human experience and other ways of doing things the organized forms of human life will tend to stagnate. "What is needed, therefore, is a continual readiness to recognize that every view is particular to a certain definite situation, and to find out through analysis of what this particularity consists."[4]

That there is an antagonistic "will to single morality" in some Western critiques and discourses is borne out by the all-too-recent fact that Jürgen Habermas makes "a claim to *universality* with [regards to the] *Occidental understanding of the world*." This is part and parcel of his profound "irritation" at the "mythical understanding of the world."[5] The claws of Western science and scientific-empirical rationality might be more carefully hidden beneath the paws of 'objectivity' and 'disinterest' but they exist nonetheless. But, such claims of unilateral objectivity and universal relevance (truth) in Western rationalism are humanly impossible. More importantly, they are profoundly undesirable and morally irresponsible, especially when they are made in a global-village world in which many conflictive cultural systems co-exist— brought together by science and technology (the airjet, fax machine, and satellite communications) and yet kept very far apart by human ignorance and intolerance.

With or without reference to the imaginative context of the global village:

> it has become extremely questionable whether, in the flux of life, it is genuinely a worthwhile intellectual problem to seek to discover fixed and immutable absolutes. [Whether it] is [not] a more worthy intellectual task perhaps to think dynamically and relationally rather than statically.

To think dynamically and relationally is to articulate human experiences multisubjectively and multiculturally. It betokens the recognition that "whatever human beings think and do and produce [in their specific contexts] concerns all other human beings."[6] To understand human experience relationally and dynamically is to consider it from the perspectives of its many contextual and historical manifestations. It means not conceiving the fact of difference or unfamiliarity to mean false, wrong, distortive, or deviating from what is universally and essentially right. All human beings make choices and pursue actions that they think or hope will fulfill their fundamental desires, and they often validate these choices and action circularly, in terms of their own way of seeing and acting in the world. This is unavoidable; without the selection and validation of all eventuality and happenstance as necessary and right, the sheer volume of possibilities and actualities of experience overwhelm the human mind and incapacitate the will to act.

Unfortunately, the circular validation of what has already been selected as the true or right form of actual or imagined human experience often involves the repression of the peculiar or self-serving choices and forms (representations) of other selves-and-worlds. But, recognition and admission of the essential partiality and particularity of different forms and systems of human self-and-world production and reproduction should make us recognize ourselves in others and others in ourselves. Then, and only then, can we overcome the tendency to make arrogant and myopic claims of universality in our self-and-world representations, especially when this has palpable consequences in relation to these others. The will to single morality and rationality might be replaced by a more humble view of the contextuality and temporality of the forms and claims. This, in turn, might minimize the oppressive and repressive force one system of representation often directs against another or others just because they are different and/or unfamiliar.

The multisubjective and multicontextual approach to the understanding of human experience that comes to be in the wake of the dismantling of univocalism and universalism could also lead, beyond mere recognition, to the active encouragement of the existence of multiple forms and systems of human experience in the same or relatively homogenous world-context. This is because the self or world so inclined dares accept what Nietzsche calls the "resolute reversals of accustomed perspectives and valuations." This human self or world wants "to see differently in this way for once"; it is important "to *want* to see differently" because seeing is an activity that is loaded with cultural and ideological priorities. In endeavoring to see differently, one can reverse one's accustomed perspectives and in this way prepare the human "intellect for its future 'objectivity.'" This kind of objectivity must be "understood not as 'contemplation without interest' (which is a nonsensical absurdity), but as the ability to *control* one's Pro and Con and dispose of them, so that one knows how to employ a *variety* of perspectives and affective interpretations in the service of knowledge."[7]

The kind of objectivity, or rather multisubjectivity (perspectivism) Nietzsche proposes and this book endorses remains eternally "on guard against the dangerous old conceptual fiction that posited a "pure, will-less, painless, timeless knowing subject." It works:

> against the snares of such contradictory concepts as "pure reason," "absolute spirituality," "knowledge in itself"; these always demand that we should think of an eye that is completely unthinkable, an eye turned in no particular direction, in which the active and interpreting forces, through which alone seeing becomes seeing *something,* are supposed to be lacking; these always demand of the eye an absurdity and a nonsense. There is *only* a perspective seeing, *only* a perspective "knowing"; and the *more* affects we allow to speak about one thing, the *more* eyes, different eyes, we can use to observe one thing, the more complete will our "concept" of this thing, our "objectivity," be. But to eliminate the will altogether, to suspend each and every affect, supposing we were capable of this—what would it mean but to *castrate* the intellect?—[8]

The following sections of this chapter will be geared toward bypassing empirical-minded demonizations of unfamiliar and uncanny *(Unheimlich)* forms or systems of representation as ideology as a way of reaching toward a fuller understanding of human experience. Beginning with Francis Bacon's theory of idols, generally regarded as their common origin, this chapter will illuminate the will and affects that underlie empirical-positivistic Western critiques of ideology. The premise here is that each and every mode, form, means of thinking, doing, and producing ideology adds something to the general store and story of concept-phenomenon. Hence it asks each of the critiques investigated to contribute something toward a syncretistic or mythopoetical view of ideology in which the concept simply appears to be a rubric for potentially unlimited forms and systems of human experience.

The Legacies of Francis Bacon's "Theory of Idols," the Common Origin of Western Critiques of Ideology

> Philosophical systems . . . are but so many stage plays, representing worlds of their own creation after an unreal and scenic fashion.
>
> —Bacon

Bacon's "Theory of Idols" is commonly regarded as the origin of Western Enlightenment critiques of ideology; Karl Mannheim, for instance, writes that "Bacon's theory of *idola* may be regarded to a certain extent as a forerunner to the modern conception of ideology." He warns, however, that "it cannot be claimed that there is an actual relationship, directly traceable through the history of thought, between this [theory] and the modern conception of ideology." Hans Barth's more unequivocal claim in *Truth and Ideology* is that the eighteenth-century French Enlightenment commentators on ideology availed themselves of Bacon's "famous theory of idols" as "set forth" in his *Novum Organon*.

> What Bacon called idols was termed prejudice by the French Enlightenment, whose fight for reason was a fight against the idols or prejudices of mankind. Ideology described the right technical procedure to be followed in the formation of ideas, whereas the theory of idols was charged with exposing the fallacies of thinking and the misuse of man's intellectual powers. By accepting the first book of the Novum Organon, ideology entered into a momentous alliance with Bacon's theory of idols, the consequences of which were to become fully apparent only with Feuerbach and Marx.[9]

The prime objective of Bacon's *Great Instauration* (whose first part is the *New Organon* in which he posits his famous theory of idols) was to create a kind of system of knowledge termed "natural philosophy" or "science." This philosophy is founded on "natural history," defined as "an observational and experimental study of nature" and justified by its quest to create sensuous-material "fruit and works." In the preface to the *Great Instauration,* Bacon stresses that he "is not [creating] an opinion to be held, but a work to be done"; he is "laboring to lay the foundation, not of any sect or doctrine, but of human utility and power." "Of all signs," Bacon writes, "there is none more certain or more noble than that taken from fruits. For fruits and works are as it were sponsors and sureties for the truth of philosophies." The Christian underpinnings of Bacon's overall agenda is evident in his *A Refutation ofPhilosophies.*[10]

At one point, however, Bacon contradicts his commitment to the service of fruits and works when he suggests that "from experience of every kind [we] must first endeavor to discover true causes and axioms; and seek for experiments of Light, not for experiments of Fruit." This apparent contradiction is a sign of his indecision between serving the "Creator" (the gnostic realm of 'Spirit' and 'Light') and serving the sensuous-material needs of humanity (the avatars of 'Flesh' and 'Darkness'). Fulton H. Anderson believes

that Bacon is basically inclined to "exclude all that is transcendental and admit nothing that could be deemed a priori" and that in his:

> naturalistic scheme there is no place for a knowledge which has for its
> purpose mere contemplation—the activity assigned by Aristotle to the
> metaphysician. The aim of all knowledge is action in the production of
> works for the promotion of human action and the relief of man's estate.
> Through inductive science man is to recapture his dominion over na-
> ture long forfeited and long prevented through the efforts of erring
> philosophers and men of learning.[11]

Bacon himself insists that the basis of his philosophy, "natural
history. . . . ought to be esteemed the great mother of the sciences." But his description of this "naturalist scheme" betrays an
ultimate deference to the metaphysics of Christian theology. "Of
Natural Philosophy," he writes, "the basis is Natural History; the
next stage the basis is Physic; [and] the stage next the vertical
point is Metaphysic." The aim of natural philosophy is to illuminate
the "glory of God" by uttering "the three acclamations, *Sancte,
sancte, sancte* [Holy, Holy, Holy]; holy in the description or dila-
tion of his works, holy in the connection or concatenation of them,
and holy in the union of them in a perpetual and uniform law."
In consonance with his avowed "hatred of darkness" (the gnostic
equivalent of fleshly existence), Bacon seems to subjugate the
domination of nature and the production of fruit and works to the
expression of "humility toward the Creator." In the idea of Christian Charity, however, the conflict between service to the Creator
(God) and humanity seems to be reconciled.[12]

In contrast to the putative inclination toward fruits-and-works
in his natural philosophy, "all received systems" are in Bacon's
view "barren of [fruits and] works." By all received systems,
Bacon meant all precedent Greco-Western philosophies, but he
reserves the brunt of his "disgust" for Aristotle, whom he labels
the "evil begetter" of "barren" or "scholastic philosophies." According to Benjamin Farrington, Bacon's "early disgust to Aristotle" is "one of those adolescent moments of moral insight which
determine the whole course of a life." The primary point on which
Bacon hangs his difference to Aristotle is that the latter's "writings
were 'barren of the production of works for the benefit of man.'"[13]

However, the loaded contrasts Bacon makes between his practical and useful works and the merely theoretical character of "all
received systems" distorts a more complicated picture of the relationship between theory and practice in these precedent philoso-

phies. In *Theory and Practice,* for example, Nicholas Lobkowicz demonstrates exhaustively that "the Greek version of the opposition between 'theory' and 'practice' originally amounted to an opposition between two 'ways of life,' political life and philosophic life." Those ancient Greek rational "philosophers who strove for something which they knew was above man considered themselves aliens among men."

> The philosopher was a "stranger among men." *Qua* philosopher, he felt himself closer to the divine than to his politically minded fellow men, and the latter quite naturally reciprocated by considering him either a madman or an egoist.
>
> At the same time, however, the philosopher could not avoid being a man who lived in a society with others. . . . "Theory" and "practice," philosophy and politics, no longer were separable simply because the philosopher was a man, and a man had to remain in the public realm even though, *qua* philosopher, he strived for something radically transcending the political order and thus the human level.
>
> To later Greek philosophers this unity of "theory" and "practice" will be so obvious that . . . they will support the ideal of a life composed of both philosophy and politics.[14]

Like Socrates and Plato before him, Aristotle believed that theory or philosophy (the contemplation of ideals and/or the face of God) is a higher endeavor than practice/politics (intervention in the human lifeworld). He allowed, however, that "any man was capable of embracing philosophy and philosophic life," that is, if he could afford the leisure to pursue such in life. In his philosophy, therefore, "'theory' and 'practice' were two dimensions or poles of human existence" that corresponded to "an opposition between what was strictly human and what was divine in man."[15] The same opposition underlies Bacon's "great instauration," the work in which he makes his blanket rejection of "all received systems" as "idols" self-aggrandizing at best.

Bacon excluded the works of the Pre-Socratics from the class of false and distortive received systems. In Democritus, particularly, he "saw a philosopher who was fortunate in being free from the doctrine of final causes and in discerning a formed and active matter, which was not the indeterminate, deprived, and inert abstraction he had met in the writings of Plato and Aristotle." Nevertheless, Bacon's own natural philosophy defers to "Divine Revelation" and thereby genuflects to a "Being qua Being" or an "indeterminate, deprived and inert abstraction" not unlike Aristotle's *Theos.*[16]

The tripartite division of the spheres of human experience by Bacon also preserves the deference to divinity and theology in his representations of human experience.

> Man, according to Bacon, belongs to three kingdoms, the Kingdom of God . . .; the political kingdom in which initiative in sovereignty, justice, and law is given by God to ruling powers; and the kingdom of nature over which man at the Creation has been given dominion. . . . For the understanding of the first and second of these kingdoms one must go to the revelation given in the scriptures; [only] knowledge of the third is attainable through the exercise of human faculties.

Bacon suggests that "the ethical direction of the divine part of man is to be found in the placets of revelation," and yet he closes off investigation of "the area of Divine Revelation" as "beyond the purview of natural philosophy." In spite of being "also a partaker of the Divine Image[,] . . . Man the investigator of nature . . . [is] a natural creature with faculties by nature limited." Thus, humanity is unable to

> attain to a knowledge of the transcendent mind and nature of God, or anything else that is divine. A metaphysics which pretends to this knowledge, like the Peripatetic ontology, . . . is in philosophy pretension and in theology heresy.[17]

Bacon's quarrel with "the Peripatetic ontology" is part and parcel of his resistance to the "demonstrations of truth" in the English scholarly tradition of his time. He rebelled "against this method of testing and examination," which he saw as "a bequest from the magisterial Aristotle." Such demonstrations of truth were "conducted according to the rules of syllogistic logic" and composed "largely of a collection of propositions traditionally taken from the physical, ethical, political, and metaphysical works of Aristotle." To Bacon, "it was no more than verbal gyration, elevated and refined by the Peripatetics into an art" that makes the demonstrator very much "like a playwright making a play with little, if any, foundation in fact." In his theory of idols, therefore, he places all "received systems" under the rubric of "idols of the theatre," which he defines as deliberately perverse conceptions of human experience.[18]

For all his ostentatious hostility toward Aristotle, Bacon owed a lot to him; it was "from Aristotle, and from Plato too," that "Bacon acquired the opinion that the tasks of politics are occupations appropriate to a philosopher." Even his "congenitally expansive tastes," "his always living beyond what persons with natures less lavish than his considered more than adequate means" can be traced to his acceptance of "Aristotle's contention that the fully virtuous citizen will have within his magnanimous disposal the products of husbandmen, mechanics, artists, and scientists." In fact, he "first admired and later envied the Stagirite [Aristotle] for his having at his disposal, while relatively a young man and tutor of Alexander at the court of Macedon, a host of helpers in collecting data suitable for natural histories."[19]

Bacon seemed to resent Aristotle largely because his lifelong search for support for his own naturalistic endeavors was met with indifference at the royal courts, the churches, and the halls of Cambridge. He blamed the predominance of Aristotle's philosophy in the schools, churches, and courts of England for this state of affairs. In his early writings, among them the *Advancement of Learning* of 1605, he had taken care not to attack Aristotle for fear it might alienate "a learned sovereign and the learned subjects in Court, church, and the universities." However, when his self-restraining was not rewarded with "royal or other support for his instauration" Bacon decided to be more open in his attack on all received systems and, especially, Aristotle. In his famous and influential *New Organon,* published in 1620 when he was a very ripe sixty years old, Bacon attacks all received systems or precedent human self-and-world representations as "errors" or "phantoms" and names Aristotle their "evil begetter."[20]

In his theory of idols, Bacon identifies "four classes of idols which beset man's minds"—"for distinctions sake"—"calling the first class *Idols of the Tribe;* the second, *Idols of the Cave;* the third, *Idols of the Market-Place;* the fourth, *Idols of the Theater.*" He suggests that these idols or perversities by "which the mind is occupied are either adventitious or innate." "Innate" idols consist of idols of the Cave (which are rooted in individual human nature) and idols of the Tribe (which arise from the "false assertion that the sense of man is the measure of all things"; that is, from Western humanism). "Adventitious" idols also consist of two classes of idols, the first of which he terms idols of the Market Place and view as created through the "commerce and consort of men." He labels the second "Idols of the Theater" and conceives it as created through intellectual rationalizations and systematizations of commonsensical or vulgar human notions.[21]

"The most troublesome idols of all," Bacon believes, are those "which have crept into the understanding through the alliances of words and names." These are idols of the Market Place:

formed by the intercourse and association of men with each other.
. . . For it is by discourse that men associate, and words are imposed
according to the apprehension of the vulgar. And therefore the ill and
unfit choice of words wonderfully obstructs the understanding. . . .
Words plainly force and overrule the understanding and throw all into
confusion, and lead men away into numberless empty controversies
and idle fancies.[22]

Idols of the theatre are very much like idols of the market-place
in that they are "not innate, nor do they steal into the understanding secretly; but are plainly impressed and received into the mind
from the playbooks of philosophical systems and perverted rules
of demonstration." Idols of the theatre "have immigrated into
men's minds from the various dogmas of philosophies, and also
from the wrong laws of demonstration." Bacon calls such representations "idols of the theater, because in my judgement all the received systems are but so many stage plays, representing worlds of
their own creation after an unreal and scenic fashion." He observes
further that "in the plays of this philosophical theater you may
observe the same thing which is found in the theater of the poets,
that stories invented for the stage are more compact and elegant,
and more as one would wish them to be, than true stories out
of history.[23]

Bacon seems to believe that theatricalizations of human experience in "stories invented for the stage" are more seductive to human beings than "true stories out of history." Indeed, he contrasts
his allegedly "methodical" *"interpretations of Nature"* with the
"rash or premature" "Anticipations of Nature" in other representations of human experience, for example, and sadly concludes that
"for the winning of assent anticipations are far more powerful than
interpretations." This is because:

they straightaway touch the understanding and fill the imagination;
whereas interpretations, on the other hand, being gathered here and
there from various and dispersed facts, cannot suddenly strike the
imagination; and therefore they must needs, in respect of the opinions
of the times, seem harsh and out of tune, as the mysteries of faith do.[24]

Still, because he is already predisposed toward interpretations
Bacon makes these superior to anticipations of nature. He argues
that the latter representations are vulgar because they pander to
mass "assent" and "general opinion" and because "nothing pleases
the many unless it strikes the imagination, or binds the understanding with bands of common notions." In fact, he goes even further

to adopt a polemical, antiplural position that suggests that "if the multitude assent and applaud, men ought immediately to examine themselves as to what blunder or fault they may have committed."[25] Clearly, Bacon is unwilling and/or unable to credit the validity of a position other than his own, which is why his work is ideological in the narrow pejorative sense. The prior predisposition against popular or general representation of human experience seems to be what accounts for the bulk of myopia and bias in his view of human experience.

Ultimately, Bacon's own conceptions of the idols that allegedly beset the human understanding compromise the very means he proposes for overcoming their idolatry, if not exactly ideology. He suggests that while adventitious idols "are hard to eradicate" innate idols "cannot be eradicated at all." In the case of innate idols, therefore, the "inductive method" he borrows from none other than Aristotle and institutes as the most viable or effective means with which, "with a religious care," "to eject, repress, and as it were, exorcise every kind of phantom" is inoperative.[26] Moreover, insofar as he views adventitious idols as systematizations of innate idols, the irrepressible existence of innate idols assures the continuity of adventitious idols. As such, neither class of idols can be eradicated with the inductive method, and, in the final light, the whole project of overcoming idolatry/ideology becomes questionable.

Even Bacon's quest to parallel his career on that of this publicly villified but secretly admired mentor, Aristotle, was not successful; at least not during his lifetime. The ritual parricide by means of which he intended to arm himself with the powers and methods of this ostentatious other, Aristotle, did not achieve its end until after Bacon's death. Thereafter, "a generation was to elapse before scientists, at home and abroad, hailing Bacon as a 'new Aristotle' undertook . . . the collecting of myriad natural histories."[27] In other words, when time and death had healed the parricidal wounds inflicted by Bacon 'the son/successor' on Aristotle the 'father/predecessor' the parallels and affinities between them, nay, their quintessential identity, is revealed. In time and death, the veils of self-differentiation disintegrate and Bacon is revealed as the "new Aristotle" who is also the ritual murderer of the old Aristotle.

The concealment of profound affinity and identity behind the veils of ostentatious difference underlined in Bacon's relationship to Aristotle also characterizes the symbolic relationship between ideology and critiques of ideology. The pacification of a palpably other self or form of representation prior to its consumption and concealed emulation is indeed the basic mechanism of self-empowerment in ideologies. "Matter," as Newton's First Law of Thermodynamics has it, "is neither created nor destroyed." The necessity of economy in human existence and representations of experience ensures that nothing is really created or destroyed. Instead, everything is strategically transformed to fit the new or changed circumstances.

Karl Marx's Theory of Ideology and the Field of Problems it Delimits for Subsequent Critiques of Ideology

> The ugly is the form things assume when we view them with the will to implant a meaning, a new meaning into what has become meaningless.
>
> —Nietzsche

> Ideology is the name critique gives to a system of representation it intends to displace.
>
> —Anonymous

By Karl Mannheim's account, "the modern conception [of ideology] was born when Napoleon, finding . . . his imperial ambitions [opposed by the eighteenth-century French *philosophes*], . . . contemptuously labelled them 'ideologists.' Thereby the word took on a derogatory meaning which . . . it has retained to the present-day." He goes on to suggest that "during the nineteenth century the term ideology," used to deny the "validity of the adversary's thought because it is regarded as unrealistic . . . gained wide currency."[28] Karl Marx's narrow pejorative conception of ideology, I believe, belongs to this nineteenth-century tradition. With Marx, the field of ideology is narrowed even further to apply almost exclusively to the ideas of a mythical "ruling class" whose interests and representations are opposed to that of the equally mythical working class. Marx championed the latter class, and this prior investment underlies his view of what forms are true and false representations of human experience. Plainly stated, Marx's theory of ideology proceeds from a prior predisposition toward the mythical working class.

Marx's affinity for the masses contrasts with Bacon's more elitist sympathies, but the defining elements of the latter's rejection of other forms of representing human experience as idols can be found in Marx's critique of ideology. In fact, Marx considered Bacon "the first theorizer of vulgar materialism and the 'real founder of all modern experimental science.'" Ralph Ley also locates Marx's inheritance of Bacon's general hostility to scholasticism in the "claim that *theoretical* knowledge has to prove itself by 'fruits and works.'" At least, such a propensity underwrites Marx's "Theses on Feuerbach" (1845), a work Engels calls a "brilliant germ of the new world outlook." In this work, Marx proclaims that "the dispute over the reality or non-reality of thinking which is isolated from practice is a purely *scholastic* question." In the oft-quoted eleventh thesis, moreover, Marx insists that before him "the philosophers have only *interpreted* the world, in various ways; the point, however, is to *change* it." For Marx, the "historical" or "scientific materialism" he espouses is the only form of representation suited for this crucial project of change.[29]

The theory of ideology Marx propounds in the *German Ideology* (1845) serves a larger project of overcoming the so-called alienation of the postcapitalist Western self-and-world. To quote Robert Tucker, Marx viewed human "history, particularly under modern capitalism" as "a story of man's alienation in his life as producer" and his overriding desire was to restore "Man" to himself, a project he believed could only be accomplished in a state of "communism." Communism, Tucker writes, is "presented as the final transcendence of alienation via a revolution against private property." Marx himself sees communism as:

> the *positive* transcendence of *private property*, or *human self-estrangement* and therefore as the real *appropriation of the human* essence by and for man; communism therefore is the return of man to himself as a *social* (i.e., human) being—a return become conscious, and accomplished within the entire wealth of previous developments.[30]

For Marx, there is a basic relationship between human thought and the forms of social-material life; as he puts it:

> The ideas of the ruling class are in every epoch the ruling ideas: i.e., the class which is the ruling *material* force of society, is at the same time its ruling *intellectual* force. The class which has the means of material production at its disposal, has control at the same time over the means of mental production, so that thereby, generally speaking, the ideas of those who lack the means of mental production are subject to it.[31]

Marx conceives his championed working class as an undifferentiated or nonconflictive totality, as opposed to the ruling class which
is split into two sub-classes of actors and thinkers. He submits that
the division of labour of "classical economics"

> manifests itself also in the ruling class as the division of mental and
> material labour, so that inside this class one part appears as the think-
> ers of the class (its active, conceptive ideologists, who make the per-
> fecting of the illusion of the class about itself their chief source of
> livelihood), while the others' attitude to these ideas and illusions is
> more passive and receptive.

This internal "cleavage can develop into a certain opposition and
hostility between [its] two parts," but any such schism "automatically comes to nothing" as soon as this "class itself is endangered."
Faced with an outside challenge, the ruling class conceals the internal rift within itself, but the dire consequence is that "the sem-
blance that the ruling ideas were not the ideas of the ruling class
and had a power distinct from the power of this class" "vanishes."
In other words, the defensive front of unity this class erects to
protect itself is precisely what betrays the parochial character of
its ideas. The moment of critique and contestation therefore dis-
closes the presence of ideology; or, as Habermas has been quoted
to say, "ideology is a product of the critique of ideologies."[32]
Ironically, Marx's conception of the ruling class as two groups
that become one in times of crisis makes this class more dynamic
and more resistant to the challenges posed by other classes. In
Marx's words, "the individuals composing the ruling class possess
among other things consciousness and therefore think." The unspoken conclusion is that, precisely because it is said to be an
undifferentiated mass, the working class lacks "its active, concep-
tive ideologists, who make the perfecting of the illusion of the class
about itself their chief source of livelihood." Without this capacity
for self-representation, this class can neither be aware of itself and
its interests nor be the vanguard of its own revolution. Therefore,
it is no wonder that in orthodox Marxism members of the ruling
class are expected to commit "class suicide" and become the vanguard of the working-class revolution. Marx's own self-
appointment as chief spokesman for this class is perhaps another
sign of this lack of its own thinkers.
Marx's commitment to the working class makes him shrink from
pushing his own arguments to their logical ends, especially where

they might jeopardize the interests of this class. For instance, he claims that:

> each new class which puts itself in the place of one ruling before it, is compelled, merely in order to carry through its aim, to represent its interest as the common interest of all the members of society, that is, expressed in ideal form: it has to give its ideas the form of universality, and represent them as the only rational, universally valid, ones. The class making a revolution appears from the very start, if only because it is opposed to a class, not as a class but the representative of the whole of society; it appears as the whole mass of society confronting the one ruling class.

"Appears" is obviously the keyword in the foregoing quotation; the "class making a revolution" pretends that its parochial interests are universal or, at least, representative of the context "merely in order" to win the support of other classes and "to carry through its aim."[33]

The pretense to universality, or at least cross-sectionality, seems to be a necessary feature of representations of human experience, if Antonio Gramsci's arguments in his *Prison Notebooks* are anything to go by. He suggests that:

> Every philosopher is, and cannot but be, convinced that he expresses the unity of the human spirit, that is, the unity of history and nature. Indeed, if such a conviction did not exist, men would not act, they would not create new history, philosophies would not become ideologies and would not in practice assume the fanatical granite compactness of the "popular beliefs" which assume the same energy as "material forces."[34]

Hans Barth suggests in *Truth and Ideology* that "were one to treat" Marx's idea "of the self-restoration of man in a classless society . . . in the same way as Marx treated the political and philosophical ideologies of feudal and bourgeois society, . . . the ideology of the proletariat, too, would have to be unmasked as the interest-conditioned ideology of a single class." Marx attempts to dodge this logical end of his argument by counter-proposing that "every new class . . . achieves its hegemony only on a broader basis than that of the class ruling previously." As such, the procession of parochial self-and-world representations ("ideologies" in his terminology) "comes to a *natural end* . . . as soon as class rule in general ceases to be the form in which society is organised." Naturally, the working-class revolution is for Marx the event that brings class rule to an end. He expects that in the communist state instituted after this revolution "*the* idea" of "*Man,* . . . [as] concept developing in history" will overcome its proliferation as "various ideas."[35]

After the successful revolution against private property, Marx believes, the "working class" becomes the ruling material and intellectual force in society; it represents the Highest Good simply because it is the largest group in society. In the interest of the working class, Marx makes scapegoats of the ruling class by projecting sin, error, and falsity into it. He routinely excludes this demonized class from active participation in the working-class utopia. Over and above this, his division of Western capitalist society into two mutually exclusive and essentially conflictive classes is undesirable. Parts and segments of human-phenomenal existence are not as categorically defined or as exclusive as he makes them out to be; there are always overlaps and included middles. Gramsci is right to observe that on the level of their "implicit assumptions" and "common sense" notions the members of working class may be the best champions of dominant/ruling-class ideas. In a world of opinion polls in which what pleases the masses is what is most valuable and/or relevant common-sensical or popular notions are in fact ruling ideas: "The question is, will it play in Peoria?" In such a case, working-class consumption of ruling-class ideas is not at all "false consciousness," as Marx claims, but rather a profound awareness of their best interests.

In the *Prison Notebooks,* Gramsci argues that the "common sense" ideas of the working class constitutes a "popular philosophy which is only a fragmentary collection of ideas and opinions." The term *ideology* can be applied to these notions only "on condition that the word is used in its highest sense of a conception of the world that is implicitly manifest in art, in law, in economic activity and in all manifestations of individual and collective life." Pared of its "bestial and elemental passions" and "instinctive and violent impulses," and thereby left with only elements that are "conscious," "critical," and of "good sense," spontaneous or popular philosophy can become the "healthy nucleus" of a "more unitary and coherent . . . philosophy of praxis."[36]

For Gramsci, the "philosophy of the intellectuals" is high thought as opposed to the low one of "common sense" or "popular philosophy." The critique of this high philosophy of the intellectuals, he suggests, is the proper concern of the philosophy of praxis. Such a critique is:

not a question of introducing from scratch a scientific form of thought into everyone's individual life, but renovating and making "critical" an already existing activity. It must be a criticism of the philosophy of the intellectuals out of which the history of philosophy developed and which . . . can be considered as marking the "high points" of the progress made by common sense, or at least the common sense of the more educated strata of society but through them also of the people.

There is, therefore, a linear-historicist relationship between high and low representation, and this "relation between common sense and the upper level of philosophy is assured by 'politics.'" In "the philosophy of praxis," the intellectual, the primary agent of politics; "does not tend to leave the 'simple' in their primitive philosophy of common sense, but rather to lead them to a higher conception of life."[37]

For Gramsci, "philosophy in general does not in fact exist. Various philosophies or conceptions of the world exist, and one always makes a choice between them." This choice is made from the standpoint of "real activity," because *all action is political*" and because "the real philosophy of each man is contained in its entirety in his political action." Thus, the "contrast between thought and action, i.e., the coexistence of two conceptions of the world, one affirmed in words and the other displayed in effective action, is simply a product of self-deception." Gramsci views the question of the reality and/or unreality of different forms and systems of representation as a context-historical one and suggests that the disclosure of the existence of "various conceptions of the world" (that is, of potentially conflictive ideologies) occurs only at points of crisis or "abnormality" in a given context. These, he writes, are "the exceptional (and hence potentially revolutionary) moments in history in which a class or group discovers its objective and subjective unity in action." At this same moment, the "submission and intellectual subordination" of nondominant groups is also revealed.[38]

Gramsci and Louis Althusser are common figures of departure in post-Marxist and/or cultural materialist critiques of ideology such as those collected as *On Ideology* by the Centre for Contemporary Cultural Studies. These essays, the editors of this collection suggest, attempt to weaken considerably the "iron laws of determinism" that underwrite Marx's conception of the relationship between the economic "base" and the noneconomic "superstructures" of modern (Western capitalist) society. The basic assumption they make is that Marx "fails to account for qualitative—if not logical—differences between the different contexts and forms of ideas and practices." In the light of viewing as "axiomatic the close, if not causal, relation between ideas, institutions, and societal context," the essays in *On Ideology* conclude that the "natures of the two concepts—ideology and culture—[are] not the kind to demand a theoretical choice between them." Culture in such a framework is constituted by "diverse elements which cross different theoretical terrains only one of which is that of a theory of ideology." By means of a "more specific analysis of some areas of culture, the collected essays attempt to reach "a deeper knowledge than is at present available."[39]

Culture is, in my view, as much a subset of ideology as ideology is a subuniverse of culture; culture is a body of choices and practices legitimated by ideology; culture and ideology, both, make things not only thinkable (as opposed to being unthinkable or taboo) but also eminently "do-able." Both mark some things as values ("dos") in contrast to others that are taboos ("don'ts") and make their doing not only felicitous but also necessary. In the name of such cultural and ideological imperatives, coercion and group pressure are brought to bear on the deviant individual or group. At best, both culture and ideology make things easier to do by investing their doing with divine metaphysical and/or atavisic comforts.

Ideology is an activity that exists under the umbrella of culture and yet can form and conform to it. Ideology is a means of rationalizing and organizing either the paramount ideas, values, norms, and conventions within a given culture or merely those that pertain to parts or decoupled spheres of activity within that culture. The operation of ideology does not always reflect empirical or tangible necessity. Different cultures (as it will soon appear) appeal to different forms of ideological justification and persuasion and coercion. By extension, ideology is eminently plural and metaphorical in its forms and modes of operation. This is perhaps why many Western empiricists and rationalists who want univocal and taxidermic simplicity in representations of human experience find it perverse. Yet in their own writings and utterances these univocalists do not necessarily escape the far-ranging clutches of ideology.

In the wake of growing recognition of the infelicity of the Marxist conception of ideology, some Western critiques have proposed symbolic and metaphoric approaches to the concept *and* phenomenon. Because they allow a more comprehensive and multicontextual perspective, such approaches are germane to the basic perspectivism of the present work. The first example of such

symbolic-metaphorical descriptions of ideology is Clifford
Geertz's "Ideology as a Cultural System." In this work, Geertz
conceives ideology as a feature of human existence that underlines
the fact that:

> The tool making, laughing, or lying animal, man, is also *the incom-
> plete—or more accurately the self-completing animal.* The agent of
> his own self-realization, he creates out of his general capacity for the
> construction of symbolic models the specific capabilities that define
> him. Or . . . it is through ideologies, schematic orders of social order,
> that man makes himself for better or worse a political animal.[40]

In a similar vein, Joseph Campbell writes that "it is now a com-
monplace of biological thought to observe that man, in his character as animal, is born at least a year too soon, completing in the
sphere of society a development that other species accomplish in
the womb." "Man's capacity for play animates his urge to fashion
images and organize forms in such a way as to create new stimuli
for himself." Other "animals are without speech . . . [and] without
art" because of their "inability to play with forms."[41] It would seem
that Aristotle's conception of mimesis in chapter 4 of the *Poetics*
as the basic representation whose operational variations result in
forms as diverse as mythology, ritual, art, metaphysics, religion,
and science had anticipated both Geertz and Campbell's position
by many centuries.

In Geertz's cultural-symbolic framework, "the function of ideology is to make an autonomous politics possible by providing the
authoritative concepts that render it meaningful, the suasive images by means of which it can be sensibly grasped." Over and
above politics in the narrow sense, ideology weaves "an intricate
structure of interrelated meanings—interrelated in terms of the
semantic mechanisms that formulate them." "A template
or blueprint for the organization of social and psychological processes," ideology conceptualizes and organizes variegated desires,
choices, and actions of diverse peoples and groups into a coherent
system of self-and-world representations. Ideology is quintessentially metaphorical, if not a metaphor in and of itself, and metaphor,
Geertz writes, is "the power where language, even with a small
vocabulary, manages to embrace a multi-million things." The struggle to unify diverse terms and to create unity-in-diversity seems to
define and link ideology and metaphor. "In metaphor one has, of
course, a stratification of meaning, in which an incongruity of sense
on one level produces an influx of significance on another."

The power of metaphor derives precisely from the interplay between the discordant meanings it symbolically coerces into a unitary conceptual framework and from the degree to which that coercion is successful in overcoming the psychic resistance such semantic tension inevitably generates in anyone in a position to perceive it.[42]

In Paul Ricoeur's metaphoric-symbolic approach as espoused in his *Lectures on Ideology and Utopia,* ideology is a form that creates representations greater than the sum of its parts. The very necessity of ideology lies in the fact that "the belief of the ruled must contribute more than is rationally warranted by the claim of the governing authority." Ideology creates "surplus values" that "provide the needed supplement to belief that will fill [the] gap" between authority claims and their acceptance. It "compensate[s] for [any] discrepancy" between hegemonic claims and belief in them. As such, it needs to be conceived in terms that are "more radical than the distorting, dissimulating function." Ricoeur, therefore, proposes to "set aside" views of "the concept . . . as opposed to science and return to what may be the most primitive concept of ideology, that opposed to praxis." His opposition of ideology to praxis is still unfortunate because ideology is equally directed toward praxis and theory. Besides, necessary as they might be to human thinking, any categorical distinctions between theory and practice distort the complex relations between these constitutive forms of human experience.[43]

In Ricoeur's approach to ideology, George Taylor suggests:

All social action is already symbolically mediated, and it is ideology that plays this role in the social realm. . . . It is, in fact, only on the basis of ideology's integrative function that its legitimative and distortive function may appear. "Only because the structure of human social life is already symbolic can it be distorted" (Lecture 1). Distortion would not be possible without this prior symbolic function. Ideology becomes distortive at the point "when the integrative function becomes frozen . . . when schematization and rationalization prevail."[44]

As such, ideology is not intrinsically wrong; it only appears so when its metaphorical reconciliations of constitutive opposites in human experience are outstripped by circumstances of time and place. As soon as it is unable to comprehend, assimilate, and satisfy the new desires and needs in its referent lifeworld ideology appears false and distortive, losing its authority and persuasive force. Incidentally, a similar eventuality attends human and superhuman figures (heroes, rulers, and gods) who often serve as the sources of power and meaning in human cultures.

Ideology Beyond the Boundaries of Western Thought: The Affinity of Ideology, Magic, and Charismatic Mythmaking

Ideologies undersee symbolic and metaphoric reconciliations of constitutive opposites into an effective-affective body of representations.
—Anonymous

The foregoing discussion on ideology has necessarily been limited to *written* Western critiques, but I do not share the prejudicial belief of some Western writers that the *concept* applies only to predominantly literate (as against oral) Western societies. On the contrary, I believe that insofar as ideology is concerned with the justification of otherwise arbitrary human choices and actions, it can, and does, obtain in any human culture. This is why I extend my discussion to cover the question of "charisma" and "charismatic leadership" in a primarily oral non-Western society. In investigating the role of Okomfo Anokye and Osei Tutu in Asante folkloric history, my aim is to demonstrate that ideology does not necessarily have to be written or based in empirical facts.[45]

In *Ashanti Law and Constitution*, Robert S. Rattray calls Okomfo Anokye the "maker of modern Ashanti," and the text of one Asante libation-incantation seems to support this view: "Komfo Anotche . . . made the Ashanti nation, and he made many laws for us [chiefs; rulers] that we might rule the people."[46] In reality, Anokye was the spiritual/magical part of a duo of actors credited with transforming the Asantes from a disparate band of "clans" into a mighty nation. Osei Tutu was the material or 'political' double of Anokye, the ruler/warlord with whom the priest/medium teamed up and, thereby (to us Gramsci's words), united the nature of that self-and-world with its history.

Anokye is said to have effected the political "amalgamation of the other clans . . . under Osai Tutu" "by means of his medicines." By "medicines," the Asante primarily means "magic" or "sorcery," and magic is, indeed what underwrote the ethico-political and cultural representations Anokye crystallized around his charismatic friend, Osei Tutu. However, "medicine" also connotes intimate knowledge of the forces of nature and culture; it implies an understanding of the animate and inanimate surroundings of the human

animal. Okomfo Anokye appears to have been a great statesman
and law maker: "Sir Francis Fuller, a former British Chief Commis-
sioner of Ashanti," calls him "'the Cardinal Wolsey' of Ashanti."
Rattray himself applauds the "genius of Komfo Anotche in concili-
ating captured enemies, and giving them important positions near
the King." In doing this, Anokye shows his awareness of the *Real-
politikal* fact that naturalized or assimilated others tend to be more
loyal than natural-born citizens precisely because their loyalties
are always in question. Still, not one to leave anything to chance,
Anokye also compelled every member of the Asante nation to take
the "Great Oaths" or *Ntam Kese,* oaths broken at the very cost of
one's life.[47]

The most common response Rattray received to his enquiries
about the origin of the intricate body of laws and customs with
which the Asantes governed themselves was: "'We do not know;
Komfo Anotche made this a law.'" In his view, it is:

> highly improbable that Anotche was the originator of any of these
> rules. What he probably did was to establish, by edict, long-existing
> customs which were possibly already beginning to disappear. In any
> case, we may be assured, by the success which attended his efforts as
> a legislator, that his utterances and codes of conduct were based upon
> a profound knowledge of the past of the scattered tribes, whom by his
> genius he welded into a nation.[48]

To all intents and purposes, Anokye did not only construct and
interweave Asante past and present, but also predicted its future.
He is said to have "foretold that when an Ashanti King should
break his laws, the red man would come and take the Ashanti
people, and this prophecy is also fulfilled."[49] The "red man" is, of
course, the white colonizer whose arrival on the African continent
signalled the beginning of the destruction of its autochthonous cultures. Whether or not Anokye uttered all these predictions and/or
performed these sublime acts of reconciliation is immaterial. Did
Methuselah live for nine hundred years? Did Jesus Christ really
ascend into heaven? What matters is that to the Asante being who
constructed his or her life-defining choices and actions in those
terms Anokye was the central I, Eye, and Aye of his or her self-
and-world representation. What matters is that as the central figure
or fountainhead of ideology, Anokye made and kept the disparate
ethnic groups within the Asante self-and-world one.

The most effective act Anokye performed was to conjure the
"Golden Stool" *(Sika 'Gua)* out of the sky (high heavens). This
stool was generally considered "the shrine and symbol of the

[Asante] national soul." Even the invading British imperial forces believed enough in the symbolic-unitive force of this stool to expend countless human lives on trying to capture it. They seemed to believe that without it they would not be able to break the back and spirit of Asante resistance. To the Asantes themselves, the Golden Stool was so complete a symbol of their essence and unity that "the supposed desecration or destruction of" this stool at one point in time threw "the Ashanti people into national mourning." On another occasion, to stem fears that the triumphant British might demand the Golden Stool to sit on, an Asante Queen Mother ("Amma Sewa Akoto") had a "Silver Stool" sent to "H.R.H. the Princess Mary, Viscountess Lascelles, on the occasion of her wedding." In the letter that accompanied this preemptive gift, the Queen Mother writes that:

> It may be that the [English] King's child has heard of the Golden Stool of Ashanti. That is the stool which contains the soul of the Ashanti nation. All we women of Ashanti thank the Governor exceedingly because he has declared to us that the English will never again ask us to hand over that stool.
> This stool ["Silver Stool"] we give gladly. It does not contain our soul as our Golden Stool does.[50]

Theatre and magic, both performative in essence, were the means by which Anokye accomplished his ultimate symbolic feat of unifying the multiethnic Asante self-and-world into a mythical-symbolic whole. Before a gathering of heads of the five major clans of Asante and their allies, he is said to have conjured the communal spirit of the new Asante nation out of the skies, captured it, and placed it at the centre or core of a stool made specifically for the occasion. Beside this collective Asante essence, Anokye placed the heart of Ntim Gyakari, King of the Denkyiras, and greatly feared other of the Asante self. In his palpably majestic otherness, Ntim Gyakari demonstrated the essential incompleteness of the Asante self; he and the imperial nation he headed were what had to be consumed to make this self complete and whole. In more material terms as a foe and bitter rival, Denkyira needed to be pacified in order to preserve the safety of the Asante self.

The terms in which Rattray recounts Anokye's crowning symbolic act do great service for the ritualistic-metaphorical description of ideology offered at the end of this chapter. These symbolic interpretations are placed in parentheses in the following quotation.

A log [a single origin] was cut into two [dual division or 'doubling' of origins]; that part which had grown nearest to the roots [earth/low; material-political] was made into a Stool for Osai Tutu, the other half [sky/high; spiritual or transcendental] into a Stool for Komfo Anotche. . . . After the Stools had been carved, Anotche became possessed and danced [the body; dance-theatre; nonverbal representations]. Something descended from the sky [the communal-collective 'spirit' of Asante nation] which Okomfo Anotche caught. This, and the heart of Ntim Gyakari [the mythical feared-yet-desired Other], which had become ashes [now pacified and assimilated into the Self, thereby augmenting its own force], we put into the central part of the Stool.[51]

Obviously, the symbolic-metaphorical integration of the outwardly conflictive elements of the Asante self-and-world is the empowering act accomplished in both the carving and investing of the Golden Stool. Perhaps the most important of these acts is the symbolic sympathetic-magical merging of the communal spirit of Asante self with the essence of its most dreaded-yet-desired other, Ntim Gyakari. As king or 'dominant I' of Denkyira, (the national opponent of Asante), Ntim Gyakari represents its essential force. To be as total or absolute as possible, the Asante nation had to comprehend (embrace and consume) this national other as well as its chief representative. Indeed, it seems that to be empowered and empowering the acts and concepts that facilitate human existence must be or pretend to be relevant to both the self and the other. Thus, the empowered Asante national self is one that has comprehended (understood, embraced, and consumed) the essence of its mythical other self-and-world, people and nation.

The legitimacy and authority of the symbolic or sublime reconciliations Anokye makes between Asante nature/essence and its history/material lies in the force of "his medicines" and/or magic. Furthermore, he uses dance and theatre, two forms of representation often said to be predominant in oral or primitive societies, to cement his claims and actions. One might say, therefore, that the bases of legitimation for Anokye's claims are as appropriate to his primarily oral, magical-realist context as Bacon's appeals to inductive reasoning and natural history (but in the name of God and Divine Revelation) are to his early capitalist world. Similarly, Marx's appeals to science and materialism seems to carry the appropriate, persuasive weight in his late capitalist context.

The Agonistic Description of Ideology

What redeems the illusions of ideology is their allusions to desired ends

—Anonymous

The fundamental human need to invest choices and acts with pre-ontological and metaphysical value is the point of departure for the pluralistic framework on ideology described in this section. Such an approach shares Martin Seliger's view that ideology "covers a set of ideas by which men posit, explain and justify ends and means of organized social action, and specifically political action, irrespective of whether such action aims to preserve, amend, uproot or build a given order." In his view, ideology "has always denoted sets of attitudes and ways of behaviour which can be observed in the real world"; it is "action-oriented thought."[52] However, the attunement to reality and action in ideologies does not necessarily make them political in the narrow sense; neither does it make empirical and tangible ends the ultimate proofs of their legitimacy. The notions that most empower ideologies (such as Good, True, Just) are often intangible and circular; they are also often nostalgical-atavistic in that they are traced to old parchments and to the utterances of such celebrated figures of original choices and actions as heroes and gods.

Ideologies transmute their temporality and parochiality into a more effective and affective universality by pretending to unite the nature and history of their referent self-and-world. This has been demonstrated in the works of Marx and Gramsci. Gramsci's explanation of this necessity, worth recalling here, is that if representations did not pretend to unite human "history and nature" "men would not act, they would not create new history, philosophies would not become ideologies." Obviously, the need for action is what makes philosophies ideologies; action concretizes human thought, often at the cost of transgressing and compromising ideal-metaphysical boundaries and values. Because it rationalizes plural, often conflictive, terms of human experience, ideology bridges and breaches the distances between outwardly or empirically opposed terms. This is why it is best understood metaphorically and ritualistically.

The view of ideology in Western Enlightenment critiques as false knowledge or consciousness, in polemical opposition to an allegedly true philosophy or science, conceals the profound similarities between them. The demonstrable relationship between ideology and philosophy, if any such distinction is at all valid, is one in which outward hostility is belied by veiled or concealed cooperation. At the point of emergence of the narrow pejorative manifestation of ideology, two simultaneous acts take place. In the first, diseased parts of an old worn-out body of representations are demonized as ideology or false consciousness; in the second movement, unfalsified parts of this body are gathered and formed into the nucleus of a new body of suasive and authoritative concepts and images. This ritual-act of self-division, self-differentiation, and partial recuperation of ruins and dregs is, indeed, the fundamental motion and emotion of ideology. The connection between ideology and the critique of ideology also lies in this ritualistic-symbolic act.

Habermas' claim that "ideology is the product of the critique of ideologies" can be framed in the perspective of the relationship between philosophy and ideology to mean that "ideology is the product of the timely and/or untimely critique of pathologized or demonized philosophies." Philosophy here is merely the name given to self-and-world representations *before* they lose credibility and belief, and ideology are these representations *after* this fact. Ideology, in yet another light, could be the name given to a form or system of representation with the view to deconstructing and displacing it. But, insofar as they conceive and represent the world in ways that serve the implicit or explicit interests of some select subjects or groups, critiques of ideology are themselves ideologies. Approached comprehensively and relationally, therefore, there is no real or strict distinction between ideology and critique. However, heuristic needs and/or the limitations of human thinking might require the preservation of such a distinction.

Ideology can be conserving as well as transforming of representations of human experience, depending on whether or not the particular utterance or claim seeks to support or contest dominant or subordinate interests in the referent lifeworld. The same goes for critique. Both ideology and critique can be "ideological" and "utopian" in the senses defined by Mannheim in *Ideology and Utopia*.[53] Ideology and utopia are merely two sides of the same Janus-faced phenomenon; one face or phase supports the status quo while the other attacks it. The ideological attitude stresses integration and cohesion, which is not to say that it is incapable of supporting a disintegrative and sundering function.

The "utopian" tendency in ideology and critique supports and valorizes restless, skeptical critique, but this is not to say that such a tendency cannot support stability and fixity. In fact, the fixity sought by utopian forms of ideology tends to be more nostalgic and atavistic than those sought in openly integrative tendencies. The best example of the utopian extreme of ideology is perhaps Marx's critique of ideology, which is marked by a desire to institute both nostalgic communism and populism. On the whole, the utopian tendency in ideology tends to paint present states of existence in the worst possible light so as to reach toward a future state of being that is more often than not a paradoxical return to a nostalgic past.

Generally, the assumptions one makes about human experience, and especially one's attitude to prevalent social-existential circumstances, greatly influence the kind of ideology and critique one practices and endorses. Some find the narrow pejorative view of ideology too mistrustful and limiting, while others regard the integrative and cohesive view of ideology as too naive and untroubled by the power principle.[54] While one position may be more permissive and comprehensive than the other, neither the integrative nor the disintegrative tendency is right or complete in itself. Taken together, these contrary tendencies give a fuller picture of the quests and questions of ideology and its double, critique. Both of them can serve a parochial will to power; each one presents a perspective on human experience that is tied to the implicit or explicit interests it advocates and the brave new world it seeks to institute.

At points of crises in any society or culture, the adherents of an embattled body of representations are forced to defend it, to argue that it represents the best interests in and of that self-and-world. They paint those who seek to change those representations as irresponsible saboteurs and extremists. On the other hand, the advocates of change dismiss the embattled order and its body of representations as false, parochial, if not downright oppressive. The simple truth underlined by these vociferous claims and counterclaims is that at critical points in human existence the regnant forms and systems of representation begin to fail and are challenged by another or other forms that often carry the banner of critique and change. Naturally, the regnant ideologies mount their own defense and when the dust clears the old order's forms have either been restored or been torn apart by triumphant critique.

But even where the latter scenario obtains, some parts of the old or torn system that are still considered powerful and acceptable parts can be recuperated and used to create a new body of images and concepts. The new images and representations are said to better fit the changed and changing circumstances. Incidently, this process of dismemberment or disembodiment, followed by restoration and transfiguration into transcendental symbols and fountainheads of ideology is the primary act in the agonistics or body-histories of such ritual-religious and mythological figures as Dionysos, Jesus Christ, Anokye, and the Yoruba Ogun. These figures were all initially killed or torn apart only to later become original actors and cores of powerful self-and-world representations.

The ultimate view of ideology in this work is as an agonistic or dialectical phenomenon articulated between two polar extremes that are, in fact, rubrics for plural terms and possibilities. The first constitutive pole of ideology is the focal point of a collection of allegedly fixed or eternal essences. I term this the locus of "morality" because there human ideas, actions, or phenomena that are deemed complete and perfect, or as close as possible to completion and perfection, are gathered together. The realm of morality is therefore not unlike the realm of socratic-platonic "ideal-forms" from which all phenomenal things were said to originate. Compared to this realm, phenomena are mere appearance, and desirable or not, the fulfillment of human desire and the self through the pursuit of right or good action needs and/or presupposes such ontological-teleological and metaphysical fixities.

In the constitutive sphere of morality, present-contingent or arbitrary choices and actions are invested with notions of pleasurability, meaningfulness, goodness, rightness, truth, and so on. Here human choices and actions become infused with metaphysical-transcendental comforts and putatively lasting values by means of circular appeals to and identifications with such celebrated a prioris as God/Divinity, the Ancestors, the Founding Fathers, and so on. In a post-Enlightenment context appeals to such humanist concepts as Rationality, Universality, Freedom, Democracy, Liberty, and Equality might be what invest human choices and actions with moral comfort and value.

In phenomenal life, beginnings often explain and justify destinations and the arc described by such teleological motions give life the appearance of completion and fulfillment. Morality is the primary means of originating and completing human desire, of closing the circle of existence; it defines the ideal ends or the nostalgic pasts toward which human actions are eternally directed. Of course, these ideal-metaphysical objectives are never quite reached, but no moralist or ideologist worth his or her salt would admit this fact. For the sake of life, which is best manifest as action, human beings will pretend that their ends are reachable and that the particular form of representation they employ is the best means of reaching universally correct and absolute moral ends. Marx's "communism" is a state of morality in the wake of whose coming all human division and alienation comes to an end and humanity recuperates its wholistic or totalistic past. The same desire or assumption underlies most of the searches for social-cultural future-pasts and past-futures in the works of the writers discussed in this book.

Moral systems are often systems of economy to the extent that they legitimize and limit the form and range of human expenditure. Notions of right and wrong, possible and impossible, and so on, in moralities are means of conserving total human effort by placing limits on wasteful experimentation and restless trial and error. The economic thrust in morality is evident in Nietzsche's description, in the *Antichrist,* of the creation and institution of "immortal Law" in human cultures. He writes that:

> At a certain point in the development of a people, . . . the [stratum] which sees farthest back declares the experience according to which one should live—that is *can* live—to be concluded. . . . Consequently, what must now be prevented above all is further experimentation, a continuation of the fluid state of values, testing, choosing, criticizing values *in infinitum.* Against this a double wall is put up: one, *revelation,* the claim that the reason in these laws is not of human origin, not sought and found slowly and after many errors, but of divine origin, and hence whole, perfect, without history, a gift, a miracle, merely communicated. Then, *tradition,* the claim that the law has existed since time immemorial and that it would be irreverent, a crime against one's forefathers, to raise any doubt against it. The authority is founded on the theses; God *gave* it, the forefathers *lived* it. The higher reason in such a procedure lies in the aim, step by step to push consciousness back from what had been recognized as the right life (that is *proved* right by a tremendous and rigorously filtered experience), so as to attain the perfect automatism of instinct. . . . *To that end, it must be made unconscious:* this is the aim of every holy lie.[55]

Morality, in other words, is a holy lie. Because stability and fixity are crucial preconditions for human choice and action in the phenomenal world, ideological representations often hide the plural possibilities and actualities of human experience behind the reposeful veils of metaphysical fixities. To aptly describe life, however, one must throw aside these protective moral-metaphysical veils to reveal the restive appearances and happenstances beneath them. This is how one reaches the realm of expediency, the sphere of history as opposed to nature or putative essence. Expediency is the pole at which the transcendental truths and ideals and fixities of the human self-and-world are unveiled and shown to be arbitrary and temporal. In the realm of expediency, human actors deliberately alienate or distance themselves from the present self-and-world so as to better see it and work to change it. Changes and revolutions are consciously pursued at the pole of expediency yet the paradoxical aim of such disclosures is to create new purities, ideals, and fixities. For in human terms, there cannot be endless change and revolution.

Changes pursued in the sphere of expediency are precursors to the creation of new stabilities, even if the seekers of change pretend to be the agents of the endless revolution. In phenomenal reality continuity and change are inseparable; change is the beginning of a new continuity, and continuity is only feasible if it allows latent changes and assimilations. Even the almighty Christian God (in the ideological representations of the Christian Bible) recognizes the continuity of old and new representations of human experience. When he dissolved the old world in a flood he replaced it with a new one, and even though he fashioned a New Testament his adherents still looked to the old one. Indeed, both old and new texts or covenants exist in the putatively holy Christian Bible, and either one is invoked as expediency sees fit.

Already internally conflictive because of the coexistence of old and new testaments, the Christian Bible is periodically overwritten and re-formed by texts representing the interests and representations of newer Christian sects. The Book of Mormon, for example, calls itself "Another Testament of Jesus Christ." As a matter of fact, there always was multiplicity with regard to the original central figure of the Christian ideology. The central actor in the representations of the New Testament of the Christian Bible is a symbolic trinity composed of Father, Son, and Holy Spirit, each one of which can manifest itself apart from the others. The Son on earth can cry out his pain to the Father in heaven and the Holy Spirit can come down in the form of a bird to His descended Son.

The bifurcated Bible with its trifurcated actor has been much invoked in the ubiquitous quest for human futures that are in fact recuperations of simple nostalgic pasts. This is perhaps because it promises and predicts a violent Second Coming ("no more water, the fire next time") of Christ the Son, an Armageddonal return that will spell the end of the separation of Heaven (spirit; morality; essence) and Earth (flesh; events; history). In its wake, humanity will for the last time be redeemed from the original Fall from Grace that occurred in the Garden of Eden and become one with divinity. Like Marx's communist state, the postarmageddonal state (St. Augustine's "City of God") is said to be final.

Until these Marxian or Christian utopias are attained, however—if it is at all wise to look forward to such a dead end—humanity must needs be resigned to the essential incompleteness and temporariness of all its self-and-world representations. Until this fateful day, no form of human self-and-world representation could honestly claim to be universal and final and it cannot justify its oppressions of others on any such ground. Until this unwelcome day, the potentially limitless forms of representing human experience (such forms as philosophy, ideology, religion, testament, covenant, history, myth, and so on) must go on jostling and succeeding one another tirelessly and endlessly. For, in phenomenal or sublunar life, in life before the final state of God or of humans with God-like pretensions, the end of ideology must, of necessity, be a long long way away.

2

The Ancient Feud between Philosophy and Poetry, or the Question of Mimesis and Theatre (Tragedy) in the Representation of Ancient Greek Experience

> One of man's distinguishing marks is that he is the most mimetic of all animals, and it is through his mimetic activity that he first begins to learn.
>
> —Aristotle

> Is not the most naïve form of representation mimesis?
> —Jacques Derrida

The disagreement between Socrates/Plato and Aristotle on the nature of mimesis and theatre is ultimately a debate on the fundamental question of what forms are valid, true, or useful representations of the ancient Greek self-and-world. Mihai Spariosu rightly observes that "Plato disguises the power-principle under the transcendental values of Good, Love, and universal Justice" in his arguments against mimesis and theatre in the *Republic*. Similarly, Gerald Else submits that in Socrates/Plato's arguments art is never treated "for itself, [but] always in the multiple context of morals, politics, education and metaphysics." Such an observation is supported by the fact that despite being essentially opposed to art and theatre, Socrates/Plato offer to allow them and readmit their creator-makers into their ideal republic provided someone other than an artist or a poet can prove that these forms are "not only delightful but useful for constitutions." Else suggests that in adopting this functional approach to art and theatre, "Plato" was being "faithful to the traditions of Hellas, for which literature had always been, in one way or another, a public concern. But he was also—no doubt deliberately—behind his time."[1]

The arguments Aristotle makes on behalf of mimesis, art, and theatre in the *Poetics* are generally regarded as counterstatements to Socrates/Plato claims in the *Republic*. His conception of mimesis as the fountain head of all human knowing and being seems to return the concept-phenomenon to a pluralistic or mythopoetical framework that seems contrary to the unitaristic-idealistic-philosophical perspective that underwrites the *Republic*. The present chapter reopens this ancient debate and endorses Aristotle's views over those of Socrates/Plato in order to reach an overview on mimesis and theatre that can comprehend their variegated conceptions by the writers and movements discussed in this book.

In Book Three of the *Republic,* Socrates/Plato conceive mimesis as habitual impersonations and imitations that "settle into habits and . . . become nature if they are continued from early youth, in body voice and mind." They want to control such imitations if only because these contradict Socrates/Plato's belief that "one man could not imitate many things as well as he could one thing." Socrates/Plato insist repeatedly that the essence of the human being is "no more than one," but they also admit that the human soul is "laden with thousands of such contradictions which exist all at once." Still, they are convinced that "the same part of the soul could not possibly hold contrary opinions at the same time about the same things." In line with that conviction, Socrates/Plato reject phenomenality in its entirety because in it "contrary *appearances* are shown at the same time about the same things." "The work of the reasoning part of the soul," which to them is "the best part of the soul," they submit, is to minimize the proliferation of experential and existential forms.[2]

Interestingly, the only evidence Socrates/Plato produce to support their axiomatic claim that the essence or truth of being and phenomena is "no more than one" is taken from Greek mythology. In an obviously paradoxical move, they appropriate the mythological "tale of a mighty man, Er, son of Armenios" to support a rational philosophy that is involved in a struggle to the death with mythology, poetry, and other nonphilosophical representations of human experience. Er's return from the land of the dead and the unborn (where judgments are passed on human "souls" and "punishments and penalties" meted out accordingly) is in itself nothing short of miraculous. The tale he tells implies that human essence and fate/destiny is one and not many. Er describes the weaving of the destinies of human souls about to descend into the sublunar world on a "spindle" "turned on the knees of Necessity" by eight "Sirens." These eight Sirens turn the spindle of Necessity and also turn with it, "singing one sound, one note, so that from all eight there was one concord." "Three daughters of Necessity, the Portioners" of human Fate, named "Lachesis and Clotho and Atropos," sing "to the concord of the Sirens, Lachesis the past, Clotho the present, Atropos what is to come." Human souls about to enter "another cycle of mortal life that leads to death" appear before these daughters of Necessity, pick up "lots, and little models of lives, lying upon the lap of Lachesis," and choose their "own Destiny." This Destiny is a single one and to it they "shall cleave of necessity" when they descend into the sublunar world. Whatever destiny the human soul chooses, and whatever life it lives on earth, "the blame is for the chooser; God is blameless."[3] In this way, God, the source of all essences and chief occupant of the noumenal realm of ideal-forms is freed from responsibility for the uncertainties and unforeseen eventualities of human phenomenal existence.

The well-ordered city or republican utopia in the interest of whose foundation Socrates/Plato make their unitarist arguments in the *Republic* is one in which different spheres of human activity are rigidly separated. There, "we shall find the shoemaker always a shoemaker and not a pilot in addition to his shoemaking, and the farmer always a farmer and not a judge in addition to his farming, and the soldier always a soldier and not a moneymaker in addition to his soldiering, and so forth." This utopia is also joyless in that it sacrifices poetic-artistic beauty to social-political function; it will deny admission to the clever and accomplished poet and instead:

employ the more austere and less pleasing poet and storyteller, for our benefit. He should imitate for us the speech of the good, and should tell his tales on those patterns for which we made our laws at the beginning, when we were trying to educate the soldiers.[4]

"Soldiers" are the "ideal citizens" of Socrates/Plato's well-ordered utopia. They are to be selected from elite social groups, given military training, and kept pure and apart from other segments of the society by not being "allow[ed] to imitate a woman . . . nor . . . slaves whether men or women, doing what slaves do." Neither are they to be permitted to "get into the habit of making themselves like madmen in word or act." The toiling and working groups in this utopian society, as well as their immediate superiors or overseers, are declared unworthy of imitation or emulation by the privileged ideal citizen-soldiers. They are also excluded from meaningful participation in the nucleic activities of the well-ordered city. It is therefore fortunate that this elitist Socratic/Pla-

tonic state is merely "described and founded in words." Socrates
does "not think it exists anywhere on earth," but then again, "it
matters nothing whether it exists anywhere or shall exist." It is
enough for him if "in heaven, perhaps, a pattern of it is indeed laid
up, for him that has eyes to see, and seeing to settle himself
therein."[5]

Socrates/Plato's otherworldly bias makes them view all poetic-
mimetic representations as "three moves away from reality, and,
thus, something easy to make without knowing the truth." They
insist that "poems are appearances and not real," and that poetic
representations are nothing more than "images of virtue and whatever [poets] put in their poems." Such forms "do not lay hold of
truth." A painter can "fashion an apparent cobbler, although he
knows nothing of cobbling himself" and, as such, cannot impart
any useful knowledge about this craft to "his viewers." Similarly,
an artist is merely a maker of images, an imitator of phenomenal
forms that are themselves mere approximations of "ideal forms."
Hence, "the craftsman is on a higher stage than the imitator" or
"maker of the image" who "as we say, knows nothing of the real
thing, but only appearances." His art or "imitation is a kind of
play, not earnest."[6]

To Socrates/Plato, "imitative art is an inferior uniting with an
inferior [part of the soul] and breeding inferior offspring;" it lacks
the reasoning of rational philosophy. The plurality of art makes it
appear too much like ancient Greek mythology, a form of self-
and-world representation Socrates/Plato and other ancient Greek
rationalists reject because of the arbitrary, contradictory, and often
immoral acts of its pantheonic first actors and subjects. By its very
nature, mythology means the contamination of forms and essences
Socrates/Plato would rather have pure and apart. Nonetheless,
they are not altogether blind to the pleasurability of mixed forms.
They agree with Adeimantos that the "mixed style [of representa-
tion] is delightful too," and that it is "much the most delightful to
children and tutors" and to "the world at large." Still, their final
word is that the mixed or pluralistic style of representation "would
not suit our state, because man with us is not twofold or manifold,
since each does only one thing."[7]

Obviously every selection and argument Socrates/Plato make in
the *Republic* is influenced by the quest to establish a well-ordered
city based on the a priori and teleological assumption of the oneness of all forms of human experience. They suppose a one-to-
one correspondence between art and whatever it represents and
demand that all art must be directly productive or purposeful. All

art and representation must serve the constitutional and acculturative needs of their ideal city; they must lead to better health and
government. It is very damning to art, Socrates/Plato believe, that
none "of the poets, ancient or modern, is said to have cured people,
as Asclepios did." Equally damning is the fact that no "city was
ever governed better because of [Homer's descriptions of state-
craft] as Lacedaimon was because of [the practical statemanship
of] Lycurgus."[8] To them, the putative lack of immediate or direct
usefulness makes any form of representation undesirable and
useless.

Since to Socrates/Plato mimesis is inherently perverse, what
their view of theatre as its exemplary form means is that it is
simply the most debased and vulgar form of mimesis. Theatre (or
"dramatic representation") they suggest, is the "poetic imitation"
of "men in action," of men "acting freely or against their will, and
believing themselves to have done well or ill from the action, and
in all this feeling grief or joy." Like Aristotle after them, Socrates/
Plato concentrate their discussion of theatre mainly on tragedy,
which they viewed as its exemplary form. The editors of the *Great
Dialogues* suggest that "Plato often uses 'tragedy' as a general
expression, as we might use drama, or poetry." However, it is also
clear that what they mean by tragedy is a perverse form of theatre
that makes a public display of the "lamentation and brooding" of
a "decent man" or, worse yet, "one of the heroes."[9]

By condescending to make a spectacle of the mournings of a
"decent man" who has "lost a son or something he prized very
well," Socartes/Plato argue, tragedy eschews "deliberation" and
"reasoning" and becomes "unreasoning and idle and the friend of
cowardice." Its primary concern with the representation of turbu-
lent actions is to them unmistakable proof of its vulgarity and de-
basement. Tragedy represents violent people and actions, they
argue, because "the wise and calm character, being nearly always
the same and self-composed, is not easy to imitate, and when imi-
tated is not readily understood, especially by a festival assembly
of all sorts and conditions of men gathered in a theatre."[10]

The tragic poet, Socrates/Plato submit, is "like the painter in
making things which are inferior in point of reality" and "in being
intimate with an inferior part of the soul, not the best part. Thus
we are justified at once in refusing to let him into a city which is
to be ordered well; because he arouses and fosters and strengthens
this part of the soul, and destroys the rational part." Like "the
imitative poet," the tragic poet lacks a sense of measure and bal-
ance; he "establishes an evil constitution in his soul, he gratifies

the unthinking part of it which does not know the difference between greater and less, but believes the same things to be now
great and now small, by imaging images very far away indeed from
the truth."[11]

Socrates/Plato's arguments against mimesis, art, and theatre in
the *Republic* come in the wake of the documented decline of the
ancient Greek tragic stage during the late fifth and early fourth
centuries B.C. This fact is dramatized, comically, in Aristophanes's
play *The Frogs* (c. 405 B.C.) where Dionysus, the central character,
embarks on a journey to Hades to find "a poet who can *write*."
Dionysus calls the contemporary writers of tragedy "insignificant
squeakers and twitterers, like a lot of swallows. A disgrace to their
art."[12] Besides its writing, the acting and performance of tragedy
had also degenerated by the time Socrates/Plato make their arguments in the *Republic*. The ancient Greek histrionic tradition at
this time had fallen to the general level of shameless pandering to
the lowest tastes and the most vulgar elements of the audience.
This is why even the first defender of theatre, Aristotle, is compelled to exclude performance from his list of necessary elements
of theatre and tragedy.

To those ancient Greek rationalists who were ideologically opposed to theatre and to all nonphilosophical representations of
experience, the political consequence of theatre is mob misrule. A
term that has been used to describe this is "theatrocracy," coined
and defined by Socrates/Plato in Book III of the *Laws* as "the
mania of a citizenry intoxicated with complete and varied kinds of
music, licentious in its tastes, complacent in its lawlessness." In
other words, theatre or theatrical representation is seen a perverse
and vulgar form of self-and-world representation. Socrates/Plato's
proclamation of "an ancient feud between philosophy and poetry"
was, therefore, a call to all right-thinking people (rationalists) to
do battle against the mythopoetical plurality and seeming vulgarity
of art and theatre.[13]

Like his former mentors, Socrates/Plato, Aristotle had a nostalgic-functional view of art and theatre. The difference is that Aristotle conceived the functionality of art in ways that were more
indirect than those of Socrates/Plato. The nostalgic-functional view
of art and theatre seems to have been an integral part of the traditions of Hellas. In *The Frogs*, for example, Aristophanes gets both
Aeschylus and Euripides to agree that art must teach a lesson and
create better human beings. Aeschylus observes that "from the
very earliest times the really great poet has been the one who had
a useful lesson to teach" and Euripides suggests that "a good poet"

should have "technical skill" and "he should teach a lesson, make people good citizens."[14]

Similarly, "in defending tragic art," Else writes, "*Aristotle was defending something that hardly existed in his day*"; besides, he looks at mimesis in the limited perspective of theatre, and theatre in the rarefied light of ancient Greek tragedy of the sixth and fifth centuries B.C. Incidentally, this period was the "Golden Age" of Greek culture and civilization. Even further, Aristotle limits his discussion to the "best" tragedies of this Golden Age, using examples drawn mainly from the celebrated works of Homer, Aeschylus, Sophocles, and Euripides. Some commentators even believe that Sophocles' *Oedipus* is the sole model for Aristotle's treatise on ancient Greek art and theatre.[15]

The most serious charge Socrates/Plato had brought against tragedy in the *Republic* was that, by means of performance, it pandered to the tastes of the lowest segments of the body politic. The only way Aristotle could combat this context-historically justified claim was to exclude performance from his list of the "necessary" or "essential elements" of tragedy. In doing so, however, he rarefies his perspective on this putatively exemplary form of theatre even more. On the whole, Aristotle rejects the claim that "the epic appeals to a cultivated group of readers who have no need of an actor's posturings, while tragedy appeals to masses—which means that is a vulgar thing and therefore plainly inferior." He insists that "this censure should be directed against the acting rather than the poetry; for in the recital of epic, too, a minstrel can overdo the gestures. . . . This has been the objection to Callipides, as well as to certain actors of our own day who enact a gentlewoman as though she were a slut." He concludes that "tragedy, no less than the epic, may produce its proper effect without being acted: we can judge its quality quite well by reading it."[16]

Perhaps the most effective defense Aristotle mounts on behalf of mimesis is to conceive it as the most basic form of expressing or representing human experience and to suggest that its exemplary manifestation is theatre. To Jacques Derrida's query, "Is not the most naive form of representation mimesis?" Aristotle's answer would be a resounding "yes." For, in chapter four of the *Poetics*, he writes that:

Broadly considered, the origins of poetry may be traced to two causes (*aitia*), each of them inherent in man's nature. On the one hand the desire to "imitate or represent" is instinctive in man from childhood; in fact one of man's distinguishing marks is that he is the most mimetic of all animals, and it is through his mimetic activity that he first begins to learn. Moreover, such imitating and representing is always a source of delight, as experience plainly shows. . . . The reason for this is that learning gives the keenest pleasure—not only to philosophers but even to the rest of mankind despite the scant attention they bestow on it.[17]

Aristotle's philosophy (that is, the way in which he formalizes human-phenomenal experience as an interrelated body of concepts and activities) is not without its fair share of a priori assumptions, teleological desires, and advocacies. But then again, nothing pertaining to human and phenomenal experience can be without such wills, effects, and interests. What makes Aristotle's system more germane (to my interests at least) is that it comprehends the infinite forms and possibilities of human experience better than Socrates/Plato's unitarist-purist philosophy allows. Aristotle's view of mimesis valorizes mythopoetical profusion and the formal reconciliations of opposite terms and elements in all representations. This sublimative or sublative plurality in and of representation is precisely what Socrates/Plato reject in their arguments against poetry and theatre. Socratic/Platonic reason or rationality decrees that different terms and forms cannot and should not mix. They justify their arguments against poetic-artistic representations on the grounds that "it was *reason* which led us on. And lest [poetry] condemn us as rather harsh and rough, let us tell her that there is an ancient feud between philosophy and poetry."[18]

Obviously, the kind of reason or rationality that supports such a project of fundamental exclusion is narrow, and, as Socrates/Plato own arguments demonstrate, idealistic. In such a framework of rationality, Wheelwright suggests, "truth, together with its object, Real Being, must be rational, i.e., characterized by perfect self-consistency." To Socrates/Plato, human-phenomenal experience cannot contribute to this ideal-perfect process; human "sense-experience does not reveal *Real Being* but only Appearance, and thus does not give truth, but only opinion." Their ideal state is what redeems the lowly human senses; its careful nurturing of the ideal citizen makes the "experience of sense give rise to 'sound opinion' *(orthê doxa)* which must serve as [the] starting-point in any subsequent investigation of truth."[19]

Having decided to oppose the idealistic arguments of Socrates/Plato, "Aristotle's problem was to formulate a theory of *being* and a theory of *change* that" could "avoid the metaphysical extravagance of the platonic doctrine of archetypes." His solution to this problem was to assume that the human mind is capable of apprehending the truth without the sanction or guidance of any state, ideal or otherwise. "Man is an animal, and along with all other animals he possesses a 'power of sense-discrimination' *(aesthêsis)*," which can be systematized through the "power of memory." "To know a thing is to group its 'articulable meaning' *(logos)*—i.e., what can be *said* about it," beginning with its immediate form or "specific thinghood" *(ousia)*. To Aristotle, "form *(eidos)* is not anything apart from particular objects, it is inherent in their very matter *(hylê)*." Through the "power of memory" the human being makes connections between immediate and mediated perceptions of things and comes to discern "the universal characteristics shared by them. This is the original inductive or abstractive process . . . by which, as we carry it forward to embrace still wider classes of particulars, we come to apprehend the general characteristics or 'forms' *(eidos)* of things, which serve as the 'first principles' *(archê)* of our subsequent demonstration."[20]

In the Aristotelian framework, human knowledge is a dynamic process, a process of reaching toward ends that eternally recede. In such a light, Being eternally remains Becoming and Becoming never becomes fixed in unchanging Being and Form. As Wheelwright phrases it, Aristotle believes that "there is no absolute becoming, except in a relative sense."

> Among mortals at any rate, perfect completeness or complete perfection is never found. In each actual embodiment there is always, to a greater or less degree, a 'falling short' *(sterêsis)* of what the thing ideally (i.e., by definition) is. The definition of a thing . . . merely [states] its 'general formal character' *(eidos)*. This formal character of a thing indicates, from a purely logical standpoint, the species under which the thing immediately falls; while from a 'natural' *(physikos)* standpoint it indicates the goal *(telos)* toward which all members of that species tend naturally to move. Form, then, is not, for Aristotle, a Platonic archetype existing independently and apart from the matter that it shapes. Form is implicit in matter; or, from a converse standpoint, the matter of anything is its potentiality *(dynamis)* of receiving or becoming a certain form.[21]

In Book Twelve of the *Metaphysics* Aristotle suggests that "it is through wonder that men begin to philosophize" and that "even the myth-lover *(philomythos)* is a sort of philosopher *(philosophos)*, for a myth is composed of wonders." For him, mythology is simply another, more inclusive form, of thinking and/or cognition. Mimesis is the most primary form of thinking, and "thinking *(noêsis)* is the initiating principle" of all human experience. "We desire because of our opinions rather than form opinions because of our desires,"[22] Aristotle writes. In truth, the relationship between desire, mimesis, and thinking is not linear, as Aristotle suggests, but circular.

Aristotle considers rationality an inalienable feature of being human, and human culture as a web of norms and forms constructed in the face of some fundamental context-historical possibilities, probabilities, and necessities. To him:

> Man as a rational creature has a 'natural' (i.e., living and for him conscious) tendency to love reason and to bring his conduct into conformity with it. Rational principle thus plays a double role: (1) on the objective side, it is the ideal by which the rational soul desires to be guided by the unmoved mover of the rational soul [God]; (2) on the subjective, it is the rational soul's own inherent power *(dynamis)* to act rationally. Rational principle, then, is at once: (2) an intimate part of man's own rational nature, which he brings into active expression through the effort of 'moral choice'; and (1) a genuine archê of choice and of action, self caused and not entirely dependent on anything external. . . . It is as an unmoved mover, then, that the soul performs, and is responsible for moral action.[23]

If a rough, "modern" account of the political differences between Socrates/Plato and Aristotle be made here, it will be that the former's position is statist and elitist, even repressive, while the latter's is individualist, populist, and even liberal. Socrates/Plato do not trust the intelligence of the ordinary human being as far as they could thow it, while Aristotle seems to believe in the inherent ability of each and every being to make rational and enlightened choices. This distinction cannot be taken too far or viewed as absolute, however, because, in point of fact, Aristotle endorsed, or at least did not explicitly reject, the holding of slaves in Athens or Greece. Thus, his apparent "liberal-humanism" is limited; it applies only to those who are already free, privileged, and Greek or granted these by birth or law.

My own "political" stand reconciles both Aristotelian and Socratic/Platonic positions in the sense that it allows that a measure of state or collective guidance is needed in every human society if the rational or irrational natural penchants of the individual are not to lead to untempered egoism and anarchy which ultimately mean the death of both the individual and society. Be that as it may, when it comes to the question of the representation, I see Aristotle's mythopoetic and pluralistic view of rationality as allowing for better understanding of multifarious human experience than does the narrow view held by Socrates/Plato, particularly in the *Republic*. This is the main reason behind the ever slight inclination toward Aristotle in this book. Of course, the eternal question is how much of any state or collectively imposed guidance, control, or limits on individual freedom is enough or too much. Still, it is better to allow for many ways of accomplishing the same goal than to deny a host of possibilities in the name of one very narrow way and a small body of adherents.

In the light of Aristotle's pluralistic view of rationality, the "ancient feud" Socrates/Plato proclaim between philosophy (idealistic truth) and poetry (poetic or phenomenal truth) appears as an expedient, if not noble, lie or pretense. Poetry and philosophy are "axiological co-conspirators" in the representation of human experience. A telling sign of this is Socrates/Plato's appropriation of myth to legitimize the claims they make for philosophy in the *Republic*. Poetic-artistic representations of human experience might seem more comprehensive in range than Socrates/Plato's ideal-formal philosophical representations, but neither is complete or sufficient in itself. Poetry and philosophy are simply different forms of representation and rationalization, each one capable of underwriting the perpetual motion of human being and/as becoming in the phenomenal or sublunar world. Like "metaphysics, morality, religion, science," philosophy and poetry are, as Nietzsche puts it, "various forms of lies" that enable one to "have faith in life."[24]

Different forms of representation, be they poetic, philosophical, or otherwise, can act as motive and emotive forces *(energeia)*; they can initiate and sustain the "process of achieving . . . fulfilment" in human phenomenal existence. Aristotle "defines motion *(kinêsis)* in general as the fulfilment of a potentiality quâ potentiality," and "change *(kinêsis)* . . . as movement from a 'starting point which is also a determining principle' *(archê)* to an 'end which is also a goal' *(telos)*." Human life traces such a motion from a beginning toward an end, and it can be served by different forms of representation, as long as these forms appear capable of reconciling extreme possibilities in human experience. This powerful intertwining of constitutive opposites is demonstrable in ritual, which transplants originary/past events into present contexts—that is, reconciles past and present—through periodic reenactments. It is also implicit in the conception of the sublime in terms of manifest reconciliations and sublations of such primary opposites as being and nonbeing, order and chaos, beautiful and ugly, and so on.[25]

The constitutive terms of Aristotle's philosophy are interpenetrative or sublime. His philosophical system as a whole is marked by a fundamental vacillation between a bipartite and a tripartite division of the spheres of human activity. In it, Wheelwright writes, the "various fields of 'knowledge, or science' *(epistêmê)* are classified according to the primary distinction between the contemplative *(thêorêtikos)* sciences and the 'practical or moral' *(praktikos)* sciences." Contemplative sciences are primarily concerned with "what cannot be otherwise than it is" or putative essences and forms. Yet, they are not "limited to . . . what happens by necessity"; they "also study what happens 'usually'" and, in other words, deal "with the realm of probable occurrences."[26]

"Besides the sciences," Wheelwright continues, there are the arts *(technê)* which have to do with making *(poêisis)* and involve a productive *(poiêtikos)* use of reason." Diotima of Mantineaia, the mythical prophetess whose mask and voice Socrates/Plato borrow to make their uncharacteristically mythopoetical arguments in the *Symposium,* provides the best definition of the operational sphere of *poiêsis.* She suggests that "in all cases where anything passes from not-being into being, the cause is *poiêsis;* so that [in a sense] the works produced by all the arts are acts of *poiêsis* and the makers of them are poets." Insofar as its constitutive extremes (being and nonbeing) are the basic poles of human experience, *poiêsis,* as Diotima defines it, covers the total range of human self-and-world productions and reproductions. As such, even Socratic-Platonic philosophy falls under its umbrella.[27]

In Aristotle's philosophy, human experience is articulated in terms of a constitutive conflict between "the goal of man" and "man's political nature." Aristotle suggests that the goal of man is "happiness *(eudaimonia),* [whether] real or imagined," but such happiness cannot consist in "transient pleasures." Each material-based guise or form of happiness "requires for its realization too many extrinsic conditions; it lacks self-sufficiency *(autarkeia).* Only the life of mind in contemplation can be called self-sufficient; it alone, therefore, constitutes happiness in the true and full sense of the word." To Aristotle, contemplative life "approximates more closely to self-sufficiency than any competing ideal" but it "does not mean isolation" from the world. "Man is naturally political *(politikos),* and cannot lead the good life nor find happiness entirely apart from his fellows, . . . he becomes to that degree responsible to the society in which he lives."[28]

The seemingly irrepressible conflict between contemplative *(philosophia)* and practical life *(politikos)* underwrites Aristotle's "view of the 'tragic.' For, the essence of the tragic is an irreconcilable conflict between man's nature and his fate [or goal]." In the *Poetics,* Aristotle takes up Socrates/Plato's offer to "allow to those other champions of [poetry] who are not poets but poet-lovers to rise to plead for her in prose, that she is not only delightful but helpful for constitutions and human life." Spariosu believes that in so doing, "Aristotle only consolidates and systematizes his master's work," that he takes Plato's claim that "literature 'tells lies'" and builds "his entire *Poetics* on it."[29]

Aristotle does indeed suggest in the *Metaphysics* that "bards tell many a lie," but he does not consider the poetic-artistic fictions artists create wrong or useless. On the contrary, he applauds such fictions as attempts to come to terms, in a rational and organized way, with human experience. He observes, for instance, that "Homer more than anyone else has taught poets the art of poetic fiction. It consists in the skillful exploitation of a fallacy *(paralogismos)*" in a way that stands beside and illuminates human experience. As the most celebrated "epic poet, but also precursor and in a sense inventor of the drama," Homer serves the "greater cause . . . of poetry as a whole, of which tragedy is the exemplar and Homer . . . the first prophet."[30] It is interesting to note that in Book Ten of the *Republic* Socrates/Plato trace "tragedy to its leader Homer." But, insofar as Homer was the great writer of epics, it is all of fiction that comes under attack in the *Republic,* and to that extent all of fiction that Aristotle defends in his *Poetics*.[30]

By way of Homer, Aristotle suggests that the lies told in poetry are akin to the necessary or "noble lies" told in the glorified philosophy of Socrates/Plato and the ancient Greek rationalists. Such lies are, in Else's words, "lies told *comme il faut*," which is to say that they are not merely symptoms of a "sinful craving of mouth and ear" (as ancient Greek rationalists viewed mythology) but valid, and perhaps more able, means of rationalizing and fulfilling life. As such, the edifice Aristotle builds on the premise he borrows from Socrates/Plato (that poetry tells lies) ultimately redeems and valorizes art. His position on art anticipates Nietzsche's suggestion that "Truth is Ugly. We possess art lest we perish of the truth."[31]

Like Socrates/Plato, Aristotle viewed theatre as the exemplary form of mimesis, but since to him mimesis was a legitimate means of representation, the exemplariness of theatre was positive rather than negative. Aristotle seems to valorize theatre because it articulates human experience in the quintessential terms of choice and action, and "action," Hegel writes in his notes on tragedy, "is rather essentially the manifestation of human life." Aristotle also viewed tragedy as the highest form of theatre or dramatic representation, but unlike Socrates/Plato he defines it as the representation of human actions that are serious and of some magnitude whose ultimate objective is the purging or sublation of pity and fear, which are elemental but debilitating human emotions. In fact, Aristotle defends poetic-mimetic and theatrical forms of representation in the *Poetics* from the elevated and august perspective of tragedy.[32]

Aristotle's *Poetics* shares Socrates/Plato's premise that "men in action is what poetic imitation imitates," which is why he constructs the operational nexus of ancient Greek tragedy around the dramatic plot (*mythos* in the original Greek). He describes this central element of drama and tragedy as the causal arrangement of events and actions, and at many points in his treatise stresses that human action is pivotal. Else believes that this emphasis on action underlines Aristotle's conviction that:

> Human life and action belongs to the 'practical' sphere and have nothing to do with metaphysics. *Our world,* except in so far as we live the theoretical life of pure reason, is a *realm of contingency and approximation.* It has principles, but they are valued 'only for the most part.' . . . That, in fact, is why Aristotle so carefully uses the double formula 'according to probability and necessity' throughout the *Poetics;* for necessity cannot be absolute in the sublunar world."[33]

Tragedy, Aristotle suggests, "is a representation (*mimêsis*) of an action (*praxis*) that is serious, complete, and of a certain magnitude . . . arousing pity and fear in such a way as to accomplish a purgation (*katharsis*) of such emotions." It presents or represents human experience "in the form of actions directly presented, not narrated," using six formative or "necessary elements," of which "the most important" "is the structure of incidents." "Tragedy is a representation essentially not of men but of 'human action' (*praxis*): i.e., of human life, its happiness and its misery." Its "proper end" is to represent "a mode of action" and not to display "some sort of [human] quality." The persons or characters of tragedy "will be of one sort or another according to their several characters, but" they must primarily be shown to "achieve happiness or misery according to their actions." The "characters" or humanlike figures of tragedy "are developed as subsidiary and instrumental to their action. Hence the incidents and the story or plot are the real end of tragedy; and the real end is of course our principal concern."[34]

To further emphasize the centrality of plot, Aristotle declares that "while there cannot be a tragedy without *action,* there may be one without character." It is "in the plot that we find those elements whereby tragedy achieves its most powerful emotional effect, namely 'reversals of situation' *(peripeteia)* and recognition scenes." Plot is "the 'initiating principle' *(archê)* and, so to speak, the soul of tragedy; character being second in place. Tragedy is the representation of an action; and it is principally in carrying out this function that it represents agents likewise." Thus, it is "manifest that the poet [which is to say the 'maker'] is primarily a maker of plots rather than of verses, for he is a poet by virtue of the representing that he does, and the object that he represents is actions." The representation of patterns of human action in the tragic plot, Else suggests, makes "the paramount duty of the poet . . . the uncovering of a true relation which already exists somehow in the scheme of things."[35]

Incidentally, the same word, *mythos,* refers to both the tragic plot and the tales of ancient Greek mythology, and this might be an indication of a fundamental relationship between ancient Greek tragedy and mythology. Gilbert Murray argues against such a view when he writes that Aristotle's use of the term *mythos* to describe the plot of tragedy is anachronistic or "unsuited to the tragedy of the fifth century." But temporal incongruity aside, there are salient etymological and semantic justifications for Aristotle's use of *mythos*. Plot is the arrangement of significant actions and events into a meaningful body of representations, in the same way that mythology is a collection of heroic and originary superhuman acts and events into a coherent body. James Boon's suggestion that "Music is to sound *(sons)* as Myth is to meaning *(sens)*" throws light on the fact that mythology and tragedy are both "webs of signification."[36]

At the very least, "the drama and the myth were simply two different expressions of the same religious kernel," and religion is, of course, one of the most obvious and naive forms of self-and-world representation. Thus, the first and most primary source of acculturation in tragedy is the religious kernel which it shares with mythology. Secondly, Aristotle anchors the artistry of the tragic poet in the "skillful handling" and translation of "traditional stories" into a present context.[37] Transplantations of the past into present and juxtapositions of these two temporal frameworks can make both of them appear strange and unfamiliar. In its quintessential rearrangements and representations of stories of the mythical-mythological past in a present framework, therefore, tragedy opens up the possibility that alienation effects (the precursors to all human knowledge and consciousness) can be obtained. The concern with "events inspiring fear and pity," that which differentiates tragedy from other artistic-theatrical forms, also makes it akin to shock therapy and adds to its potential store of alienation effects.

"Tragedy at its best," Aristotle writes "will not have a simple but a complex type of construction, and it will also represent actions arousing pity and fear." Catharsis, the central effect of tragedy, is "best produced when the events are at once unexpected and causally related. For thereby they stir our wonder more than if they happened by themselves or by mere chance. Even coincidences appear most remarkable when they have some appearance of design." Esle is convinced that *"Aristotle can accept the tragic emotions, especially pity, because he considers them to be affiliated with reason."* To him, moreover the reconciliation of necessity and accident in Aristotle's conception of catharsis is:

> one of the most pregnant remarks in the entire *Poetics*. . . . For the essence of the tragic is an irreconcilable conflict between man's nature and his fate. Aristotle does not speak of such a conflict. . . . Nevertheless, . . . it plays its role in his theory in the guise of the fearful and the pitiful.

Else reads Aristotle's conception of tragedy and catharsis as his "attempt to make the best of two incompatible worlds. The tragic, the inrush of demonic powers upon a man's happiness, becomes merely the 'unexpected,' the unforeseen, and in this *guise* the Tragic is wedded to causality."[38]

In the wake of the wedding of accident to necessity comes the revelation that it is not so much the *arousal* of pity and fear that is the central objective of tragedy as the transcendence or sublation of such disabling emotions and emotional elements. What is made irrelevant at the end of tragedy is not fear, but the fear of fear itself, not pity, but the disabling of human choice and action in the face of the unexpected, the unknown, and the unfamiliar. Human action is the central desire as well as problem in tragedy, as it is in ideology. The birth of tragedy or a tragic view of life occurs with the recognition that the elevated ideas or concepts that underwrite human existence and facilitate both choice and action are not eternally fixed, right, and inviolable. Tragedy is born out of the recognition that metaphysical notions and comforts are open-ended and unstable, and that a particular choice or course of action that appeared to be good and right at some point in time can turn out to be the beginning of error, terror, and tragedy.

In tracing the fundamental uncertainties of human choice and action, tragedy questions the elemental body of dos and don'ts (values and taboos) according to which most human beings and cultures organize their phenomenal existence. From the vantage of tracing the consequences of the transgression of some basic norm or taboo in a given world, it shows that the forms of human existence are impermanent. To Socrates/Plato, this means that tragedy vulgarizes elevated concepts and cheapens the emotional experiences of the noble or heroic human beings, laying them at the feet of the festive rabble gathered in a place of seeing and representation (theatre). But to Aristotle this unavoidable lowering of the elevated is not the point of tragedy, which takes very seriously its exploration of the profound ambivalence of human action. To him, the central question of tragedy which is "To Act or Not to Act" ultimately translates into "To Be or Not to Be."

I find the fundamental ambiguity of human action and experience well-illuminated in two often-juxtaposed Akan-Ghanaian proverbs. The first *(Nea wo pe dodo ni nea eku wo)* suggests that "What you love most is ultimately what kills you" and is almost immediately cancelled out or sublated by the second *(Ye be wu nti ye nda?)* which provides that "For fear of death shall we banish sleep?" Tragedy illuminates the fact that "whatever you set your mind to, your personal total obsession, this is what kills you. Poetry kills you if you're a poet and so on. People choose their death whether they know it or not."[39] In the service of life, however, tragedy sublates this initial pessimism or fatalism with a final acquiescence to the necessity of action: *Amor Fati.*

Nietzsche's searing insights into tragedy in the *Birth of Tragedy* are based on a similar view of its representations and sublations of initial appearances of pessimism. He suggests, for instance, that Shakespeare's Hamlet resembles his "Dionysian man" in that:

> both have looked truly into the essence of things, they have *gained knowledge, and nausea inhibits action.* . . . Knowledge kills action; action requires the veils of illusion: that is the doctrine of Hamlet, not the wisdom of Jack the Dreamer who reflects too much and, as it were, from an excess of possibilities does not get around to action. Not reflection, no—true knowledge, an insight into the horrible truth outweighs any motive for action, both in Hamlet and in the Dionysian man.[40]

Tragedy turns against its own initial pessimisms, sublates the unripe view of the uncertainly of human action, and validates the pursuit of action in the interest of fulfilled being—in spite of the looming spectre of self-pity and fear. To appropriate terms in which Michel Haar interprets Nietzsche's concept of *amor fati,* tragedy endeavors to "shatter the traditional concept of necessity" so as to "encompass" and reconcile "those logical contraries that are Chaos and Form, chance and law." In Nietzsche's telling words, "the *metaphysical comfort*—with which . . . every true tragedy leaves us . . . [is] that life is at the bottom of things, despite all the changes of appearances, indestructibly powerful and pleasurable."[41]

In his compendious commentary on Aristotle's *Poetics*, Else "puts *catharsis* in the center of a nexus of concepts with which it is organically connected: *pathos, hamartia,* recognition, pity and fear, and (perhaps) the tragic pleasure." He suggests that catharsis is "a purification of the pathos," and that "the agent of the purification [sublation] was the 'imitation,' that is the plot," and not the internal movements or emotions of the audience. Tragic action begins with the transgression of some preconstituted limits by the protagonist(s), which is to say that "*hamartia* is the precedent condition, the premise upon which the (complex) dramatic structure is predicated."[42]

The protagonist of tragedy can only "win pity and forgiveness" in the end if his or her hamartia is "caused by ignorance of particulars" rather than by the "ignorance of general principles." But genuine and innocent or not, the initiating tragic mistake (hamartia) leads logically, causally, even inexorably to the pathetic (fearful and pitiful) climax or *pathos* which, Else submits, is in fact the "premise on which the plot is built." Aristotle suggests that the "kind of situation the dramatist should look for" in making his plot is one in which "the 'tragic occurrence' *(pathos)* takes place between friends," or in which "some such crime as murder is done or planned by brother against brother, or son against father, or son against mother or mother against son." As Else points out, however, the "real function of the pathos is not to shock the audience by its physical occurrence"; "in itself, merely qua act of violence or destruction, it has only low emotional quality. The pathos rises to the genuine tragic level when it involves 'dear ones' and to the highest level only when the act is based on a *hamartia.*"[43]

Violence committed against dear ones or blood relations is taboo violence, a palpable transgression of the Greek *Talion.* Incidentally, some such blood crime is the initiating action or hamartia of Sophocles' *Oedipus,* Aeschylus *Oresteia,* and Euripides' *Medea,* three of the plays Aristotle places on his list of best tragedies. The *pathos* or pathetic event is what connects the archic *(hamartia)* and telic *(catharsis)* extremes of ancient Greek tragedy into a ritualistic-symbolic total picture. The protagonists of tragedy are at one and the same time breachers and bridgers of chtonic gulfs and of totemic or taboo boundaries. By the very nature of their actions, they step across limits and commit transgressions that often lead to their destruction in the name of the security and continuity of the world in which they live.

However, these protagonists of tragedy can hardly make Learian claims of being "more sinned against than sinning." Tragic action extends beyond narrow notions of sin and sinning—it often signals a fundamental shift in elevated norms that once seemed so stable and unchanging. Tragedy reveals the existence of a schism between what has come to be and what was originally thought to be Good, True, Right, Beautiful, Necessary. To the extent that God is often said to be the source of the Good, True, Right, and so on, it often appears to humanity in the grip of tragedy that God is dead or has moved and left no forwarding address.

The state of a world abandoned by God to the clutches of tragedy is a world not unlike Thebes faced with the riddling Sphinx in Sophocles' *Oedipus*. The proliferation of contagion and phenomenal ills ("the numberless plague") in Thebes calls to mind the "rotten" state of Denmark in Shakespeare's *Hamlet*. Tragedy underwrites the fact that the placid surface of sanctified appearances is belied by as-yet-unformulated, unassimilated, and unpacified eventualities. Humanity cannot help but make and unmake its existence endlessly because existence (defined in terms of choices to action) can never be posed, composed, or reposed in unchanging perfection. This inexorable fact makes tragedy an eternal feature of human experience.[44]

One of the controversies touching tragedy is that the actions of its protagonists or central actors can be equally traced to individual Freewill or choice and group- or god-ordained Fate/Destiny or predetermination. Some recent commentators see Sophocles' *Oedipus* as a vehicle or mechanism of scapegoat violence on the grounds that it deals carelessly with the crucial question of the guilt or innocence of Oedipus in the murder of Laius. Ancient Greek tragedy, as a whole, has been excoriated as a system of representation that valorizes victimization and evil-projection. To these liberal-humanists, the fact that Sophocles' play *(Oedipus)* does not pursue the question of responsibility for its hamartic transgression to an unambiguous source makes it a vehicle for scapegoat violence. They find Oedipus's summary inculpation, self-flagellation, and ultimate banishment extremely unpalatable in view of the fact that the question of responsibility for the murder of Laius remained undecided between the One (presumably Oedipus) and the Many (the faceless band of brigands first blamed for the regicide).[45]

It is true that Sophocles' *Oedipus* is convicted on the strength of circumstantial, oracular evidence; evidence produced by the very institution whose authority is inversely related to his fate. Oedipus appears to have been summarily convicted and exiled in order to preserve the authority of the Delphian oracle and the continuity of Thebes itself. But it is the conjunction of accident and fate in the play that created the appearance of truth *(paralogismos)* and made Oedipus the most logical or natural culprit. It is worth recalling that Aristotle had suggested the conjunction of the expected and the unexpected, the caused and the uncaused, as the crux of catharsis, the central effect of tragedy.

After the source of numberless plague in Thebes had been traced to the uninvestigated and unavenged death of the former king, the testimony of the Corinthian shepherd made the crucial question in the play that of whether one person (Oedipus) or many people (the unidentified band) was responsible. Subsequently, the reluctant testimony of the Theban shepherd had subordinated the once-pivotal question of numbers to that of tribal and filial identity of Oedipus. The testimony of the Theban shepherd made Oedipus a Theban, the son of Laius, and, as such, the person preordained by the oracles to murder his father and marry his mother. In the wake of this conjunction of accident and fate, the initially pivotal question of the "one" or the "many" is displaced and prostrated by the question of who exactly is Oedipus. Even Oedipus, the so-accused himself, drops his pursuit of an answer to the question that could have freed him, and was, in fact, his best defense. Perhaps the primordial fear of incest and parricide militated against the pursuit of empirical-jurisprudential questions; all everyone could see and hear and feel is the horror, the horror. This overwhelming emotional, rather than logical, experience of taboo transgression, the fact of blood, was all the evidence needed. Oedipus himself does not only punish himself horribly by gorging out his own eyes, he also submits to the Thebes- and Creon-sanctioned punishment of dethronement and banishment.

Living is acting, but in acting the protagonists of tragedy bridge and breach the fundamental notions on which their actions impinge and often infringe. These figures of tragedy often become set apart from other human beings and are, sometimes, if ambiguously, destroyed. Thus, victimization happens in tragedy, as it does in actual human existence, but like any other facet of tragedy, it is treated as a problem rather than a fatih or dogma. Tragedy does not celebrate "surrogate victim[age]" the way René Girard suggests that it does in his *Violence and the Sacred*.[46]

The symbolic functions of tragedy are assured in its exploration of the gaps between claim and belief, between belief and transgression, and between celebrated notions and their less-glorified manifestations in human action. Indeed, if ritual and carnival are authorized periodic violations of the high notions and taboos of human societies, tragedy is a dramatization of the unauthorized transgressions. Yet, in spite of this apparent concern with deviance and sin, in fact, because of it, tragedy co-operates with the inscriptions and reinscriptions of the elemental "dos and don'ts" of the human lifeworld. By reenacting or representing the mythical-legendary or originary transgressions of the significant norms and values of a past and pacified lifeworld within a present or actual framework, tragedy becomes a giant alienation effect that generates new insights and points toward possible change. It can also act as a homeopathic system that creates ritualistic serums with which present or actual humanity is inoculated against the timeless dangers it encounters.[47]

Perhaps the paramount alienation effect of tragedy obtains in its juxtaposition of contingent worldviews and/or forms or systems of representation. In its marking of the disjointure between the old and new, tragedy traces some possible and probable responses to the pressure of change. Else, for instance, reads Aeschylus's *Oresteian Trilogy* as a dramatization of the clash between the "Atavism" of 'old' religion and the "Equity" of the new 'rational law.' He writes that, even though it is the more contemporary, rational law "does not usurp the place of religion, it offers no substitute for the cathartic rites, if they are required; but it is the authority which decides whether they are required." If we want to understand this conflict of laws and moralities in Aeschylus's work, Else suggests:

we have to reckon with two different and potentially conflicting principles in the consciousness of Athenians: (1) the immemorial horror of blood-pollution, with all its consequences for the murderer, his family, . . . and the state; and (2) the positive right of men, in a court of law duly assembled, to judge whether pollution has been incurred and to what degree. In this battle between those two principles—for it was a battle, or rather a war, with the new one steadily making in-roads upon the old—we must regard Plato's Laws as marking one station, and Aristotle another.[48]

According to Aristotle, tragedy does not give "any random pleasure, but only pleasure that is proper to it"; it aims "to produce
through *mimêsis* the kind of pleasure that comes from responding
with pity and fear." However, most critics view "tragic pleasure" as
an oxymoronic monstrosity. "One of the most striking paradoxes in
the realm of literary art," P. K. Guha writes in *Tragic Relief,* "is
presented by tragic drama. It deals with pain and suffering and
yet, like all forms of art, it serves as a source of pleasure." Aristotle
himself mentions the concept only twice in his treatise without
really explaining it either time. Similarly, in more than six hundred
pages of astute commentary on the *Poetics,* Else mentions "tragic
pleasure" only twice and then only to dismiss it each time as "triv-
ial and distracting."[49]

Nevertheless, tragic pleasure is not an aberration in Aristotle's
otherwise rational view of tragedy. Tragic representation is about
ambiguity, paradox, and reconciliations of contrary terms and as
such it can see both the initial evocation and ultimate sublation of
pity and terror as pleasurable. Tragic pleasure is essentially oxymoronic, and very much in accordance with the conjunctions of opposites in naive or fundamental representations of human experience.
In tragedy or tragic representation principles of power, pain, and
pleasure cooperate to make human existence thinkable, do-able
and, if to a lesser extent, comfortable.

3

The Ubiquity of Theatre and Theatricality in Representations of Human Experience

As a mode of representation, theatre seems to inform and illuminate the basic processes of human self-and-world representation, and yet, in concrete terms, it means different things to different people. Marvin Carlson notes in his Foreword to *Approaching Theatre,* for instance, that "in terms of its interpenetration with the rest of our lives, theatre should be the most approachable of the arts." But, "the very ubiquity of the theatrical in human life and culture—and, conversely the apparent ability of theatre, as a human activity, to absorb all other human activities into itself—make it so varied and complex a phenomenon as to test the limits of any mode of critical understanding."[1] It seems to me that the ability of theatre to test and extend the limits of only one mode of understanding is a valuable one and its very plurality of theatre can be a boon to comprehensive thought.

The manifoldness of theatre can be simplified in a variety of ways to aid not only its own self-understanding but also the role it can play in the representation of everyday human experience. Perhaps the most immediate way to approach theatre is through the description of its constitutive or formative elements and the conventions that underwrite their organization. This is the basic approach in Aristotle's *Poetics,* although chapters twenty-four and twenty-five also address the vexed question of the validity of poetic-theatrical truth. Aristotle lists and describes six formative elements of theatre (dramatic representation): namely, Plot, Character, Thought, Diction, Music and Song, and Spectacle. Plot, in his definitions, is the caused or deliberate arrangement of actions, events, and/or situations that constitute the play; it is to him the most primary and important element of drama and theatre. Drama is essentially an enactment or reenactment of events or situations and plot is what organizes them into a coherent body.

Character is a term that refers to the human or humanlike agents whose basic desires, motivations, and pursuit of happiness drive the actions and situations of the dramatic/theatrical plot. Thought/ Dialogue applies to the totality of linguistic or rhetorical devices that reveal the basic desires and drives (motivations) of the various characters. By extension, thought/dialogue drives the dramatic plot. Diction refers to the choice of words and use of linguistic and rhetorical gestures by specific characters. In Austinian terms, the play or drama is a speech-act continuum in which the said and done are often indistinguishable and inseparable.[2]

Music and Song seem to be recessive traits carried over from the ritual origins of theatre; elements that were crucial to the ritual forms that preceded the ancient Greek tragic drama on which Aristotle based his discussion of art and drama/theatre in the *Poetics*. Music and song refer to the aural aspects of staging, and join with spectacle (the sixth formative element) to constitute the performance of drama/theatre. Aristotle distinguishes the fifth and sixth elements of drama/theatre from the four preceding elements, which he labels "literary" in the sense that they pertain to the written text of drama/theatre. Stripped of performance (visual-aural realization) and composed of the four literary elements alone, theatre becomes drama in the restricted sense of dramatic text. Drama in this sense is not theatre because theatre is completed by direction, performance, and production.

Spectacle originally referred to the visual aspects of drama or theatre, but it has come to connote the whole province of theatre production. The necessity of spectacle or performance to the realization of theatre is a controversial issue, even to defenders of theatre and theatricality. The most damaging charge Socrates/Plato had brought against the theatre in the *Republic* was that by means of performance, it pandered to the lowest and most vulgar segments of the human lifeworld.[3]

Much as he disagreed with Socrates/Plato on the question of the value and validity of art and theatre to the representation of human experience, Aristotle, perhaps because he shared their fear of the masses, found it necessary to exclude performance or "spectacle" from the list of "necessary elements" of theatre. Writing from the perspective of what he considered the highest form of theatre, Aristotle submits that "the 'essential power' *(dynamis)* of tragedy is independent of a 'stage representation' *(agôn)* and of actors." As such, he represses that aspect of theatre which made it most accessible to the *hoi polloi*. One consequence of this removal of performance and the spectacular aspects of theatre from the list of its necessary elements is that "traditional theatre scholarship has privileged the dramatic text" over the more complex and comprehensive theatrical work.[4]

Placed in the larger context of the representation of the everyday human self-and-world, the question of theatre extends into the light of truth and ideology. Here, the question of the necessity of performance to the realization of theatre becomes a question of the validity or truth of theatrical representations of human experience. The two diametric positions held on this question of theatre can be described as "theatrical" and "antitheatrical." The antitheatrical attitude towards theatre is the predominant prejudice in Western Enlightenment thought and rationality, and in it theatre is said to be the exemplar of plurality and/or proliferation of mythopoetic forms and systems. With Socrates/Plato and Francis Bacon, the alleged perversity of theatre is linked with the superior appeal or seductiveness it has for popular or mass segments of the human self-and-world. From its very first Western beginnings, therefore, the antitheatrical bias has supported an antipopulist and antidemocratic (elitist) prejudice toward the representation of human experience. It is underwritten by fear of or adversion to the plurality and multiplicity inherent in poetic and mythological (mythopoetic) forms of self-and-world representation. It bespeaks a prior predisposition toward a unitarism and purism and often endorses forms and systems of representation aimed at establishing idealistic and monological utopias.

Jonas A. Barish says of the antitheatrical attitude that "looked at attentively it comes to appear to be a kind of ontological malaise, a condition inseparable from our beings, which we can no more discard as shed our skins." But he adds that on the whole "attitudes towards the stage, quite plainly come fraught with passion and charged with contradiction."[5] Even the most divergent or diametric attitudes toward theatre share the common view of it as the most exemplary form of mimesis and representation. But whether this exemplariness is considered desirable or undesirable depends on the basic attitude to mimesis of the person making the judgment.

Like Aristotle, the writers and movements discussed in the following chapters of this work view theatre as the most effective means of representing and transforming human experience. How exactly this claim is made and defended will be shown in part two of this book. On the other hand, Socrates/Plato, Francis Bacon, Jean-Jacques Rousseau, and Nietzsche (in his the later, post-Wagnerian works) oppose any such valorizations of theatre and reject all theatricalizations of human experience. But, whatever passion is displayed in the face of theatre is often based in an intimation of the close and uncanny resemblance between its fictional stage and that of the world at large. As Shakespeare's Jaques puts it in *As You Like It,* "All the world's a stage, and all the men and women merely players; They have their exits and their entrances; and one man in his time plays many parts." Paradoxically, therefore, even the most passionate or violent reactions against theatre (antitheatricality) serve to confirm its seductiveness and greater appeal to the mass of humanity.

Socrates/Plato sowed the first seeds Greco-Western antitheatricality, but Bacon was the first Western thinker to systematize this bias by collecting and grouping all forms of representation ("all received systems" in his own words) he found unacceptable under the rubric of "idols of the theatre." Following him, Karl Marx made ideology an umbrella term for the ways in which ruling classes represent, or rather misrepresent, human experience and relations in the material world to serve their own interests. Like Bacon before him, Marx tended to view any form or system of representation that was not his own scientific or historical materialism as perverse and distortive of real human experience (ideology).

All in all, positions adopted with regard to the question of theatre in human self-and-world representations are predicted in prior ontological-teleogical assumptions and desires. Theatricality and antitheatricality are simply the two most basic positions, both influenced by prior assumptions and definite intentions toward the dominant conditions in the referent self-and-world. It is often apparent from the works of antitheatrical writers that they do not so much reject theatre *sui generis* as resist what it means in a given context. Socrates/Plato, for instance, would allow poetry and theatre into their ideal republic if they could prove capable of conforming with its constitutional and acculturative imperatives. Similarly, Jean-Jacques Rosseau strictly contextualizes his answers to the question of the validity of theatre vis-à-vis the representation of human experience. In fact, at different times and under different circumstances the same critic or observer can manifest a theatrical or antitheatrical attitude to the representation of experience. A case in point is Nietzsche's early endorsement of Richard Wagner's musico-mythico-theatrical agenda as opposed to his hostility to theatre and the theatricalization of human experience in the wake of his disillusionment with Wagner.[6]

Written at a time when Nietzsche was much taken with Richard Wagner and his music-theatrical mythmaking, *The Birth of Tragedy* uses Wagnerian music drama as a circular way of understanding ancient Greek tragedy. Nietzsche comes to understand the acculturative possibilities of ancient Greek tragedy in the comparative light of Wagner's music-drama form. This is his way of obviating what he calls the "danger of the direct questioning of the subject about the subject." The way Shakespeare's Polonius would sum up this strategy is: "By indirections find directions out." In obtaining valuable insights indirectly, from the distance of a familiar, one minimizes the possibility of being lied to. For, it serves the interest of the directly questioned subject-object to put on a flattering mask and lie about itself to the questioner.[7]

Walter Kaufmann seems to miss the point of the strategy of comparison and indirection in *The Birth of Tragedy,* for, he proposes to cut out the sections that contain Nietzsche's endorsements of Wagner's music-dramas. He laments that this work "does not end with Section 15, as an early draft did, and as the book clearly ought to. . . . The heart of the book is found in Sections 7 through 15, which deal with the birth and death of tragedy. This is by far the best part of the book and can probably be understood fairly well by itself. Sections 16–25 are [not] worthy of Nietzsche." He continues that the *Birth of Tragedy* "is marred by the faults Nietzsche enumerates in his 'Attempt at a Self-Criticism.'" But if Nietzsche labels the *Birth of Tragedy* an "impossible book: . . . badly written, ponderous, embarrassing, image-mad, image-confused, sentimental, . . . without the will to logical cleanliness, very convinced and therefore disdainful of proof," he also praises it as "a book for initiates, 'music' for those dedicated to music." In the end, even Kaufmann cannot help but admit that the *"Birth of Tragedy* is, for all its faults," "one of the most suggestive and influential studies of tragedy ever written."[8]

A great part of the value of the *Birth of Tragedy* lies in the searing insights it offers on the acculturative relationships between theatre, myth, and culture. And it obtains those insights by way of its juxtaposition of Greek tragedy and Wagner's music-dramas. Nietzsche confesses that "the great artist to whom [his book] addressed itself as in a dialogue . . . [was] Richard Wagner," whose music-theatrical myth-making was an important one in the context of late nineteenth-century Europe. The music-drama form was Wagner's contribution to the widespread quest, in the late nineteenth and early twentieth centuries, for a "total work of art" (*Gesamtkunstwerk*) that could reconcile the disparate elements of Euro-Western self-and-world. As Modris Eksteins explains, "the search for the *Gesamtkunstwerk*—for the holy grail that is the 'total art form—was actually a universal one by the end of the nineteenth century."[9]

The conception of music in Wagner's *Gesamtkuntswerk* is also well placed within the late nineteenth- and twentieth-centuries' romantic tradition in which music was considered the paramount means of Western-European self-and-world disalienation and reintegration. Nietzsche's arguments in the *Birth of Tragedy* follow a similar logic, but in it art and music seem equally empowered. The basic *premise* in this early work is that "it is only as an *aesthetic* phenomenon that existence and the world are eternally *justified*." Art, Nietzsche argues, is "the great means of making life possible, the great seduction to life, the great stimulant of life," and the "complement and consummation of existence." In its most sublime form, art is a manifestation of the inordinate longing for "oneness of man with nature," a desire that "*must* necessarily be found at the gate of every culture." Nietzsche believes that "all that we call culture is made up of . . . stimulants," such as "the socratic love of knowledge" and "art's seductive veil of beauty," that seduce "creatures in life to compel them to live on."[10]

To Nietzsche, therefore, socratic philosophy, art, religion, metaphysics, as well as the "more powerful illusions" created by means of mythology all serve culture, acculturation, and the human will to life. To him, "the highest goal of tragedy and of all art" obtains in the sublimation of formless or disorderly Dionysian "flood and excess" by the more formed and ordered (organized) processes of Apollinian consciousness. In the wake of this fundamental reconciliation, "Dionysus speaks the language of Apollo; and Apollo, finally the language of Dionysus."[11]

The near-miraculous reconciliation of constitutive opposites in sublime forms of art and representation is the operative mode of mythological and, as previously argued, ideological formulations of human experience. To Nietzsche, myth is "a concentrated image of the world that, as a condensation of phenomena, cannot dispense with miracles." Myth organizes the disparate elements of phenomenal experience into a coherent whole, thereby circumscribing existence; it makes things both whole and holy. Hence:

> Without myth every culture loses the natural power of its creativity; only a horizon defined by myth completes and unifies a whole cultural movement. Myth alone saves all the powers of the imagination and of the Apollinian dream from aimless wandering. The images of myth have to be the omnipresent demonic guardians, under whose care the young soul grows to maturity and whose signs help the man to interpret his life and struggles. Even the state knows no more powerful unwritten laws than the mythical foundation that guarantees its connection with religion and its growth from mythical notions.[12]

When Nietzsche became disillusioned with Wagner, he just as passionately rejected his theatrocatic-acculturative project as he had previously endorsed it. Thus, his demonization of theatre and theatricalization of human experience are an integral part of his apostatic rejection of Wagner. Significantly, the titles of the two works that contain his antitheatrical views are *The Case of Wagner* and *Nietzsche Contra Wagner*. In *Nietzsche Contra Wagner*, Nietzsche conceives theatre (as Socrates/Plato, Bacon, and Rousseau had conceived it before him) as a vulgar form of representation that panders to mass or popular opinion and tastes.

> What is the theater to me? What, the convulsions of [Wagner's] "moral" ecstasies which give the people—and who is not "people"?—satisfaction? What, the whole gesture hocus-pocus of the actor? It is plain that I am essentially anti-theatrical: confronted with theater, this mass art par excellence, I feel profound scorn at the bottom of my soul which every artist today feels. *Success* in the theater—with that one drops in my respect forever—failure—I prick up my ears and begin to respect.[13]

The violent passion and with which Neitzsche rejects theatre equals the passion of his acolytic involvement with Wagner; for him, it seems theatre and Wagner are one. But even in the heat of passion, Nietzsche's antitheatrical passion seems very conscious of its Greco-Western antecedents; his use of the term *theatrocracy* to describe Wagner's music-dramatic representations, for instance, invokes a term coined by Socrates/Plato to describe "the mania of a citizenry intoxicated with complex and varied kinds of music, licentious in its tastes, complacent in its lawlessness." To this anti-populist definition of theatre Nietzsche adds his own qualification that in "declining cultures, wherever the decisions comes to rest with the masses, authenticity becomes superfluous, disadvantageous, a liability. Only the actor still arouses *great* enthusiasm."[14]

His dismissals of theatre notwithstanding, Nietzsche's philosophy is profoundly aesthetic, performative, and theatrical, especially in its endorsement of "perspectivism" as the only viable and valid form of objectivity. In Nietzsche's definition, a perspectivist objectivity is one that is constituted by a series of subjects and subjectivities. Such an objectivity or pathos of distance is theatrical, insofar as theatre is considered, often lamentably, as the avatar of plurality and multisubjectivity. Jean-Jacques Rousseau's rigorous contextualization of his antitheatrical arguments in *Politics and the Arts, Letter to M. D'Alembert* also recognizes the plurality of theatre and the necessity of perspectivism in any attempt to question the validity of theatre for the representation of human experience. He writes that "to ask if the theatre is good or bad in itself is to pose too vague a question. . . . The theatre is made for people, and it's only by its effects on the people that one can determine its absolute qualities."[15]

Like many Western antitheatrical commentators before him, Rousseau "does not limit himself to a discussion of the theatre narrowly conceived, but is investigating the moral effects and correctness of all pleasures of the eyes and ears with particular regard to their most sophisticated form, the drama." Still, he does not so much reject theatre as question the wisdom of establishing it in a small, unspoiled, or ideal republic such as he imagines Geneva to be. He believes that theatre is a symptom of decline or decadence, and that "when the people is corrupted, the theatre is good for it, and bad for it when it [the people] is itself good."

> It follows from this that, in order to decide if it is proper or not to establish a theatre in a certain town, we must know in the first place if the morals [manners] are good or bad there . . . However that may be, all that I can admit about this is that it is true that the drama will not harm us if nothing at all can harm us any more.[16]

Theatre, Rousseau might say, is not good in the natural or primitive state; indeed, its very presence is a sign or symptom of the alienation of humanity from this original or undomesticated state of nature. The only people to whom theatre poses no danger whatsoever are those who are already irretrievably lost or alienated. Rousseau seems to contradict his former views when he suggests:

> that the general effect of the theatre is to strengthen the national character, to augment the natural inclinations, and to give a new energy to all the passions. In this sense it would seem that, its effect being limited to intensifying and not changing the established morals [manners], the drama would be good for the good and bad for the vicious.

In any case, like Socrates/Plato and Bacon before him, he declares that "reason has no effect in the theatre" and that there is no real freedom of choice for the author of a play. "Far from choosing . . . the passions which he wants us to make us like," the playwright "is forced to choose those which we like already." This is because theatre reflects national-civic prejudices:

> At London a drama is interesting when it causes the French to be hated; at Tunis, the noble passion would be piracy; at Messina, a deli-

cious revenge; at Goa, the honor of burning Jews. If an author shocks
these maxims, he will write a very fine play to which no one will
go. . . . Thus the theatre purges the passions that one does not have
and foments those that one does.

None of the following perspectives on theatre is complete in
itself nor free of interpenetrations by the other perspectives and
approaches. Each view or vantage contributes something to a
somewhat total or comprehensive picture of theatre as institution,
idea, and metaphor. The first simplified perspective on theatre is as
a discursive system employing a dialogical or dialectical imaginary.
Theatre, in this sense, is constituted by the interlocutions and contestations between two dominant, often conflictive or strategically
opposed, terms of representation or figures of action. The agonistic
exchanges between these diametric or dialectical figures and terms
circumscribe the totality of the theatre-work.

The second dialectic or dialogic in this perspective of theatre
obtains in the traditional division of the theatre building or simply
the space of performance into two distinct spaces, called the stage
and auditorium. These seemingly distinct spaces are connected
and mediated by two sets of theatre conventions. As described by
Elizabeth Burns, "authenticating conventions" govern the internal
coherence of the theatre-work while "rhetorical conventions" or-
chestrate the relationship between the fabricated play and its real
or actual audiences. The reciprocities between these two sets of
conventions underwrites a more comprehensive and, indeed, complex socio-aesthetic space shared by the creators (writer and performer) and consumers (spectators) of theatricalized self-and-
world illusions.[18]

The dramatistic framework on theatre has been variously employed by a host of writers—among them Davignaud, Gurvitch,
Irving Goffmann, Victor Turner, and Kenneth Burke—to theorize
the formation of both individual human identity and being-in-the-
phenomenal-world (social being). In *Role Playing and Identity,*
Bruce Wilshire criticizes some of these theories, particularly Goffmann's. But his own arguments appear very much like those he
criticizes.[19]

In a more complex sense, theatre is a potentially limitless dance
of augmentations, contestations, and mutual deferences between
plural subjects and symbolic systems. Such a perspective underlies
recent philosophical or theoretical-metaphorical appropriations of
the concept-phenomenon. In an allied sense, theatre is a fecund
metaphor or trope that traces the Gnostic necessity of the holy

(one) Word becoming Flesh. This gnostic view of theatre is pronounced in the works of Adolphe Appia and Antonin Artaud, but also implicit in the works of the other Western writers discussed here. In such a light, theatre appears to some commentators as something that prostrates or demystifies the holy Word. Through performance, it seems to present or represent this Word, and the elevated notions founded upon it, to the unwashed and unenlightened masses. The making Flesh (materialization or embodiment) of ideality (or elevated human notions) is, therefore, regarded as both a cause and a symptom of decadence and decline.[20]

In some religious or mystical discourses, the materialization of phenomena in this (as against other) world betokens the fall or alienation of transcendental notions from their original purity and grace. Hence, the ubiquity of the secular-religious trope of the Fall in Western discourse. This view of material existence as a fall or deviation from ideality is perhaps the unspoken reason for the repression of theatre and performance in many religious and even secular discourses and movements. But, the desirability of oneness (uniformity or unitariness), and its equation with stability and continuity, in most representations of the human self-and-world might be what makes the quintessential plurality of theatre most troubling. In any case, it is in the unspoken name of stabilizing sameness or oneness (the most effective facilitators and precursors to human action) that theatre is demonized in some antitheatrical representations of human experience.

Theatre can be approached in yet another perspective as (i) a specified or localized place at which a particular form of human activity takes place; (ii) as a cultural-aesthetic institution with its own self-legitimizing and self-authenticating conventions; (iii) and, finally, as an activity whose affinity to the constitutive and formative elements of everyday life makes it a powerful metaphor and via indirecta to the understanding of human experience. This indirect understanding or circumlocution of human experience by way of theatre is not at all simple. Theatre is a particular kind of recreational activity that takes place in a place designated or marked as such by the observance of certain rules and conventions. It articulates experience in terms of human-like agents (characters) performing actions they hope will fulfill their basic, self-defining desires. These agents are impersonated by actors before a gathered group of people called an audience. At the very least, the assumption is made during the creation of a play or piece of theatre that it would, ideally and/or ultimately, be performed before a gathering of people called an audience. Some commentators have therefore defined the quintessence of theatre as the relationship between actors and audiences. Wilshire, for example, regards "Eric Bentley's attempt to condense theatre to its essence: A impersonates B for C." as "an 'obviously' true description of theatre that nevertheless conceals fundamental problems."[21]

The fundamental problems Wilshire sees in Bentley's dialogic or dialectical conception of theatre turns around the word "impersonates." Yet, it is difficult to see Wilshire's point precisely, especially in the light of the fact that his own arguments of role-playing in the creation of human identity plays out on a not dissimilar ground. In any case, it is possible that its occurrence in a place specially marked as or simply called a theatre or playhouse might be what best labels an activity as theatre or theatrical. The reverse is also possible in the sense that many gymnasiums and open spaces have been converted or transformed into ad hoc theatres by dint of the activity taking place in them. More essentially, it seems that theatre happens because an audience accepts what they see and hear in a certain space as theatre. Through this acceptance, the audience mark the space in which the twofold activity of playing and watching occurs, for the duration that it occurs, as a theatre or playhouse.

Bruce Wilshire attains a perspective on theatre initially similar to the foregoing, but which ultimately reaches beyond its simple dialogic or interactive character, when he approaches normal or traditional theatre by way of experimental theatre. In his words:

> Our encounter with experimental theatre reminds us that the "world" of the play requires the participation of the interpreting viewers and auditors—as well as artists—and that these persons are located in a theatre standing in the actual world. The "world" of the play must be nested within the world in complex ways before the event of theatre can occur. "World" is progressively checked against world, and world against "world." . . . Our hypothesis is this: theatre is a mode of discovery that explores the threads of what is implicit and buried in the world, and pulls us into a compressed and acknowledgeable pattern before us in its "world." Theatre discovers meaning, and its peculiar detachment reveals our involvement.[22]

The value of theatre to the representation of human experience is first anchored in the fact, observed by Wilshire, that "theatre is life-like. Primarily it is so because, as the mimetic art par excellence, it reveals certain aspects of our mimetic reality as human beings. Offstage we imitate others deliberately and undeliberately, consciously and unconsciously, and are authorized and unauthorized by our models." Wilshire goes on to say that "theatre is an aesthetic detachment from daily living that reveals the ways in which we are involved in daily living—particularly our empathetic and imitative involvements. Theatre is the art of imitation that reveals imitation." On the other hand, "human life is theatre-like, and . . . to understand the theatre-like we must understand theatre. Theatre—from the Greek word theatron—means literally a place for seeing. We must devise a way of seeing this place for seeing."[23]

Seeing bespeaks ways of seeing that are grounded in cultural and ideological constructs or paradigms. Seeing is related to Being, and the question of how best to articulate and contextualize human being-in-the-world is the fundamental basis of human cultures, as of all systems of thought and action. "Perception," Wilshire suggests, "always involves interpretation"; perception is "absence given presence." Theatre, is a vehicle of appearances and presence, and "as Karl Kerenyi has pointed out, in ancient Greek theoria, or its equivalent, meant 'to look god in the face.' Appearance is not mere appearance, or appearance set over against reality, but it is the revelation of the ultimate powers and inexhaustible being of things." The fundamental relationship between theatre, theory, and theology is anchored in the fact that:

> Theatron, the word for theatre, is related to theoria, spectacle, but this can also mean speculation and theory. Thus it is suggested that theatre, at its origins, was its own mode of speculating and theorizing about human nature and action. It is not identical with philosophy's mode of speculating and theorizing, for what it presents directly to histrionic perception—the conditions for the coherence of a life or lives—is argued for by philosophy.[24]

The nature of the fundamental relationships between seeing (in a theatre) and action-propelled formation of an actual or real human self-and-world is important to the present work. Such a concern is phenomenological, insofar as "phenomenology is the systematic attempt to unmask the obvious." Like Wilshire, I assume that "theatre is already an implicit phenomenological variation on the meaning of human being and doing, and it has sprung up between actual persons in the world." However, rather than concentrate on the creation of individual human identity or self via role-playing standings-in between actor and audience, as Wilshire does, I emphasize the more comprehensive questions of self-and-world creation and transformation as nestled in the underlying assumptions and overriding desires of theatre.[25]

The experience of theatre and performance is as much an involvement with humanlike characters as it is an appreciation of the conventions of theatre and performance, with or without reference to the elements of life. Of all art forms, theatre comes closest to capturing and duplicating the essential character of human experience. The basic material of theatre is humanlike beings acting and interacting in line with deep-seated desires and dreams of self-fulfillment. These beings come into conflict with others or even with other parts of themselves and they resolve or fail to resolve these conflicts. Human action and being-in-the-world (be it the playful or unreal world of theatre or the serious or real everyday world) are both anchored in role playing. In fact, the works discussed in this book demonstrate that the ludic or playful representations of theatre can be as serious as everyday presentations of the human self-and-world. Both serious and playful role playing can be manipulated to satisfy the fundamental human desire for self-and-world fulfillment. Thus, the distinction between theatre and life come apart at the point where the serious is playful and the playful is serious; that is, in the indeterminate and endless dance of self-and-world being and becoming. The very concern of theatre with appearances and surfaces that can either reveal or conceal deep-seated feelings and desires plays on the quintessential ambiguity of human experience. Shakespeare has one of his dramatic characters say that "there is no art to find the mind's construction in the face." Still, theatre struggles, heroically, against this and tries to find a few ways in which one could find deep truths in the superficial appearances of phenomena.

Beyond the experience of individual human selves and identities, theatre offers the experience of possible and probable worlds, with or without reference to the actual or present world. The issues raised in a play or theatrical work have their own worth, whether or not they have any relevance to the present and actual experience of the audience. The value of theatre as a metaphor or idea is, therefore, twofold; in the first place, it illuminates the creation of individual human identity through role playing; in the second, it provides indirect access to the symbolic processes by means of which collective human conventions and cultures are created.

Modalizations of theatre into such forms or genres as tragedy, comedy, and so on can be the outcome of particular attitudes to human existence. In the *Poetics,* Aristotle views comedy and tragedy as polar forms of theatre created by poets or artists with fundamentally divergent ideological inclinations. On the other hand, he praises Homer as a sublime genius who is able to create both comedies and tragedies. Forms or genres can also be the result of different combinations of the formative elements of theatre and of its collaboration with other performing and nonperforming arts such as music, dance, masks, and, very recently, electronic media. Some of the hybrid forms of theatre that have resulted from its interaction with other art forms are music-drama, opera (which comes very close to the Golden Age Greek tragedy Aristotle wrote about), dance-drama, the masque, comedia d'ell arte, and, of course, the contemporary ugly duckling, performance art. The countless innovations of dramatic form in the history of Western theatre suggest that the process of self-differentiation within theatre is open-ended.

The possibility of genetic variation through interactions with other forms and through the readjustment of internal elements exists for all arts, and for all phenomenal things. But the fundamentally permissive character of theatre seems to make it singularly susceptible to this syncretic-mythopoetic tendency. This inclination toward willing self-contamination and impurity seems to be what has made theatre particularly unacceptable to purity- and unitarity-minded commentators, the first of whom were Socrates and his disciple Plato. Much the same reason (or rather unreason) motivates the antitheatrical tendency in Greco-Western theatre and thought.

In the history of Western theatre, innovations and hybridizations have often meant appropriation and exploitation of scientific-technological advances in the conception and production of theatre. The *deus ex machina* of the ancient Greek stage, gas and electric lights, and a host of other modern innovations made possible by modern science and technology had a profound effect on subsequent innovation of forms and production of theatre in each context. New ways and means of conceiving and articulating human experience also affect the innovation of forms, genres, modes, and the production of theatre. The common ground on which novel forms of theatre are justified is that they make it more present and, thus, more suited for the representation of contemporary subjects and ideas. The explosion of artistic and theatrical forms, modes, and manifestoes (such as realism, naturalism, symbolism, expressionism, impressionism, surrealism, absurdism, modernism, and now postmodernism) in the Euro-Western world since the late nineteenth century is often explained as a quest for forms, modes, and models that are more apt for the representation of experience of that period. Incidentally, Western science and technology advanced in dizzying leaps and bounds during the same period.

There is, therefore, a connection between a historical context and its formal artistic and theatrical innovations, but it is not always a linear or direct one. The introduction of new forms of work and industry in a given time and place does affect the forms of play and leisure deemed relevant to or reflective of that context. As such, it serves us well to consider how new or present-day forms of drama and theatre reflect on the age-old question of theatre in the representation of the human self-and-world. The most conspicuous forms of theatre in the Western world today are multimedia performance art and the essentially non-discursive postmodernist theatre devoted mainly to the representation of surfaces, disconnected images, ersatz impressions, and solipsistic experience. The question one wants to ask is, what is being said or implied in the endless procession and precession of simulcra and fragmented or superficial (Warholian) images in these multimedia works.[26]

Postmodernist theatre tends to be zealously scientistic-technological to the extent that it employs, without criticism, electronic multimedia that often dwarf the other, more human and more fragile, elements of the representation. It also operates on multiple levels of action, and tends toward a troubling Benetton-like use and abuse (uncritical and unreciprocating consumption) of surfaces. Postmodernist theatre appears to apotheosize fragmented, decontextualized forms and artifacts taken undiscriminately from various cultures and societies. Most postmodernist works of theatre seem to me to be neither concerned with meaning and communication nor with the logical or sociable rationalization of human experience. The existence of any such eventualities in them appear more accidental than planned.[27]

The view of art as the objectification of human subjective experience and of artistic endeavor as a heroic striving to make the particular more general and thus intelligible to the receiver-consumer of that work is largely abandoned or actively rejected in postmodernist works. The relationship of the artist-performer to the audience is often indifferent, if not downright hostile. Born out of the erroneous belief that any form of limit or closure is oppressive, is the manifestation of an undesirable power principle, postmodernist theatre often appears to be overburdened with situations and impressions that find no outlet and/or no end. Still, being overloaded with many forms, subjects, and perspective does not necessarily mean that theatre, or any form of representation for that matter, obviates closure and power-laden selection. For all its inclusions, postmodernist theatre and representation excludes something because they select from the irrepressible and potentially limitless multiplicity of actual or imagined phenomenon. The fact is that selection is basic to all formalizations of human experience, and no amount of inclusiveness can repress this human, all-too-human, fact. Sadly, then, postmodernist forms of art and theatre often sacrifice the traditional elements of pleasing unity and coherence of form without fulfilling their desire for all-inclusion and/or the absenting of the power principle from representations of human experience.

Cast in the light of the planned obsolescence, conspicuous consumption, or commodity fetishism that sustains Western capitalist industry, the ceaseless innovation of new forms in Western art appears consumerist. New manifestos in both art and industry trumpet forms and products that are said to be new and more powerful or suitable than other products and forms. Such claims often elevate particular ways of seeing and doing things over some palpable other or others. The saliency of particular artistic-theatrical forms and -isms is founded in the alleged superiority of the ways in which and means by which they respond to the need to formulate human experience. These ways and means are said to be most effective and relevant to the particular or target self-and-world, but more often than not, such claims are merely said and apparent only to the claimant(s).

The widespread view of art forms as differentiations, and, more importantly, distantiations, of ritual forms that once served certain symbolic-efficacious ends underscores the profound relationship between the forms of work and play. Ritual is a serious form of play in that its enactments are seen as having an immediate effect on the life of the human community, even if this effect or efficacy is more symbolic-magical than concrete-tangible. Ritual is a means of instituting and maintaining the norms, customs, and traditions of a community, together with the narrative-historical or mythological means by which they are created. Some commentators on art and ritual have argued that art, especially theatre, is differentiated out of ritual in the wake of demographic expansion, urbanization, and other forms of social change and/or trauma. Ritual becomes less efficacious and therefore less binding on a particular self-and world.[28] If this fundamental affinity between ritual and art/theatre is credited, then one more easily understand their cooperation or conspiracy in the representation of human experience.

If theatre appears multiplex and proliferative in the singular context of Greco-Western representation, it becomes even more so when other cultural-historical contexts are introduced into the picture. The *Natyasastra* ascribed to Bharata Muni is to classical Indian (Sanskrit) theatre, art, and culture what Aristotle's *Poetics* is to ancient Greek theatre, art, and culture. Both, treatises on art and theatre suggest that mythology is the common basis of the Sanskrit romantic drama *(Nataka)* and tragedy (the highest form of classical Indian drama and ancient Greek theatre, respectively). In the *Poetics,* Aristotle repeatedly underlines the mythological basis of tragedy and names the tragic plot *mythos* (myth), thereby linking mythology and tragedy even more directly. In the *Natyasastra* Sanskrit drama is conceived as a fifth Veda (Natyaveda) or mythical-religious kennel of representation that combines the essential characteristics of the other four Vedas. Moreover, it is suggested that this dance-dramatic form is intimately connected with the mythological tales and characters of both the *Ramayana* and the *Mahabharata*.[29]

In the *Natyasastra* (Sanskrit) drama is said to have been created by Brahma in answer to the request of the Indian sages and ascetics for "an object diversion [*sic*] which must be visible as well as audible," one that represents (rearranges and retells) "stories taken out of Vedic lore as well as Semi-Historical Tales." This reminds one of Aristotle's making Greek mythology the primary source of the tales and stories represented in ancient Greek tragedy. The function of Sanskrit drama, according to Bharata Muni, is to represent:

> Semi-Historical Tales *(itihasa)* which will conduce to duty *(dharma)*, wealth *(artha)* as well as fame, will contain good counsel and (collection of traditional maxims), will give guidance to the people of the future as well, in all their actions, will be enriched by the teaching of all authoritative works *(sastra)* and give a review of all arts and crafts.[30]

The common basis of ancient Greek tragedy and Sanskirt drama is "mimesis," translated in both cases as "imitation." Bharata's specification that drama is "a representation of the states *(bhava-nukirtana)* of the three worlds" had been taken to mean that Sanskrit drama imitates human states and emotions *(bhavas)* rather than concrete and discrete actions. However, such a reading overlooks the fact that Bharata quotes Brahma, the giver of Sanskrit drama, as declaring it to be "a mimicry of actions and conducts of people" who are "good, bad, or indifferent." It is also said that because of the operation of the law and principle of karma in Hindu-Indian experience, Sanskrit romantic drama cannot represent human action that is dynamic or transformative. The world of the characters of the theatrical-romantic fiction, like that of its audience, is seen as static or predetermined by an implacable karma.[31]

But, there is more than one acceptable or persuasive interpretation of the principle of karma. The actions of the dutiful or dharmic heroes and heroines of Sanskrit drama seem effective and self-and-world transforming in the moment and space in which they are performed. Besides, the quintessential ambiguity and undecidability of the question of Fate and Freewill in ancient Greek tragedy decreases the distance between it and Sanskrit drama and makes the contrast between the exemplary forms of Eastern and Western theatre not as distinct as some commentators suggest. Sanskrit drama and Greek tragedy are simply the more ideal and/or exemplary forms of Eastern and Western theatre, and any apparent gaps between them are often narrowed by other (less polarized or less extreme) forms.

Perhaps the most conspicuous distinction between Aristotle's *Poetics* and the *Natyasastra* is that the former seeks to dispense with the total realization or performance of theatre while the latter makes it of vital importance. Aristotle subordinates "the 'visual aspect of the staging' *(opsis)*" and "musical composition" ("staging and song") to "the literary elements of tragedy" (plot, character, thought, and diction) on the grounds that "the 'essential power' *(dynamis)* of tragedy is independent of a 'stage representation' *(agôn)* and of actors." By contrast, Ghosh argues that in "ancient Indian dramas the decoration (i.e. the costumes and make-up) mostly plays an important part." "Another peculiarity, . . . he adds "was their general dependence on dance *(nrtta),* song *(gita),* and instrumental music *vadya).*[33]

The essential and/or most empowered form of theatre is not the same for every culture. In non-Western cultures, dance (more than any other form) seems to be the most exemplary form of art and theatre. By extension, it is the most powerful and empowering means of self-and-world representation in these worlds. In Bali, for instance, dance-theatre is the most magic-and-power-laden form of representation, although the near-mystical puppet-theatre *(Wayang Koelit)* seems to be the form most utilized in direct traditional aetiology and acculturation. Antonin Artaud's argument of Balinese dance-theatre as total art (discussed in the chapter 5 of this book) proceeds from the view of dance as the most enabling from of theatrical representation. The historical and cultural influence of India on Bali can be found in the fact that a good deal of the story or plot material of Balinese theatre is taken from the Indian *Ramayana* and the *Mahabharata.* Direct influences of the *Natya-*

sastra are not easily found, though the importance of the mise-en-scène or total staging of Balinese theatre seems to be in keeping with the quintessential materiality and decorativeness of Sanskrit drama.

The fundamentality of the dance to the representation of the ethnic or primitive African self-and-world is argued by E. E. Evans-Pritchard in *Witchcraft, Oracles and Magic.* His conviction that dance is the primary form of reflection for Azande witch doctors comes from his observation, time and time again, that "when asked a question they will always dance rather than ponder it to find an answer." Similarly, Geoffrey Gorer suggests in "Function of Dance Forms in Primitive African Communities" that dance is the most important aesthetic and religious art and form in West Africa. It is "the chief medium which gives meaning to their lives and united [*sic*] them with the forces which people their universe." A simple explanation might lie in the fact that dance is pivotal to most African rituals, and thus, it is conceivable for African dance forms to be seen as empowered to create culture or, at least, act as stimulants of culture. The view that dance is the exemplary form of African art and representation was widely held during the period of Ghanaian-African decolonization. Despite their ideological differences, the two major factions in the Ghana National Theatre Movement (NTM) agreed on the "fundamentality of the dance idiom in Africa" when it came to "the very basic [question] of creating an indigenous and virile popular theatre" for postcolonial Ghana.[34]

Theatre appears in many different forms, guises, and disguises within and without one homogenous context, and is conceived in peculiar ways by particular writers and movements, often on the prior basis of the kind of intervention they seek to make in the real world. The theatricalization of human experience can therefore be a precursor to real action, and the deployment of theatre in their quests for self-and-world orientation and redirection is the common link between the writers and movements discussed in the following chapters of this book. It bears keeping mind, however, that the form of theatre proposed to undersee these quests is not one but many.

The following chapters offer various conceptions of theatre, all in the pursuit of one overriding objective—the re-ordering of human experience. I have often suspended questions concerning the validity of claims made for theatre by each of the writers and movements discussed in the initial parts of this work. My aim is to understand the ubiquity of such claims and to monitor the conditions under which they flower, not to prove their truth or falsity. True, valid, real, or not, these claims reveal a lot about what human beings do in the production and reproduction of their selves-and-worlds. My primary target is the varied forms and possibilities of human living and being-in-the-world. Theatre is merely one of the many possible forms in which human experience can be rationalized, formalized, and energized, but it is often said to be an umbrella or rubric for all other forms of human self-and-world representation. Theatre is an alibi for the formal possibilities of representation, and I use it as a via indirecta to other forms of representation. By means of theatre, I circumscribe the various ways in which human beings conceal the inchoate disorderliness of untamed or undomesticated experience behind the simplified and stabilized fronts of art and culture.

Empirical reality and logical consistency are not always the keys to the truth or saliency of all human experience. In many spheres what counts most is the life-enabling leap of faith that allows some human beings to make claims and representations that are believed by others. What is assumed or said by human beings is often of no less importance than what it enables them to do. Thus, what is most fascinating about the writers discussed in the following chapters is the heroic struggle they undertake to stretch art, and theatre in particular, across the tatters they see in the fabric of their self-and-world. Their quest to create symbolic patches and surplus values makes their work ideological in the comprehensive sense and justifies their investigation in this book.

4

Adolphe Appia: The Ideological and Acculturative Priorities of Wagnerian Music-Drama and Appian Living Art

Even though all the writers and movements discussed in this book conceive theatre in peculiar and startling ways, it is my inclusion of Adolphe Appia that has been met with the most consternation. The most creditable complaint is that Appia's work, particularly his theoretical writings, are "not widely known . . . and even less widely respected" (to quote the words of a recent reader). It seems to me, however, that the unstated but often-hinted-at reason for the widespread resistance to my discussion of Appia is his acolytic relationship to Wagner and his initial endorsements of Germanism. After all, similar sympathies in Nietzsche's *Birth of Tragedy* had provoked some critics to suggest the expurgation of sections of this work. There seems to be an assumption of a continuity between late nineteenth-century German national-personalism and Nazism. The general tendency in Western discourse, since the Second World War, has been to repress all previous instances of German nationalism by projecting them forward into Hitler and his infamous band of brigands, misfits, and murderers. What is not salutary or normal, this attitude seems to suggest, is best rejected totally, ostracized completely, and thus, denied even the smallest space in one's mind. The driving fear is that closeness of any kind to that pathological event might lead to contamination and seduction by it.

However, what is not grappled with (and the physical connotation is intended) will not be effectively understood, and what is not understood stands a good chance of disguising itself as something else, returning surreptitiously, and becoming more resistant to cure. To paraphrase Santayana somewhat, ignorance of the deep probabilities and necessities of a certain occurrence increases the chances of its repetition. If there is one driving force behind the present book, it is that human thought is not without will and affects, nor without blind desires and agendas. I have absolutely no patience with the notion of disinterested objectivity behind which much of the violence of Western rationalism is often concealed. I believe that all human thought does service to some ontological-metaphysical assumptions and teleological ends.

It would be a happier world that did not only set stock on the placid surfaces of uttered claims but also sought to understand the contextual-historical needs and wills behind them. The fundamental why and wherefores underlying representations of human experience are as important as their barefaced claims and surfaces, if not more important. Human thought is both freeing and constricting; in any case, all thought reduces and simplifies the quintessential complexity of phenomenal experience. The terms of thinking, the categories by means of which human experience is described and interpreted, often involve the exclusion of a plethora of other possibilities and actualities. On the list of possible exclusions are palpable human others and their own terms, forms, and systems of self-and-world representation. Thus, apparently theoretical or intellectual formulations of human experience can easily become the means of ontological and anthropological violence committed against other human beings.

This possibility of violence in theorizations of human experience lies in the human tendency to define experience in contrast to others, be they human or nonhuman. Appia's formulation of German national-personal culture in terms of a quintessential opposition to French-Latinic genius and culture is a case in point. Neo-Africanist conceptions of a communalist African personality in opposition to an allegedly individualist Euro-Western one is yet another example. Most commentators would agree that the seeds of German nationalism were first sown in the wake of the fall of Imperial Roman Empire; at least, William Shirer makes such a claim in *The Rise and Fall of the Third Reich*. For whatever it is worth, the beginnings of African nationalism were framed in terms of a resistance to the trans-Atlantic slave trade, and to Western colonialism. Only later on did it become an overriding contestation of Euro-Western hegemony as anchored in the humanistic values of the Enlightenment project.[1]

The recent eruption of ethnicisms and nationalisms in Eastern Europe and other parts of the world also suggests that this form of self-and-world representation is a concomitant of the breakup or breakdown of old empires, totalities, and utopias. In fact, the recrudescence of nationalism in Europe since the nineteenth century is generally recognized as a consequence of the failure of the cosmopolitan-universalistic dreams and claims of Western Enlightenment and capitalism. However, nationalism does not solely pertain to or obtain in the modern (post-imperial, post-capitalist) world; on the contrary, it is a phenomenon that results from the perception and exploitation of collective (ethnic-tribal) differences. It is also a consequence of conquests—"By the Rivers of Babylon, yea we sat down, and yea we wept, when we remember Zion." Symbolically or metaphorically, nationalism is a quest for Zion, an old and holy world and existence, that can be found hidden or festering beneath the placid surfaces of even the most stable moments in human history.[2]

The ubiquity of nationalism means that it needs to be understood in its various conceptions and contexts. The sobering truth is that insofar as ethnic, racial, and national differences exist in the world nationalism can never be fully domesticated, overcome, or even repressed. The very fact that it is particularly parochial and exclusionary makes nationalism very seductive (affective-affective) to present-day people and worlds. The various limited racial, gender, and biological -isms that prevail today are profoundly related to ethnonationalism, if only because of their common rejection of the old and grand Western ideologies, liberalism and Marxism among them.

What we human beings call culture is essentially a veneer of civility and sociability we create at great cost to veil our basic animality in much the same way that clothes cover our nakedness. This is not to say that animality is inherently bad, but that it has aspects (such as the violent instinct for survival and the infantile or undomesticated quest for self-aggrandizement) that cultured-civilized human beings do not want to admit or exhibit. Culture conceals the undesirable recessive features of our animality by creating taboos and taboo systems or laws and conventions that devalue these instincts and, hopefully, keep them at bay. But, like wolves, these repressed but untamed impulses keep baying at the ascendant moons of human culture and civility. In spite of its heroic attempts to uplift human existence by investing the choices made in it with notions of divinity, priority, and antiquity, human culture often fails or becomes vulnerable in moments of crisis. Like any other animal, the human being is impinged upon by its surroundings and circumstances, and in different existential circumstances the same human being can appear and act differently. Anything that threatens human biological-material survival can make short work of culture, bringing to the fore a basic animal instinct for survival that often brooks no pretenses or niceties and does not stand on ceremony.

It has been demonstrated, quite compellingly, in many human histories that a hungry human being becomes a desperate being who is not as glorious or as self-mystifying, and self-civilizing as a well fed one. In the same way, a human culture that is hungry and/or armed with a justifiable or unjustifiable grudge against the world is a threat not only to other cultures, but also to itself. Humanity or culture that is racked with what Neitzsche terms "ressentiment" or bad conscience is a dangerous one, and, incidentally, most nationalisms (or nationalistic-parochial representations of experience) are often based in cultural-collective feelings of ressentiment (bad conscience) and bad faith. In most cases, however, these negative motives are hidden beneath outwardly laudable quests for lost (nostalgic-atavistic) selves-and-worlds, totalities that are said to have existed before a certain moment and/or form of trauma. Hunger, oppression, and alienation, whether resulting from the actions of the self or others, are among the main causes of the oft-concealed ressentiment in nationalisms.[3]

Appia's career in the theatre was born out of his search for a more forceful kind of theatre that could overcome the putative fragmentation of the Euro-Western self-and-world. He was convinced that Wagner's music-drama form best serves this ideological-acculturative agenda. For him, as for Wagner himself, the music-drama form was the primary means of creating and sustaining a pre-imperial (Roman) and pre-Napoleonic (French) German national-personality and culture. The fact that Appia's works conceive theatre as a viable means of presenting and representing human experience, that is to say in the light of ideology, is enough justification for their discussion in this work. The alleged or proven obscurity of his theoretical works is beside the point; in fact, this obscurity could very well be the result of the willful repression of parts of his corpus because of their unabashed Teutonism and gnostic-mysticism. But, by comparison, Artaud's theoretical statements on theatre are more gnostic and mystical; they are also orientalistic-primitivist to the extreme. So why have I not heard any complaints about including Artaud in this book?

Perhaps the most compelling reason why the chapter on Appia is an integral part of this book on theatre an ideology is that it offers the most explicit *Western* example of the conception of theatre in the light of nationalism. It is, thus, a precursor and companion piece to my discussion of the Ghana National Theatre Movement project in chapter 7 of this book. This last chapter is, in fact, the conceptual origin of this whole endeavor. By way of Appia's writings on theatre, I stalk the concept-phenomenon of nationalism, a quarry whose centrality to the Ghana National Theatre Movement project makes it the third important subject of this book, behind theatre and ideology. Comparative understanding, such as that which obtains in my inclusion of both Appia and the Ghana National Theatre Movement in this book, brings a strategy of indirection, circumlocution, and circumnavigation to bear on any investigation; it allows one to question one's quarry indirectly and to understand it in relation to its familiars. The Appia chapter augments the chapter on the Ghana National Theatre Movement and is augmented in turn by the latter. I cannot lose was pathos of distance.

The kind of selections I make in this work reflect my basic agenda, which is to illuminate the ontological-teleological assumptions and the contextual-historical factors that underwrite theatrical forms and their peculiar formulations of human experience. Whether these formulations are good or bad, comforting or troubling is beside the point. I believe that one cannot preempt or obviate a tendency or happenstance until one has understood the implicit and explicit reasons for its existence. Understanding presupposes a coming to terms with the appurtenant conditions of the subject-object with which one is confronted, as seen and described by those involved with or closest to them. Such understanding requires some measure of sympathy for the event and the actors who participate in it so as to avoid the making of a priori judgments. It also avoids the Western scientistic pretense of being able to overstand (to stand above and beyond) both one's own interests and those of the subject-object of enquiry.

Because I tend toward this way of understanding, I let the subjects and objects of my investigation speak for themselves, for the most part, at least. I want to let them give enough of themselves for their own reasons and on their own terms. Once I come to understand the nature and elements of subject's self-presentation and its reasons for being, however, I begin the necessary process of interrogating them on my own behalf and in the interest of my own understanding. I like to think that this approach to criticism is agonistic, that it is akin to a hunter's dance with his or her prey; me being the observer-hunter and my conceptual-phenomenal quarry the prey. I recognize that my quarry has every right and every inclination to present or absent itself in a way that will place it outside my reach. In anticipation of this, I join my quarry in its dance around the fires of its naive or simple claims to truth, all the time keeping an eye on the subjective will and affects concealed beneath the smoothed fronts of its self-presentation. Ultimately, I encircle my quarry and lead it toward the lights, having reached the understanding that while simplification and exclusion might be necessary, even endemic, to human thinking and self-and-world representation, forms and systems that are over exclusive can be dangerous because they harbor the bad seed of other-erasing violence.

I do have a healthy abhorrence for oppression in any form, be it veiled as a quest to enlighten humanity (the mask of Western Enlightenment colonialism) or to redeem and purify the folk essence by ridding it of its contaminant-others (the unspoken and unspeakable desire in most nationalisms). But, above all, I fear the kind of ignorance and laziness that localizes any abnormal or traumatic occurrence in human history in a particular moment, individual, or people. Such an attitude precludes the possibility of actively understanding and obviating the recurrence of that problem or pathology. In such projections and localizations, human extremism and violence are always aberrations; Hitler and Nazism, for example are aberrations in the otherwise absolute yet noble progression of the humanistic Western Spirit *(Geist)*. The same goes for all other-denying and other-murdering historical-political forms, systems, and -isms that contradict august Western Enlightenment humanism. Freed of these pathological aspects and manifestations, Western humanism can appear forever triumphant and Western humanity itself will be seen as eternally and essentially good. Not a chance! This, in a rather large nutshell, is the reason why I insist on illuminating the West-discomfitting representations of experience by Wagner and Appia.

The Acculturative Force of Music in Appia's Early Works and their Singular Dedication to Making Wagner's Music-Dramas More Complete and Powerful

> One like me, who has felt this tragic conflict . . . the necessity of presenting music and the human body simultaneously . . . will never disavow Wagner the man, or his works, for they inspired me with compassion and set me free
>
> —Appia

Adolphe Appia's place in the canon of modern Western theatre staging and lighting is generally recognized; his ideas on staging and lighting are included with those of Antonin Artaud, Bertolt

Brecht, C. Gordon Craig, Stanislavsky, and a host of others in *The Theory of the Modern Stage*. But beyond the specific confines of staging and lighting and, particularly, where theory or the general conception of theatre is concerned, he still remains an obscure figure in Western theatre. Most commentators would not go as far as Lee Simonson to claim that "the history of staging might almost be divided by B. A. [Before Appia] as history in general is divided by B. C." To Simonson, Appia's stature is near monolithic; he is the "indubitable creator" and innovator of the fundamental principles of modern Western theatre staging and lighting. He adds that "modern designers accepted a torch without knowing who lighted it; our experiments amplified Appia's theories almost before we knew his name, had seen his drawings, or heard a quotation from his published works." Simonson also suggests, apparently in a moment of acolytic excess, that Appia is "that rare combination, a creative artist of exceptional imagination and at the same time a rigorously logical theorist."[4]

The undeniable truth, however, is that Appia's theoretizations of Western theatre are more vatic and mystical than rigorously logical. Indeed, by the account of none other than Simonson, Appia's writing is often marked by "*schwärmerei,* the bewildering mixture of philosophical concepts such as 'inner reality,'" by "romantic and mystical imagery," and by the "transcendentalism of German metaphysics." To a similar end, Beacham suggests that "beyond . . . a gift for predictions, Appia had a talent . . . for inspired *suggestiveness*" and possessed "a vital sense of purpose" that sought to "discern once again the sacred and miraculous in [the] ancient, much degraded art" of theatre.[5]

The mystical-metaphysical tendency in his works could be one reason why Appia's influence in modern Western theatre is often restricted to his more practical or realizable ideas on staging and lighting. Another possible and certainly creditable reason offered by Simonson is that even his innovative ideas on staging and lighting were not credited to him until nearly a decade after his death in 1928. But it seems hardly an accident that the repression of Appia's theories on theatre also means the suppression of his endorsements of Richard Wagner and the music-dramatic quest to create a German nationalist-personalist myth and culture *(Kultur).*[6]

H. D. Albright's suggests that "though he was in the vanguard Adolphe Appia's work was but one aspect of a much broader sweep of change . . . in the air everywhere after the turn of the century." Indeed, Appia's antirealistic approach to theatre has profound affinities with such late nineteenth century European artistic manifestos as romanticism, expressionism, and symbolism. He also tended to gravitate toward mentor figures, the most conspicuous and problematic among whom are Richard Wagner and Houston S. Chamberlain. Walther R. Volbach, Appia's official biographer, attributes this tendency to Appia's shy, retiring, and even insecure character. Appia also collaborated with many contemporaries artists, among whom are Jacques Copeau, Emile Jacques-Dalcroze, and Toscanini. His ideas on theatre often meshed with some of these mentors and collaborators; in fact, his renovations of the principles modern staging and lighting are similar to those proposed by H. Gordon Craig, a contemporary with whom he is known to have once met and exchanged ideas. Appia disagreed with Craig's view of the actor as a living puppet manipulated by an autocratic theatre-director—at least, he was more ambivalent than Craig was regarding the hierarchical relationship between the director and actor—but he soundly agreed with Craig on the need to renovate modern staging and lighting. The staging and lighting sketches he drew for Wagner's music-dramas and other Euro-Western operatic forms were very similar to those of Craig. In mythologizing Appia, however, Simonson dismisses Craig as a "plagiarist" or mere "imitator" of Appia's ideas.[7]

Appia's canonical innovations of the principles of modern Western theatre staging and lighting are, by and large, serendipities of his pursuit of ethico-political agendas under the umbrella of theatre. Thus, the suppression of such agendas from commentaries on his works leaves his ideas on staging and lighting in an infelicitous vacuum. The motivating idea in Appia's view of theatre is that modern Western society is fragmented, disunited, and alienated. He is not alone in this conviction; Antonin Artaud and Bertolt Brecht hold similar views and their conceptions of theatre harbor similar redemptive-disalienating desires. The juxtaposition of investigations of the works of these three important figures in modern Western theatre, therefore, can provide us with a comprehensive light on the various theatrical-symbolic means proposed for the overcoming of the actual or imagined ills of modern Western society. Taken together the theatrical arguments of these three writers reveal the kind of myth making that have occurred at critical moments in modern Western societies and cultures.

Appia's early works on theatre are obsessed with maximizing the ideological and acculturative (*Gesamtkunstwerk*-ian) power of Wagner's music-dramas vis-à-vis their quest to create, first, a German national-personal culture and ideology, and then possibly, ultimately, a pan-European mythology. Interestingly, Appia's career in the theatre was born out of dissatisfaction with it; the first theatrical event he attended, Gounod's production of *Faust* in 1881, was in his own words "a moral and aesthetic letdown." He found the imprisonment of the moving, three-dimensional actor-singer in the two-dimensional stage floor and painted scenery profoundly disturbing. Appia seems to have found a renewed sense of hope in the theatre, however, when he attended the "momentous" opening of Wagner's *Parsifal* in 1882. This discovery of Wagner's mythologistic work, Beacham suggests, gave Appia the sense of "a mission . . . which fulfilled both existential and aesthetic imperatives [and it] coloured and characterized his personality and work throughout his life." "In Wagner, Appia recognized an artist whose titanic genius can redeem theatre and raise it to the level of true art." As Appia himself testifies, "*Parsifal* may rightly be called *Bühnenwelhfestspiel* (holy festival of theatre), for it consecrates the stage upon which it appears. . . . Wagner accomplished a miracle in his last work. He overcame the obstacles and problems of visual realization with weapons more powerful than any technical principle."[8]

Appia believed that in creating holy works of theatre such as *Parsifal,* Wagner "seized the initiative and . . . demanded that dramatic art return to its distant sources," there to attain "once more the purity, perfection and beauty which had been its story in antiquity."

> By freeing the music from its self-centered and unnatural isolation, and by joining it with the dramatist in a fruitful union Wagner took the first, the decisive step. But he neglected the role of the body . . . [a]nd because of this lack of understanding, he subjected the human body to manifest violence from beginning to end of the productions. But now, with the liberation of the body, music is once again free. . . . This *vital* step has been taken. The poet will become the prime focus; *he alone* will consecrate the divine union of music with the human body.[9]

Appia also believed that Wagner "conspicuously failed to reform scenic practice" and thereby made impossible the holistic realization of his music-dramas. To correct this failing, he dedicates his first two publications on theatre to ensuring that Wagner's "powerful music-drama" form (already well endowed with ideality and spirituality) attains the sensuous-material consciousness it lacked. Appia's first published work was *La mise en scène du drame wagnerian* (1895). Incidentally, it was not translated into English until 1982 when it was published as *Staging Wagnerian Drama*. The second part of this work comprised Appia's previously unpublished "Notes on Staging *The Ring of the Nibelung,*" the very first essay he wrote on the staging of theatre.[10]

Staging Wagnerian Drama was written at the encouragement of Houston S. Chamberlain, Wagner's biographer, disciple, and son-in-law whom Appia had met on a visit to Dresden in 1884. But the renovations Appia proposed were not implemented at Bayreuth until 1956 when Wolfgang Wagner, Wagner's second heir and guardian of his legacy, decided Bayreuth was ready for them. Cosima Wagner (née Liszt), wife, first heir, and guardian of Wagner's legacy considered the implicit suggestion in Appia's work that Wagner's productions lacked total spatial self-consciousness nothing short of preposterous.[11]

Still, Appia remained a "passionate wagnerite" and his own aunt described him to Volbach as "the maddest Wagnerian I know. . . . Wagner has taken the place for him of religion, of love, of *every-thing.*" The extent of Appia's obsession with Wagner is evident in the fact that his first published work was devoted to staging Wagnerian drama and titled as such. Moreover "two thirds of *Music and Stage Setting*" (his second published work) "are devoted to a lengthy speculation on the future of [Wagner's] music drama." Appia's second work, originally published in 1899 as *La musique et la mise en scène,* was translated into English as *Music and the Art of the Theatre* in 1962. It treated in greater detail staging ideas that were merely sketched in *Staging Wagnerian Drama* and proposed a symbolistic-expressionistic treatment of stage lighting on which Appia's fame in the modern Western theatre rests. In it, "Appia accepts Bayreuth as the ultimate expression of German culture" but also believed that it could be the basis of a pan-European culture that will facilitate a "free interchange" or "mutual exchange" between German "Romantic Idealism" and the "Gallic capacity for objective analysis."[12]

H. D. Albright, rightly suggest that "a good starting point in examining Adolphe Appia's aesthetic system is to be found in his criticism of Wagner." To the extent that it is the seed bed of Appia's endorsements and criticisms of Wagner as well as of his conceptions of theatre in the light of nationalism or and internationalism, *Music and the Art of Theatre* will serve as the point of departure for the present investigation of Appia's early works. Of this exemplary early work Appia writes: "music has been the inspiration of this book" and "without Wagner . . . it could not exist." Wagner "the Master's work[s]" are "untried and revolutionary kinds of drama" that create "a violent revolution similar to those instigated by speeches of a social or political reformer." "Like all messiahs,"

Wagner brings "'not peace but the sword'; for every revelation is in itself a judgement of the condition which has made it necessary. Wagner is an implacable judge. In his assertions we atone for the mean lies of expediency."[13]

In a preface written in 1918 to one English edition of *Music and the Art of the Theatre,* Appia predicts that:

> The dramatic art of tomorrow will be the *social act,* in which each of us will assist. [It will take the form] of majestic festivals in which a whole people will participate, where each of us will express our feelings, sorrows, our joys, no longer content to remain a passive onlooker.

It is evident to him that "Wagner knew that he could make his intent clear only by the total domination *of the spectator,* but "he relied solely upon music to control the spectator." In correction, Appia suggests that to be able to function effectively the "autonomous artist, the composer-dramatist . . . must master and, ideally, control all the disparate elements of production."[14] In Appia's early works, the acculturative possibilities of music are inextricably linked with Wagner's genius and exceptional individualism, both of which are cast in a political light. To him, the "master-artist" must necessarily be a master politician, someone who can exercise control in the social sphere as well. It is on this level that artistic-theatrical and ethico-political agendas meet in Appia's framework of theatrical representation.

The innovations Appia proposes for the staging and lighting of modern Western are propelled by his stated hostility to "spoken drama" and to the realistic staging praxis of the late nineteenth century. This hostility becomes focused in his predisposition toward "Wagnerian," "word-tone" or "music" drama. The acculturative force Appia finds in this hybrid form of theatre lies in his view of it as a gnostic-symbolic reconciliation of the spheres of spirit/ideal (epitomized by music) and flesh/materiality (whose highest representative is the actor's body) into a holy totality. Music symbolizes the gnostic realm of ideal-spirit because its time as not real-actual or everyday, but rather inner or ideal. Music makes its own time and is, indeed, time itself; it controls the mundane elements of theatre, and, ultimately, life itself. Thus it is the singular means by which moral fixity and order can be injected into the space of concrete-phenomenal life. Music compels the conformity of phenomena to the original Word uttered by the Ideal-Spirit, as such, it is to both an alibi and the alias for the absolute master music-

Adolphe Appia

dramatist, God. The earthly representative of it is God/Source is, of course, Wagner.[15]

Appia first proclaimed the "absolute sovereignty of music" and then instituted a hierarchy of subservient elements on its behalf in *Staging Wagnerian Drama*. This became the common feature of all his works. His omnipresent quest to unify and retotalize the disparate elements of life and art is based in the premise that "every contradiction ceases from the moment that the form and the object of the expression are identical." "Music must reign as the infallible monarch over all the elements of the setting" because, in his view, "music, and music alone, can arrange the elements of production in a harmony of proportions superior to anything that could ever be conjured up by our imagination. Without music, this harmony *does not exist,* and therefore cannot be experienced." Music in itself, Appia believes, is the unity and harmony of form and content; indeed, one motto of *Music and the Art of the Theatre,* later repeated in his final work and magnum opus *The Work of Living Art,* is a paraphrase from Schopenhauer that says that "when music reaches its noblest power, it becomes form in space." More importantly, Music would be for Appia the chief means of Euro-Western self-and-world transformation (revolution) because "music and what it expresses ["ideal" or "inner reality"] is the supreme defiance hurled against the forces of materialism and utilitarianism in our century."[16]

The apotheosis of music as the paramount agent of self-and-world disalienation is not peculiar to Appia and Wagner, but rather, a dominant trope in late nineteenth-century European romanticism. Susanne Langer argues in *Philosophy in a New Key,* for example, that music was conceived as "pure" or "significant form" and as a "kind of language . . . of genuine conceptual content" in the works of Schopenhauer, Wagner, Liszt, Berlioz, and Nietzsche. This empowered and empowering view of music is not limited to that particular period and movement. Written as late as the 1960s, Louis Arnaud Reid's "Art, Truth and Reality" argues that "the musician is a creator, if ever there was one, out of natural materials, and what he creates is a new "reality", and a new vision of reality."[17]

In a less ahistorical vein, Appia insists that "if it is to have unity, a work of art must be produced in a social milieu," that there is "a close relationship between Wagner's dramatic works and the time of their creation," and that their "very existence depends upon such a milieu." Nevertheless, "every work of genius implies a conflict to some degree," which means that the attempt "to achieve the Master's (Wagner's) ideal synthesis of the arts" *(Ge-samtkunstwerk)* exists in conflict with the regnant conditions in his society.[18]

The preponderant desire in Appian representation is to inject ideality or spirituality into human existence, and Appia believes that this can only be achieved through the subordination of materiality to a "higher reality." Because he "offer[s] exclusively the view of the director" in *Staging Wagnerian* Drama, Appia insists that the "one and highest goal of the actor in the Wagnerian drama is *renunciation*." The solution he proposes for the struggle for ascendancy between the actor and the director in late nineteenth-century European theatre is that the actor defer to the *"higher role"* of the director, for, only then "finally can the audience focus entirely on the work itself: and all those worries about an 'interpretation' which, at present, are the death of drama, will be reduced to a point where it is hardly noticeable."[19]

The importance to Appia of organization and hierarchy in the relationships between the agents of theatre is best appreciated in the face of proliferation and fragmentation of customary or conventional unities, be they real or imagined. As Michael Hays argues with regard to the proliferation of theatres in the late nineteenth century, a "structural hierarchy allowed each person a position in relation to his ability to understand the director's interpretation" of the putatively unitary and unifying Word and Text.[20] The hierarchy of elements Appia institutes in his early works (and in his last one as well) seems to be occasioned by the same fundamental insight. Yet, for all its apparent deferences to unitary forms of authority, Appia's theatrical hierarchy is often underlined by internal reciprocities.

It sometimes appears in Appia's early works that the actor needs to be depersonalized or dehumanized (like Craig's living puppets) in order to best become the pure and clear medium or vessel of music. The bipolar position of the actor in Appia's hierarchy of theatrical elements is determined in one direction by subservience to higher elements (represented by music and the creator-composer) and in the other by its control of inanimate elements of production such as light and setting. All told:

> The Actor of his own, . . . has no freedom of initiative in wagnerian drama for his whole role is precisely laid down in the measures given by the music. Music is the soul of the drama. Thus, in the final instance, it is the drama that determines staging. But . . . the drama can only determine staging if it uses the actor as its intermediary.[21]

In Appia's early views on theatre the audience is largely a passive spectator uncritical of the word-tone representations it attends and consumes. The "one goal" of Wagnerian "word-tone" or "music drama," Appia suggests in *Music and the Art of the Theatre*, is "to convince the audience of the reality of life that sparks this particular drama." But he later revises this position in the 1918 preface to one English edition of *Music and the Art of the Theatre*. Here he declares that "the dramatist will never be able to liberate his *vision* if he insists upon projecting it in a space rigidly separated from the audience." His new found understanding of and respect for the "body" or concrete-materiality seems to be the reason for his revision of his original view of theatre. He declares that:

> Today, the resurgence of the human body as an expressive medium essential to our aesthetic culture is a concept which possesses many minds, animates the imagination, and gives rise to diverse experiment . . . all directed toward the same reform. We now feel that the performer tends, almost implicitly, to come closer to the spectator; we also feel . . . a mysterious involvement on the part of the spectator with the performer. Our modern productions used to force us into such miserable passivity that we veiled our humiliation in the shadowy recesses of the auditorium. But now, as we behold the body's effort to rediscover itself, our emotion is almost a fraternal collaboration: we wish to be that body on stage; our role of spectator is now a responsibility; the social instinct awakens in us, an instinct which has been heartlessly stifled until now, and the barrier between the stage and the audience now strikes us as an unpleasant and unfortunate dissociation, the result of our own egoism.[22]

The ideal space of performance in Appia's early works is clearly based on Wagner's *Festspielhaus* at Bayreuth, and as Donald C. Mullin suggests, the "Wagnerian theatre plan," like "most of the 'free,' 'mass,' and 'epic' theatre styles" of the late nineteenth-century Europe, is based in a "quasi-religious interpretation of the function of drama." It is "*authoritarian in concept*. The audience was to submit passively to the will of the producing artist, and was to be carried to supreme emotional heights which would transcend daily experience." The only difference between Appia's early ideal place of performance and Wagner's *Festspielhaus* is that he replaces Wagner's double proscenium with a single one. Appia's ideal theatre "will have no permanent feature except an auditorium, on the other side of which a fairly large area will remain empty. In this space the *drama* will come into existence . . . [and in it] technical processes will cease to play any expressive part whatever."[23]

In his last work, Appia abolishes the proscenium and unifies the stage and auditorium into one total space of performance. But this theatre, which he names "cathedral of the future," does not underplay the "quasi-religious" priorities and possibilities of theatre. Appia had designed and had built a unified theatre space for the Institute of Eurythmics at Hellerau in 1912 and, if the reports on the "festivals" held in it are anything to go by, it shared and perhaps extended, in a more collective and bodily way, the ideological agendas of the *Festspielhaus* at Bayreuth.

The innovative expressionistic theory of lights Appia formulates in *Music and the Art of the Theatre* is, justifiably, the repository of his fame. Now applied to all kinds of theatre, this theory of lights was propounded solely for the staging of nonrealistic, musical drama. The antirealistic or mystical underpinnings and ramifications of this theory are further augmented by the fact that Appia's argument of the expressive power of light tropes on the gnostic conception of God/Spirit as Light. Appia submits that like music, which it illuminates, light expresses the "inner essence of all vision"; "light is to production what music is to the score: *the expressive element in opposition to literal signs;*" indeed, "'expressive light' is *"living* light," a totalizing kind of light that is both physical and metaphysical in the sense that it "expresses night (moon or torchlight), or the supernatural." All told, Appia believes that

The sovereign power of light is undemonstrable to one who has not experienced it; to discuss its technical use is even more difficult. . . . The life of light is too simple to be analyzed. Only indirectly, by examining its misuse in our modern theatre, can we arrive more or less by induction at the normal function of light.[24]

"Light is distinguished from visibility by virtue of its power to be expressive. If there is no expression, there is no light, and such is the case in our theatres." This is the ground on which Appia banishes footlights and floodlights from his lighting plots, that they give mere "visibility" to phenomena as opposed to expressing them. Instead, he suggests the deployment of localized or motivated spotlights that could allow for subtleties of expression in the chiaroscuric interplay of light and shadow. "Light," Appia writes, "requires an object if it is to retain its expressiveness; it must light something, and encounter obstacles." In what amounts to a counterstatement of the tendency in "realistic" or "melodramatic" staging to focus lights on two-dimensional painted sets, Appia insists that the animate-materiate body of the actor is the worthiest object and obstacle to light, it is what makes light expressive.[25]

A corollary of expressive light is the multileveled yet monolithic three-dimensional stage settings Appia conceived for the staging of Wagnerian drama and other forms of music or operatic theatre. His rejection of both two-dimensional lighting and staging and painted scenery settings are an integral part of a quest to realize or embody the gnostic spirit-idea more fully in human experience. Light and sets are supposed to actively interact with the body of the actor, to facilitate as well as actively resist his or her movements and/or spatial objectives. However, the sketches of stage-settings Appia drew for Wagner's music-dramas, and for the few productions in which he was involved, tended to dwarf the human figure and render it insignificant. Furthermore, the near-darkness in which he swaddled his stage environments increased the subordination or shadowing of the human figure, the agent of drama. The monolithic stage settings and chiaroscuric light plots cooperated to create an effect of mystical and otherworldly awe. Incidentally Appia intended and lauded this very effect of his designs.[26]

In line with his mystical-metaphysical intentions, Appia suggests that at best art attempts to capture the state and logic of dreams; "the artist yearns for the dream, and his whole productivity bears its influence" because "the dream confers limitless powers." It frees up "the inner resources of our being" to "allow such free play of our latent powers" that "the life of intellect will never be able so clearly to display." "A mysterious thread is spread across our whole life in sleep, creating the unity comparable to the relationship of cause and effect in our waking hours." Appia believes that "that precious document, the dream teaches us more about the basic needs of our personality than the most scholarly investigation." Thus the "hierarchy of production" in life and art must both "be regarded as having a function equivalent to the dream—as a kind of spontaneous objectification of the aesthetic desire."[27]

That all the metaphysical and oneiric idealism in Appia's early works are directed toward very real material-political ends becomes apparent in the second and third parts of *Music and the Art of the Theatre*. Here Appia submits that "Wagnerian drama will constitute an *epoch*" simply because Wagner represents European experience "in quite a different way from that of a latin race." Wagner's specific genius seems to be nationalist-particularist to the extent that he

has created music that is *German,* in the fullest sense of the word. . . . Music had hitherto been considered a universal art, independent of language or nationality. In divesting it of its uniqueness, and thereby making it serve a higher aim, Wagner imposed on it the restrictions of the particular language of the word-tone dramatist.

Wagner establishes a "Wagnerian tongue" and a "Wagnerian thinking," yet these will be the means of creating an international or pan-European culture. This cosmopolitan or multinational culture, Appia believes, can neither "be communicated by a telegram" nor "be constrained by the lies of the press."[28]

For this new European culture (constituted by French/Latinic and German cultural-ideological extremes) to come into being, Appia insists:

> there must be a free interchange between the two races, but it must always be remembered that it is a mutual exchange and one race must not be permitted unduly to influence the other.
>
> For a long time German culture has been stifled by the oppressive effects of French Genius. Even today, this oppression is a serious obstacle to the realization of a national culture. The laborious beginnings of Bayreuth prove this.
>
> The ground on which the two cultures will be able to exchange their gifts of necessity ought to be a national one, where the dominant idea of each race will be expressed most purely; that is, wherever the inharmonious juxtaposition of the two races will not have exercised its deleterious influence.
>
> . . . What Latin culture can give to the German must first be refined by the latter before it can be accepted. The creation of Bayreuth gave the German the rare opportunity of expressing the dominant idea of his culture in a purity which seemed hardly possible in our contemporary civilization. At Bayreuth, he was able to share with the Latin the priceless treasure of the Wagnerian *idea*. Here, on this eminently national ground, he will able to accept what the Latin has to offer, for Bayreuth will act as the filter which will guarantee the purity of the foreign element and thus make it possible for the German to assimilate it.[29]

One wonders what kind of justice and fairness could be shown toward an other once it has been made a scapegoat and invested with "oppressive effects" the dominant self feels compelled to filter and purify from its representations. Appia's acolytic relationship to Houston S. Chamberlain, whom Modris Eksteins describes as "a proponent of a xenophobic germanic ideology" with "a reciprocated admiration for Adolf Hitler," also makes one wonder about the freeness of the "free interchange" and "mutual exchange" that he insists must exist between the French/Latinic and German extremes of the future European culture. It is worth noting that most national-personalist representation of human experience tend to revolve primarily around the filtering out of an other or others presumed or proven to be oppressive. Thus, one wonders most about the predilection for agonistic dualisms and other-excluding manichaeanisms in Western representations of experience, if not in human thought as a whole. One wonders if Nietzsche is not altogether correct in his observation that:

> The will to power can manifest itself only against resistances; therefore it seeks that which resists it. . . . Appropriation and assimilation are above all a desire to overwhelm, a forming, shaping and reshaping, until at length that which has been overwhelmed has entirely gone over into the power domain of the aggressor and has increased the same [self].[30]

The Collaboration with Emile Jaques Dalcroze on Eurythmics and its Influence on Appia's Ultimate Conception of Theatre in the Light of Living Art

> The theatre is but one of the forms of living art—the complete art
>
> —Appia

A curious letter Appia had written to the *Journal de Genève* in 1914 suggests that the First World War might have underscored the radical transformation of his cultural-political orientation, away from the Wagner-extolling exceptional individualism of his early works, toward the communalistic ethos celebrated in his last book, the *Work of Living Art*. In this letter, Appia reconstructs the First World War, the first great blow to Western humanist pretensions, as something that makes otiose the rugged individualism that drives Euro-Western culture. Its "loud voice shouts at us: You must suffer together; but then, like your sufferings, you must also express your joys together. Otherwise everything is futile." It is Volbach's conviction that under the "impact of the war [Appia's] admiration for Wagner lost some of the spell it had on him."[31]

If the First World War pointed the direction in which Appia was to go, his collaboration with Emile Jaques Dalcroze at the Institute of Eurythmics at Hellerau between 1909 and 1913 confirmed that direction. Before this collaboration, the first chance Appia had to implement his ideas on theatre staging and lighting was when he designed the setting alone and collaborated with Mariano Fortuny on the lighting of the 1903 production of excerpts from Bizet's

Carmen and Byron's *Manfred* at the Comtesse de Béarn's "Intimate Theatre" in Paris. The lighting design he created for this production mainly employed localized spotlights, reduced the use of footlights to the barest minimum, and was generally said to make for "stunning effects." However, Appia's innovations had limited success, while causing a great deal of controversy. Indeed, limited success and controversy were to be the mark of almost every production based on Appia's staging and lighting designs. Every single professional or semi-professional theatre production in which he was involved closed prematurely.[32] Appia describes the period of his collaboration with Dalcroze as a "marvelous voyage of discovery," adding that "without changing my orientation, eurythmics freed me from too inflexible a tradition, and, in particular, from the decorative romanticism of Wagner . . . eurhythmics determined my future progress." It was "the answer to my passionate desire for synthesis." Eurythmics is generally defined as a systematic way of training the human body to make it more responsive to and expressive of music and rhythm. Thus, it "corresponded with a new *Leibeskultur,* or 'body culture.'"[33]

Appia became acquainted with Jaques Dalcroze in 1906, but this did not yield a "noticeable change in the ideas of either artist" until 1909 when Appia presented Dalcroze with a body of designs titled "Rhythmic Spaces." Thereafter they worked "extensively on plans for the production of Aeschylus' *Prometheus.*" The Institute of Eurythmics Dalcroze founded at Hellerau was financed by Wolf Dohrn, a well-to-do businessman whom he met in Dresden while leading a workshop on Eurythmics. Dohrn was an idealist who was interested in helping "workers to overcome the threat of dehumanization in modern industry and to regain a sense of satisfaction in their work and its products." He had established an experimental factory at Hellerau ("bright meadow") on the outskirts of Dresden, in the hope that "a new utopian community could be established and nurtured . . . on principles of social equality, liberal and universal education and the revival of unalienated art and labour." Hellerau was to be, in Dohrn's words "the future centre for a spiritual and physical regeneration, out of which a broad social renewal would follow." This broad sound renewal is to "ensure that Hellerau's inhabitants would be free from the squalled and cramped land that was prevalent in the industrial quarters of most cities." Barely a month after meeting Dalcroze, Dohrn invited him to establish the institute of Eurythmics at Hellerau.[34]

By his own account, Dalcroze was "no friend of the theatre, this playing, which—usually with no conviction—is served up to blasé spectators." He "certainly [had] no intentions of establishing a theatre at Hellerau," and so he left the theatrical aspects of the Hellerau institute to Appia. One result is that "the Hall at Hellerau was constructed exactly according to [Appia's] plans." In these plans and the building based on them, Appia abolished "the proscenium arch and raised the stage, using a completely open performance space area for the first time since the renaissance." He was aiming at nothing less than ending the "unacceptable distinction between spectator and performer." The raised stage served to hide the orchestral pit Appia had retained from the Wagnerian plan. The cornerstone of the Hellerau Institute of Eurythmics was laid on 22 April 1911. In his opening speech, Dohrn proposed that annual *festspielen* (or "celebrations and festivals" of a people "widely and equally educated, and invigorated by . . . a sense of community") be held at Hellerau. Two such festivals were held before his untimely death in 1914; the possibility of subsequent ones was denied by the outbreak of the First World War toward the end of that year.[35]

The first festival at Hellerau opened on 26 June 1912, and the second took place between the end of June and the beginning of July 1913. Both of them presented selections from *Orfeo* and *Echo and Narcissus,* a variety of "school exercises and improvisations, some pantomime dances and a rhythmic representation of selections of classical music." The staging of Gluck's *Orfeo* was more complete, and "formed the centerpiece of," the second festival, which also included a display of "handicrafts, artwork and industrial products created by the inhabitants of Hellerau." Both productions "caused a sensation," much of it centering on Appia's innovative designs of the stage setting and on the lighting plot he devised in collaboration with Alexander von Salzmann.[36]

The lighting and setting designs of both festival productions pushed the productions as close to stylization as possible, causing one critic, "Arthur Seidl, professor of Music at the Leipziq Conservatory" to term them a "'lazy flight from the world' and 'fanaticism for stylisation.'" However, the general response was more favorable; Appia's design of Orfeo's descent into Hades was singled out and praised "as a revolutionary step in the development of theatre arts." George Bernard Shaw attended the second festival and described it as "one of the best performances of Gluck's *Orfee*" he had seen. Paul Claudel also enthused that the "union of music, the plastic sense, and light . . . fixes the course and direction along which [the festive-play] develops." The pronounced use of multileveled platforms and weighty draperies or curtains in the second festival staging of *Orfeo* created an "impression" Beacham describes as "solemn, monumental and austere." The chiaroscuric lighting scheme also made the production appear "somnambulistic" and "unreal," an effect Appia seemed to have intended. In a letter to his cousin he celebrates the fact that "thanks to the lighting, the characters share in this unreal atmosphere."[37]

Among the notable artists who attended the two Hellerau festivals were Arthur Granville-Barker, Max Reinhardt, Serge Diaghilev, and Nijinsky, and most of them had nothing but praise for the innovations they saw there. According to Beacham, the "success of the collaboration at Hellerau between Appia and Dalcroze was [so] prodigious" that "few who came to Hellerau failed to admire the work they saw there." Most, in fact, recognized "its startling potential for radically transforming orthodox theatre practice." Indeed, Eksteins attests that "when Diaghilev and Nijinsky visited Dalcroze at his school of eurythmics in 1912, they had persuaded Marie Lambert to assist Nijinsky in teaching rhythm to the corps de ballet [of *Le Sacre du Printemps*]."[38]

One visitor at Hellerau, H. C. Bonifas, who saw what he calls "the dawn of a new art and a new aesthetic life" came to share the "ultimate vision of a world renewed through 'living art.'" But, as Beacham points out, "Hellerau was itself a dream of sorts," and indeed, these illusions of Elysium were soon dispelled." Outside the mystical-somnambulistic confines of Hellerau the world moved relentlessly toward the First World War. The symbolic unity celebrated at Hellerau was, to all intents and purposes, unattainable in an everyday Europe marked by the proliferation of dangerously parochial nations and nationalisms. In fact, when Dohrn died in February 1914, following a skiing accident, Dalcroze was away in Geneva working on a Swiss nationalist pageant later known as the *Fête de juin*. The First World War broke out in August 1914 and precluded his return to Germany, and in November of the same year he "formally ended his connection with Hellerau." Appia was to collaborate with Dalcroze on the restaging of *Echo and Narcissus* at the new Institute of Eurythmics (Geneva) in 1920. But nothing was ever the same again, and their relationship was finally sundered in 1921. Perhaps in the hope of postponing the end of the most creative period in his theatrical career and life, Appia did not formally resign from the Geneva institute until 1923.[39]

In his "Curriculum Vita" of 1927 Appia writes that the *Work of Living Art* is "the most significant to complete expression of his ideas." He begins this self-proclaimed magnum opus with a critique of Wagner's "total work of art" *(Gesamtkunstwerk)*, a form Appia himself had once accepted as "the art form of the future." Appia argues that Wagner's "total work of art" is a "dangerous aphorism, . . . tempting because of the soothing simplification it so readily offers," but whose facile "harmonious combination or union of all the other arts" merely invites the critical sense to rest on a "pillow of idleness." The confidence displayed in Wagner's work, Appia writes, is a "nonsense" that is belied by the sordid reality of "our concerts, our art exhibitions, our architecture, our literature, [and] even our theatre."[40]

Appia's final publication is geared toward creating a quintessentially colloborative work of theatre he calls "the work of living art." The hierarchical organization of relationships between the constitutive elements of theatre adumbrated in his early works is still important, even crucial, but he devotes less time and space to them. In other words, they become naturalized or taken for granted. Reciprocity between the key elements of art and theatre becomes the most important quest and question. The two interrelated questions he attempts to answer right from the outset are: "To be organically unified—and therefore mutually subordinated— what sacrifices must the arts agree to? On the other hand, *what compensations will they offer us, in their new mode of existence?*" The point of departure towards an answer is still that:

> Mutual subordination will always remain the only substantial guarantee of the success of a collaboration. Subordination implies analysis; What am I to receive, and what must I give in return? A more or less willing neglect of this preliminary analysis lies at the root of most social and aesthetic errors. Devotion that only gives—and never takes—is misplaced devotion. . . .
> If music hopes to regulate the mobility of the body, it must first learn what the body expects from it. . . . Unless music first receives life, it can give nothing living to the body. . . . Hence, the body must deliver up its own life to the music, only to receive it anew, regulated and transfigured.[41]

The acculturative and coercive force of music remains strong in the *Work of Living Art;* "in music," Appia submits, "we possess an element, *springing from our inner selves,* whose discipline we can accept unconditionally. From music, then, will the work of *living* art be born; the discipline of music will be the principle of culture which will make the new tree fruitful—that, is on condition that we incorporate it into the roots and thus make it organically a part of the whole." In the perspective of living art, however, music is rigorously checked and balanced by the concrete body, with regard to which Appia stresses: "we mean by 'body'—the human body—the visible form of our whole being, and . . . its supreme connotations."

> The living and mobile body of the actor represents movement in space; it therefore plays a critical role. Without a text (which may be with or without music), dramatic art cannot exist; the actor is the bearer of this text. . . . In one hand, so to speak, the actor bears the text; in the other, as in a sheaf, he holds the arts of space. Irresistibly he brings his two hands together, and by movement creates the complete work of art. The living body is thus the real creator of the supreme art, holding as it does the secret of the hierarchical relations between the conflicting elements, because it stands at their head.[42]

The creative tension in Appia's ultimate work exists in the irreducibly reciprocal relationship between the ideality of music and the materiality of the body. Ideality must be bodied forth in phenomenal experience, while, on the other hand, materiality must strive toward transcendental ideality. "The body behaves at the command of material necessity. But the feelings of the soul, too, are expressed in space—through gestures." Even "inanimate forms, by opposing their solidity to the body, affirm their own existence . . . and thus close the cycle; beyond that, there is nothing."[43]

Appia suggests that as a result of the delegitimation and devaluation of individualism under Western capitalism and in the wake of the First World War, "art has no public now; the public, no art. Art has no direct reason with us anymore and more good reason." Thus, he rejects the customary representation of a human "subject" in the art on behalf of "Indication" or the "Expression" of "intelligible ideas." In his view, "to wish to represent a subject is always to forsake creating a work of art—which, in its essence, is pure and simple expression, with no regard to a given subject." In living art, "dramatic art does not exist to present the human being for *others*" for there can be no passive others. The central figure in living art is the "communal body," a living collective body that exists "imaginatively in a boundless space, with no witness but [itself]—just like Crusoe." This body creates "space and time, one through the other" and proclaims to itself as other, "I possess Art, in you! *I am art.*"[44]

The space in which the communal body creates living art is total, as well as holy; it is a "cathedral of the future," and in it "there is no auditorium, no stage, without us and beyond us. We are the play and the stage, because it is our living body that creates them. Dramatic art is a spontaneous creation of the body; our body is the dramatic author." In the totalizing or retotalizing space of the cathedral of the future, the communal body claims to have "virtually conquered Time and Space," cleared the table of history, and united the collective bodies of humanity. When this communal body triumphs, Appia suggests, it is an all-comprehending "We" or "Ourselves" who are uplifted enough to "become conscious of our power, and able to use it in *freely* creating a living work." "No longer will or antecedents be Literature and the other fine arts. Now we hold life at its roots." "We have come back to our sources; from our sources we are going to proceed." Ironically, the first step on the journey is the recognition that "like the other arts, dramatic art is the result of a modification of relationships." But it still "remains for us to find in ourselves the modifying factor." For Appia, music is still this modifying or organizing factor; "the new Being—ourselves—will be placed under the influence of music."[45]

Obviously, theatre is a metaphor and an indirect way of questioning life; in order to "arrive at a clear idea of living art (which art is possible without being necessarily 'dramatic' in the ordinary sense of the word), it was necessary to go by way of theatre, since that is all we have. However, the theatre is but one of the forms of living art—of the complete art." Life, then, is the province of living art, and its inherent plurality resurfaces the need for reciprocity and cooperation. "The Idea of Collaboration is implicit in the idea of *living* art. *Living art implies a Collaboration. Living art is social; it is, unconditionally, the social art.*" "In approaching the practice of *living* art, one finds himself in the presence of bodies—his own included," and "if the body is the creator of this art, the artist who possesses the Idea of the living body, implicitly possesses all these bodies."[46]

In the framework of Appian living art, the traditional individual artist is merely the catalyst of representation, not the chief agent. The individual artist now "possessed of the idea of collaborating in living art" "realizes that his choice of subjects can no longer be arbitrary" and that "his sense of values is being modified." "In him the eternal elements of humanity tend to predominate . . . over the particulars in which he formerly found pleasure." This artist comes to understand that "*living* art" can only "be the result of a discipline—a discipline which, though it may not affect all human bodies, will at least awaken all human souls, through the awakening of bodily feeling." Ultimately, "in every sphere of art, *living art* will serve as regulator, moderator, and liberator; for where there is living art, anarchy is impossible."[47]

Nationalism remains vital in Appia's ultimate conception of the-

atre insofar as the "patriotic festival" is *"living* art in its most
perfect purity, in its highest idealization." By means of living art,
the "eternal drama hidden beneath historical customs, events, and
costumes [is] made visible and audible to everyone." In the light
of the totalitarian nature of nationalisms, it is not surprising that
living art "needs no audience, for it implicitly contains the audience
within itself." Appia declares that no one can turn away from living
art "as though the work were unapproachable" because "to turn
away from a work of living art would be to disown our very selves."
Living art is a "great aesthetic experience" in which everyone must
join perforce; it is a search for "some connecting link that will
engender in us the divine spark." In living art, all is one, and one
and all are "artists."[48]

The aesthetic underpinnings of Appia's conception of living artistic revolution or self-and-world human redemption show him to
be a true student of late nineteenth-century European thought. For
all his invocations of scientificity and historicity, even Karl Marx
conceives the overcoming of the alienation of Western capitalist
humanity in aesthetic terms. "In Marx's prediction," Stefan Morawski suggests, "the man of the future—among, and together with,
his other attainments—[is] the aesthetic man;" "his enduring nature, then, among other endowments of zoon politicon, is aesthetic." In Marx's communist utopia, "all men would be artists to
some degree" and not only of one particular genre or form; "the
artist of the future will simultaneously be painter, poet, singer,
etc." Ultimately, "all of production can become art; and every art
can be made intimate with productivity."[49]

The fact that "in the Marxian view . . . alienation cannot be
completely superseded except with communism" is perhaps the
chief difference between Appia and Marx's aestheticization of
futuristic-utopian human experience. However, the teleological
motivations of Appia's ultimate work, the work of living art, or the
art of living, are socialistic and even communalistic. With "profound emotion," Appia "locks up all his beliefs" and "sums up his
highest aspirations" in the conviction that the communal body acts
in living art as a "creator of values." Specifically, the communal
artist invests in "humanity—his brothers" by "taking himself as
work *and* tool, and then . . . passing on his convictions to us."
Appia labels this process "aesthetic conversion" and laments
that it:

> is still unknown to the artist. Even the best intentioned ones still think
> they are promoting social solidarity and universal art by placing before

the poor spectator a work which was never destined for him, and which, moveover, he cannot comprehend in the form given.

Representational art tends to patronize its consumers, but "it is precisely the poor spectator who conditions the technique of living art; without him there is no technique."[50]

All along, the primary subject of Appia's enquiry into living art had been the communal body, a great part of which is composed of spectators. But he feared that "had he tried from the outset to present the great Unknown, he would have had to risk being misunderstood. Now, however, strengthened by the knowledge . . . gathered" to convince "the reader of the obligations impose[d] on our being and on its relation to public life," "it seems a misunderstanding is no longer possible." Therefore, Appia freely confesses that the prime objective of living art is to celebrate the "beautiful living flesh" and to make "most sacred . . . the human body." Living art restores faith in the "feeling of collectivity of human bodies" by underlining "the happiness that this collectivity insures." It emphasizes the ability to live "in common with others" in a way that opens "a window of wonder" on experience.

> To be an artist is first of all not to be ashamed of one's body—but to love it in all bodies.
>
> If I said that living art will teach us that we are artists, I implied that living art inspires in us love and respect—not love without respect—for our own body. Such a feeling is a collective one: the artist-creator of living art sees in all bodies his own; he feels in all the movements of other bodies the movements of his own. Thus he lives, bodily, in humanity; he is its expression. . . .
>
> . . . The future of our whole artistic culture—and, obviously the very existence of living art—depends on a correct bodily pedagogy. Its importance is incalculable.
>
> . . . Aesthetic Socialism is still unknown. We think we have done well for humanity when we place a work of art within the reach of all, according to the common hypocritical phrase. . . . A cake is no nearer the reach of the poor if one puts therein less butter and sugar. The very idea of placing a cake within the reach of the poor is a senseless one. It is *ourselves* that we must place, not within their reach, but where we can give to them.[51]

When informed that the masses were rioting for want of bread in events that would lead to the French Revolution of 1789, the queen of France, Marie Antoinette, is said to have promptly replied with no sense of irony at all that they should eat cake. Appia's invocation of this apocryphal naivety or indifference is very telling, but his ultimate conception of theatre as the art of life places it beyond mere sensual material necessity, beyond the "pleasure principle." Living art does not only "signify merely having the same pleasure with others," but also stresses the heroic-thanatic necessity of "suffering together." By suffering together, Appia does not mean lemminglike self-sacrifice or blind moth-to-naked-flame self-destruction. His notion of shared suffering is not party to the mass suicide (masochism) and genocide (sadism) that occurred on the killing fields of Europe during the First World War, and which Eksteins sees validated in Nijinsky's *Le Sacre du Printemps*. Appia's notion of suffering together betokens, on the contrary, "being animated throughout one's whole being—body and soul—with the same living and active flame. It means 'being afraid together' in the all-powerful embrace of beauty; it means having accepted together the creative impulse and its responsibilities."[52]

Under the auspices of living art, Appia attempts to reconceive human life as a thing of beauty and worth that ultimately resists all forms of crisis and potential devaluations of life. Living art covers the gamut of "this life-activity itself as expressed through a body—our body" and it demands self-discipline and social responsibility. The individual must "estimate for himself the place he occupies—or should occupy—within the limits of his age and social position, of his degree of culture and personal ability, in order to be a *living* artist, a representative of the *life* of art." Appia's hope is that "by developing ourselves as much as possible, then, by taking active or sympathetic parts in every manifestation of public life, by giving ourselves without reserve and without compromise, we can prepare for the joyous future of *living* art."[53]

The quest for unity and totality that had underwritten Appia's early works are restated in his final work, the *Work of Living Art*. The kind of theatre and theatrical means for achieving this singular goal had changed over time, as any dynamic phenomenal thing must, but Appia's eyes seemed to have remained steady on the prize. In his last work, he reaffirms the "imperious need to unite with others" as the fundamental drive in life and representation. He suggests *"the cathedral of the future"* as the only "place flexible enough to afford the realization of our every desire for a complete Life." In the wholistic-totalistic and all-comprehending (holy) space of this cathedral, Appia hopes that such limited forms and labels as "'concert,' 'presentation,' 'conference,' 'exhibition,' 'sport,' and so on, and so on, will be abandoned . . . forever. Overlapping in purpose and function, perhaps they will merge into one. And each of us, then, perhaps, can *live* his life in common with

everyone else, instead of watching it trickle away in diverse channels, between impervious walls."[54]

The hallowed or holistic cathedral of the future Appia suggests
as the only means of fulfilling the imperious need to unite with
others seems to be a higher return of the Geneva cathedral whose
closure at the outbreak of the First World War Appia had lamented
in his letter to the *Journal de Genève* in 1914. What he does in his
final work, then, is attempt to transform a negative event into a
positive one, to reconceive a real-historical cathedral that had been
marked with traumatic closure into an eternally open all-embracing
symbol. In fact, this futuristic cathedral is not only meant to bring
together and overcome the putative alienations and fragmentations
in the modern European self-and-world, not only the many small
and intimate theatres that came to be in fragmented Europe, but
also to redefine the different forms and occasions of play.

5

Antonin Artaud: Forms of "Total Art" and Their Peculiar Means for Disalienating the Occidental Self-and-World

There seems to be a great deal of similarity between various Western conceptions of theatre as a means revolutionizing the forms and/or reorienting the direction of human experience since the late nineteenth century. These similarities are particularly marked between Adolphe Appia and Antonin Artaud perhaps because they both tended toward a mystical-spiritual or metaphysical view of theatre. It is possible that Artaud was acquainted with Appia's work; Susan Sontag observes that "between 1930 and 1935, Artaud made numerous trips to Germany, where he saw productions by Adolphe Appia, . . . Meyerhold, Max Reinhardt, and Erwin Piscator." Appia died in 1928, so unless what she means is that Artaud saw productions done according to Appia's theatrical ideas, Sontag cannot be right. It is more likely that Artaud was indirectly influenced by the ideas of Appia by way of Jacques Copeau, whose "Théâtre du Vieux Colombier" was a model for Charles Dullin's "Atelier" at which Artaud worked and studied. Copeau collaborated, or at least consulted, with Appia on some of the productions at the Vieux Colombier; his "Visites à Gordon Craig, Jaques-Dalcroze et Adolphe Appia" of 1929 is also evidence of some acquaintance with Appia. Indeed, barely two weeks after Appia's death, Copeau published an obituary notice in *Comoedia* of 12 March 1928 in which he praised Appia as the "renovator" of the mise-en-scène of modern Western theatre.[1]

Appia and Artaud are both considered seminal figures in Western theatre: Appia is the obscure innovator of Western theatre staging and lighting, while Artaud is the more generally acknowledged seminal figure in twentieth-century avant-garde theatre. Artaud's influence extends even further beyond theatre into the fundaments of some continental deconstructive thought. But the terms in which Appia and Artaud are canonized by their exegetes are uncannily similar. For Sontag, Artaud had "an impact so profound that the course of all recent serious theater in Western Europe and the Americas can be said to divide into two periods—before Artaud and after Artaud." This compares with Lee Simonson's claim that "the history of staging might almost be divided by B.A. [Before Appia] as history in general is divided by B.C." In Richard Beacham's view, Appia's genius consists of a "gift for predictions" and "a talent (shared perhaps by Artaud and Craig) for inspired *suggestiveness*." Similarly, Maurice Saillet suggests that "Artaud's *dreams* were to have more effect in the theatre than all his work as actor and director."[2]

The common desire for a form of representation that is total and rigorous enough to overcome the actual or imagined fragmentations of the European self-and-world led both Appia and Artaud to place a great deal of power in the hands of the theatre-director or metteur-au-scène. The director is to both artists the most obvious orchestrator and controller of the theatrical mise-en-scène, which stood for more than just the visual and aural aspects of theatre. Like Appia, Artaud viewed the mise-en-scène (the audio-visual totality) of theatre as the concretization or phenomenalization of the Western/Occidental Spirit. In the "Manifesto for a Theater That Failed" of 1927, for instance, he declares that the "mise-en-scène, . . . must be regarded solely as the visible signs of an invisible or secret language." It contains "all the fatality of life and the mysterious encounters of dreams" and "aim[s at] no less than a return to the sources, human or inhuman, of the theater, [in order to] raise it from the dead."[3]

The quest to return to the sources of representation (mimesis) meshes with Artaud's tendency toward atavism-primitivism and orientalism. One of the driving presuppositions in his conception of Balinese dance-theatre as total art is that oriental ritual and art forms are the most powerful forms. Oriental forms and representations are original, ancient, and eternal, he believes, because they are unchanging. Interestingly, such atavistic-nostalgic and orientalist notions, motions, and emotions became prevalent in Western thought when many writers became profoundly disillusioned with the Western Humanism and its Enlightenment Project.[4]

Most Western discourses that work toward the radical transformation of the dominant forms of Western self-and-world representation often tend toward the restoration of nostalgic-atavistic pasts. But there seems to be no awareness whatsoever of the nostalgia or atavism at the heart of most of these discourses. No such blindness or oversight obtains in Artaud's endorsement of a surrealistic and atavistic-regressive mode of occidental self-and-world representation. His is a deliberate act of primitivism. Like Appia and many other Westerners since the late nineteenth century, Artaud believed that Western capitalist society and culture were in a state of spiritual and metaphysical decline. After much searching and experimentation, he came to regard theatre as the most effective and affective means of overcoming this self-and-world alienation. His ultimate choice of Balinese dance-theatre as the most total and totalizing form of art and the singular means for disalienating and redeeming the Western-occidental self-and-world is the root of his orientalism. Artaud regarded the masterpieces of theatre and art as moribund, but like Appia before him, he equivocated on the abolition of such masterpieces from his own theatre. Both Artaud and Appia did not only make exceptions for particular texts, but also produced and/or collaborated in the production of some Western masterpieces. In line with their projects of the retotalization, moreover, they both sought to abolish the demarcation of stage and auditorium in traditional Western theatres on behalf of creating a unified space of performance and representation. In these redeemed theatres, the safe and comforting separations of life and theatre in traditional discourse can be destroyed. Appia's "cathedral of the future, for instance," was a space in which integrative national-patriotic festivals such as the *Fête de juin* were to be produced. Similarly, Artaud's "essential theatre" was to serve the production of magical-mystical rituals and carnivals.[5]

Artaud's extra-personal endeavors were always based in very personal desires and needs; his view of theatre and representation begun as a search for some body of conventions that could retotalize his allegedly fragmented mind and at the same time, reunify the body and spirit of his viewed-as-alienated occidental world. If his own schizophrenia (his personal psychological alienation) is a symptom of the socio-cultural alienation of his occidental world then, to cure himself he first had to cure his world, and vice versa. Toward the end of his life, therefore, when he felt that he had failed to effect both of these cures, Artaud attempts to annihilate both himself and his world by regressing, not into silence, of which he seemed incapable, but into a dauntingly hermetic form of utterance—glossolalia.

On the whole, Artaud's view of theatre and representation is antisocial, anarchic, and, at best, solipsistic; he tends to elevate private-individual experience over a social-public one. Indeed, he rejects the prevalent view of social action as the most effective, if not sole, means of self-and-world redemption (revolution). He declares his "scruples in the face of action" to be "absolute," meaning by this that they are "based on a deep-seated sense of the profound futility of any action whatsoever, whether spontaneous or unspontaneous." This rejection of social action compelled him to leave the French Surrealist Movement when it joined ranks with the French Communist party in 1924. In an article marking that break, he writes that "the social level, the material level toward which the Surrealistics direct their pathetic attempts at action, . . . is for me, no more than a useless and obvious illusion."[6]

Artaud endorses revolution that is a "regression into time"; specifically, into the "essential metaphors of the way of life of the Middle Ages." Although anchored in "total pessimism," this atavistic revolution has "its own kind of lucidity. The lucidity of despair, the lucidity of senses that are exacerbated and as if on the edge of the abyss. And alongside the horrible relativity of human action, this unconscious spontaneity . . . drives one, in spite of everything, to action." That the atavistic revolution envisioned by Artaud is nothing like Marxist-socialism or communism is underlined in his claim that "the revolution invented by Marx is caricature of life" and that its agents are nothing but "toilet-paper revolutionaries."[7] By this he means that such agents serve merely the bodily needs of humanity. On the whole, Artaud resists any form of action that takes place outside the reach of individual-solipsistic reality. This much is made evident in his correspondence with Jacques Rivière regarding poems he had written as part and parcel of his early quests for a total form of art.

Lyrical Poetry as Total Art and the Question of the Validity of Solipsistic-Surrealistic Representations of Human Experience

> For me, there is no limit, no fixed forms established for appearances; and someday GOD—or MY MIND—will recognize its own.
>
> All the terms in which I think are for me . . . true terminations, borders of my mental [states], of all the states to which I have subjected my thinking.
>
> —Artaud

Artaud traces the original fragmentation of his mind and being to a traumatic bout he had with meningitis in 1901 when he was only five years old. He interprets this childhood sickness as a calculated sabotage, the attempted pilfering of his being by the occidental God/Spirit. In Jacques Derrida's words, Artaud believed that: "My body has been stolen from me through effraction. The Other, the thief, the great Furtive one, has a proper name: God." Derrida sees Artaud's celebrated railings against Language and Writing as a passionate, yet studied, resistance to occidental Rationality, *Logos,* and, God. In such a light, he appears to be a *bouffon* spitting ostentatiously in the face of the occidental God and, in a contrary wind, having much of the spittle return in his own face. The contrary wind that returns much of Artaud's defiance of all Western, (and ultimately all human) forms of order, logic, and rationality in his own face is his demonstrated desire to belong to and be comprehended by some form of collectivity. He desires conventions in both senses of needing a body of rules to guide him and a gathering of human beings with whom he can comfortably belong.[8]

Artaud equates a fulfilling and fulfilled existence with "having thought" but, characteristically, he fears that the fulfillment of this fundamental desire would end his creativity. For, the raison d'être of his creativity and writing is precisely his struggle to express himself more coherently and completely. In Aristotelian terms, the end of Artaud's basic desire must eternally recede, must be eternally unreachable, only so the process can be on going, dynamic, and eternally viable. This paradoxical desire is illuminated and amplified in Artaud's agonistic correspondence, between 1 May 1923 and 8 June 1924, with Jacques Rivière, editor of *La Nouvelle Revue Française.* Artaud had sent poems written in connection with his early experiments with "total art" to this famous magazine and in a letter dated 1 May 1923 Rivière informs him that he is "unable to publish [his] poems in *La Nouvelle Revue Française.*" However, he is "interested enough in them to want to make the acquaintance of their author."[9]

Artaud's first letter to Rivière 5 June 1923 requests that his correspondent explain why he had rejected the poems. Rivière's reasons were that they indulged in "strong images or figures of speech" and in "awkward expressions." Artaud counters that such excesses and imperfections were the very tenor of his thought:

I suffer from a horrible sickness of mind. My thought abandons me at every level. From the simple fact of thought to the external fact of its materialization in words. Words, shapes of sentences, internal directions of thought, simple reactions of the mind—I am in constant pursuit of my intellectual being. Thus as soon as *I can grasp a form,* however imperfect, I pin it down, for fear of losing the whole thought. I lower myself, I know, and I suffer from it, but I consent to it for fear of dying altogether.[10]

In view of his romantic extremism, the "literary existence" of Artaud's poems was to him a question of "their absolute accept- ability;" indeed, it was even a question of life and death. He claims to have "noticed and accepted" the tendencies for which Rivière reproaches him as "stemming from the profound uncertainty of [his] thought." He considers himself "fortunate indeed when this uncertainty is not replaced by the absolute nonexistence from which I suffer at times." This threat of "nonexistence," he insists, is "not a question of that greater or lesser degree of existence which is commonly called inspiration, but of a total absence, a real extinction" of his thought and his very being. To his mind, "the blemishes and awkward expressions" and "unevennesses" of his writings "were not sufficiently flagrant to destroy the overall im- pression of each poem."[11]

To Rivière, the "disconcerting . . . awkwardnesses and above all oddities" in Artaud's poems "seem to . . . correspond to a certain studied effort on your part rather than to a lack of control over your ideas." He finds curious the rather striking "contrast between the extraordinary precision of [Artaud's] self-diagnosis and the vagueness, or at least the formlessness of [his] creative efforts." He suspects that this formlessness is merely a literary strategy borrowed from the "Surrealist Movement" to which Artaud be- longed during this period (1923–24). Hence his suggestion that "with a little patience, even if it entails only the elimination of divergent images or touches, [Artaud] will succeed in writing poems that are perfectly coherent and harmonious." At least, he believes that with some discipline Artaud would be more able to create "a sufficient unity of impression" in his works. On the whole Rivière finds the lucidity of Artaud's letters "altogether remark- able," especially the "one [he] wrote on the 29th of January." So much so, indeed, that he offers to publish them, in combination "with a bit of [Artaud's] poetry or [his] essay on Uccello," as "a little epistolary novel."[12]

Artaud's immediate response to this proposal is indignant. He asks: "why lie, why put on a literary level something which is the cry of life itself, why give an appearance of fiction to that which is made of the eradicable substance of the soul, which is like the wail of reality." On the other hand, Rivière's offer "pleases [him], it delights [him], it overwhelms [him]." Acting on the latter impulse, he insists that his letters must be published in their entirety and in chronological order so as to give "the reader the impression that he is not involved with something fabricated. . . . We have the right to lie, but not about the essence of the thing." A literary lie might be necessary, Artaud seems to say, but it must not overshadow "the elements of the true story."[13] When it comes to representing his own "true story" or history, therefore, Artaud rejects fictionality and theatricality.

In the light of Rivière's well-founded suspicions, Artaud fights hard to ensure that his allegedly self-defining sickness (schizophrenia or psychological alienation) is not conflated with the sociocultural alienation of his occidental world. His published letters must make "The reader . . . believe in a real sickness and not in a phenomenon of the age, a sickness which touches the essence of . . . being and . . . affects the soul in its most profound reality." The letters must communicate a sickness that is "the poison of being. A veritable *paralysis*. A sickness which deprives you of speech, memory, which uproots your thought."[14]

For Artaud, the prodigious struggle involved in orienting his baroque thought is all that is required to make his efforts literature; it is not literary merit but relevance to himself that is the legitimative basis of his literary work. This is solipsism, of course. The explicit question of literature is, to him, a problem of his allegedly peculiar form of knowing and being; a question of the validity of how he sees life and how he represents experience in terms of "impurities and hesitations." He confesses that "literature properly speaking interests me rather little." It is merely a means to an end, the framing and validation of his own peculiar thought and being-in-the world. The "scattered quality of [his] poems," their "defects of form," he argues, signal "a central collapse of the soul" and, therefore, of any principle of unity and coherence. He pleads with Rivière to "accept, I beg you, the reality" of this affliction and let it substitute for conventional criteria for the evaluation of literature. His point is that "it would be a very great consolation for me to think that even though I am not all of myself, not as tall, not as dense, not as wide as myself, I can still be something."[15]

In pleading for the acceptance of his idiosyncratic form of representation (thought) and being (reality), Artaud attempts to bypass the rules or conventions that govern the game of cultural and literary composition and publication in his occidental world. He advises Rivière that "one must not be too quick to judge men, one must trust them to the point of absurdity, to the dregs." Artaud is, of course:

> aware that a magazine like *La Nouvelle Revue Française* requires a certain formal level and a great purity of content, but granting this, is the substance of my thought so confused, then, and its overall beauty rendered so ineffective by the impurities and hesitations scattered through it that it fails, from the point of view of *literature,* to exist? It is the whole problem of my thinking that is at stake. The question for me is nothing less than knowing whether or not I have the right to continue to think, in verse or in prose.[16]

The foregoing appeal underlines Artaud's awareness of the fact that in order to be acceptable and/or relevant to a certain context of experience private meaning mongering or myth making must be done according to its dominant or ruling conventions. The game of language and literature, then, can be a serious form of play. "Art," as Huw Morris-Jones suggests, is "a kind of language or symbolic system" that creates "paradigms of usage" and plays according to "public and intrapersonal [*sic*] regulations."

> To use Wittgenstein's simile, a language is a public game, it requires at least two to play it. Hence there cannot be a private language, for a player who made his own rules could unmake them as and when he wished so it would cease to be a game at all, at least the sort of game language is. A private language is a self-contradiction[,] . . . [and] the mark of irrationalism and madness. Strictly such man is neither talking nor thinking.[17]

Artaud's correspondence with Rivière can be taken to be a struggle against the probability and eventuality of his being incarcerated in the prison-houses of silence, irrationality, and madness. Madness is palpable as long as his allegedly unique mode of self-representation remains outside the grasp of his interlocutive other. This other is, of course, Rivière in the immediate sense, but, more importantly, it refers to a larger collective, the reading public whose interests and conventions are served and defended by Rivière. Without being acknowledged by these immediate and remote others, Artaud will not and cannot exist.

In ritual, symbolic terms, his letters are a struggle against "Voodoo Death," the kind of death a human being suffers when his or her consociates say through their words, actions, or averted eyes that "we don't hear you; to us you don't exist; you're dead." In Gnostic-Hegelian dialectical terms, terms with which Artaud was undoubtedly familiar, mutual acknowledgment between self and other is what makes either of them fully or completely human. Frantz Fanon understands Hegel's "Independence and Dependence of Self-Consciousness" as saying that it is only "when it encounters resistance from the other, [that] self-consciousness undergoes the experience of desire—the first milestone on the road that leads to the dignity of the spirit."[18] Artaud's attempt to compel Rivière to acknowledge and then accept the validity of his unique form of representation is the first milestone on the road to his fulfillment.

Unfortunately, what Artaud offers as his unique and predetermined mode of expression often appears like a surrealist convention. The more he attempts to distance himself from the definitive terms of this literary movement the more he gets entangled in them. He appears surrealistic when he writes that "a man possesses himself in flashes" and that even then "he does not reach himself completely." Still, he himself sees his alleged "chronic inability to concentrate on an object" as a "weakness [that] affects the whole age, as witness Tristan Tzara, André Breton, Pierre Reverdy." All these people belonged to the surrealist movement, but the difference between him and them, Artaud would have one believe, is that:

> in their case the soul is not physiologically damaged, it is not damaged substantially, but it is damaged at all the points where it joins something else, it is not damaged *outside of thought* . . . The fact . . . remains that they do not suffer and I do suffer, not only in the mind but in the flesh and in my everyday soul. This lack of connection to the object that characterizes all of literature is in me a lack of connection to life. As for myself, I can truly say that I am not in the world, and this is not merely an attitude of the mind.[19]

Because his own inclinations are antiromantic and antisurrealistic, Rivière refuses to comprehend Artaud's baroque forms and formulations of experience. He is very suspicious of the fact that the "phenomena of mental erosion" that mark Artaud's cognitive processes disappear when he himself is the subject or concrete limit of inquiry. This means to him that Artaud's literary positions and existential predispositions are surrealist poses; he believes that, like the surrealists, Artaud wants "pure thought" or nothing. As such, he warns Artaud that "romanticism aside, there is no escape from pure thought but death."[20] The desire for "pure thought," Rivière goes on to argue, characterizes the "natural [or unacculturated] mind," a mind so unfettered by conventions that

it is the "product of the immediate and, so to speak, animal func-
tionings." Such a mind "has the appearance of a vast field of ruins;
those columns which are standing are supported by chance.
Chance reigns there, and a kind of dreary multiplicity." The advice
Rivière offers in the wake of the foregoing observation is very
revealing and astute. He writes that:

> The mind is fragile in that it has need of obstacles—obstacles not of
> its own making. When left to itself, it is lost, it is destroyed. It seems
> to me that this mental "erosion," these internal thefts, this "destruc-
> tion" of the thought "in its substance" which afflict your mind are the
> result of the excesses you allow it. It is the absolute that unhinges it.
> To be taut, the mind needs a boundary and it needs to come up against
> the blessed opacity of experience. The only cure for madness is the
> innocence of facts.[21]

Rivière and Artaud's conflictive positions on representation are,
of course prefigured in incongruent a priori assumptions and teleological desires. In contrast to the solipsistic Artaud, Rivière believed in human "truths expressed with all the three-dimensionality
that can make them communicable, [and] accessible to others." To
him, "so-called normal thought is the product of chance mechanisms" and/or culturally-placed obstacles. In other words, he believes that the fundamental conventions that underwrite all human
seeing, knowing, and being (representation) are deliberate cultural
selections. From this vantage, Rivière sees the cancerous proliferation of mind in Artaud's works as a sign of "weakness," as the
absence of culture and civilization. For Artaud, on the other hand,
the very proliferation of baroque forms in his work is a "sickness
which comes from an excess of force, an overflow of power."[22]

Essays, letters, and fragments Artaud wrote during and immediately after the period of his correspondence with Rivière formulate
human experience in terms of a struggle between two existential-
homeopathic extremes, namely, health/sanity and sickness/insan-
ity. The healthy/sane extreme of human-phenomenal existence is
the pole at which the "well-balanced mind" is manifest and sus-
tained. The sick/insane extreme is, of course, the constitutive opposite of health/insanity; it is the operational sphere of the "anti-
social." the "lost by nature," "suicide, crime, idiocy, madness
"cuckoldry" and castration of mind." To this sphere of existence
and representation belong "lucid madmen, spastics, cancer pa-
tients, chronic meningitis cases, . . . [and] the misunderstood," or
"this minority of those damned by the mind, by the soul, [and]
by . . . disease."[23]

In gnostic-Artaudian representation, the health/sanity extreme is the symbolic ally of purity and perfection (God/Spirit) that is eternally compromised, contested, and contaminated by the polar elements or sickness/insanity. Sickness/insanity refers to what is placed by circumstances (such as Artaud's mythological bout with meningitis at age five) outside the dominant conventions of society and sanity. It means the alienation of the afflicted being or subject from the idea-nostalgic and/or normal self-and-world at the cost of physical and mental anguish. Sickness/insanity attends and marks the descent of elevated notions such as Spirit/Pneuma/Light into weak and compromising realm of the Flesh, materiality, and Darkness. It also marks the time of revolution and undersees the destruction or destabilization of dominant concepts and conventions as a precursor to their transformation or replacement. Framed in genetic terms, sickness/insanity introduces recessive-atavistic and/or diseased genes into a human individual, collective, or world. These combine with the normal or dominant genes in often unpredictable ways, with a view to reinforcing or transforming them. The results of such sickness/insanity and health/sanity combinations can never be fully prefigured or predicted. As in all human-phenomenal adventures and endeavors, accidents play a crucial role in the outcome of the interactions of sickness/insanity and health/sanity.

Finally, sickness/insanity is not necessarily differentiated out of health/sanity; on the contrary, it is its coexistent or simultaneous double. Either of these extremes must cooperate with its other in order to create a wholistic or totalistic framework of existence. In reality, however, health/sanity is usually valorized at the expense of its opposite. In the words of Rivière "health is the only acceptable ideal, the only one to which anyone I call a man has the right to aspire." It does not matter to him that health sanity is "given to someone from the outset" and that it often blinds him to half the world.[24]

Of course, Artaud, who locates himself at the constitutive pole of sickness/insanity and identifies with the sick/insane, considers the constituents of this existential realm true revolutionaries who serve the deeper needs of humanity. Rivière, on the other hand, attempts to lure Artaud away from his dangerous positions and threatening oppositions of healthy/sane conventions. To do this, he must pretend to understand the predicament of the sick/insane, and he often makes this claim. Yet, his last words to Artaud warn him that "there is no absolute danger except for him who abandons himself; there is no complete death except for him who acquires a taste for dying."[25]

All told, Artaud and Rivière's exchange was not fruitless. According to Sontag, "Rivière's strictures proved to be liberating. From then on, Artaud denied that he was simply creating more art, adding to the storehouse of literature." Rivière had emphasized in his letter of March 1924 that a normal existence does not "consist in a slavish imitation of the given." Still, "one must choose what one wishes to 'render' and it must always be not only something definite, not only something knowable, but also something unknown; for the mind to find all its power, the concrete must serve as the mysterious." It is, therefore, significant that in the wake of this correspondence Artaud takes his "leave from poetry" and rechannels his efforts into anchoring the power of mind and spirit in the concrete-material space of theatre. His endorsement of theatre as "total art" seems to tie in with this new objective.[26]

Before his ultimate return to theatre, however, Artaud wrote a series of articles and letters that further reveal the quintessential ambiguity and impossibility of all his efforts. As Sontag puts it, "in Artaud's fierce battle to transcend the body, everything is eventually turned into the body. In his fierce battle to transcend language, everything is turned into language." The moment Artaud intimates that "I suffer from Mind as organ," he promptly decrees that "we must get rid of the Mind." Like a child who sets itself at variance to whatever it cannot have, or in the manner of the fox who dismisses grapes that were out of its reach as sour, Artaud rejects mind and such appurtenant fruits as literature and writing. In one such instance, he declares that "ALL WRITING IS GARBAGE" and that the:

> *whole* literary scene is a pigpen, especially today.
> All those who have points of reference in their minds, . . . all those who are masters at the language, all those for whom words have meanings, all those for whom words have meanings [*sic*], all those for whom exist higher levels of the soul and currents of thought, those who represent the spirit of the times, and who have named these currents of *thought* . . .
> —are pigs.[27]

Artaud goes on to say that "those who still believe in the orientation of the mind, those who drop names, who recommend books . . . are the worst pigs of all." The ideal thing, he insists, is to have "no works, no language, no words, no mind, nothing." Without any apparent sense of irony, however, Artaud makes his own mind the

First Principle (Prima Causa or God) of phenomenal existence. "For me," he proclaims, "there is no limit, no fixed forms established for appearances; and someday GOD—or MY MIND—will recognize its own." Moreover, Artaud's prodigious output of both meaningful writings and autistic-hermetic glossolalia betray his indulgence in mind and the fruits of mind. He wrote and railed against human sense and sensibility till the last day of his life, and so well did he write, that some have acclaimed him one of the leading prose stylists of the French language! Sontag's telling summary of the central paradox in Artaud's actual and literary existence is that: "talking, talking, talking, Artaud expresses the most ardent revulsion against talk and the body."[28]

In the final analysis, because he dreaded and desired public utterance and private silence equally; because he wanted to have both the ephemerality of the word and the stability of the text; because he wanted to represent (be) and not to represent (not to be) at one and the same time; Artaud's existence and his literary work ultimately become exercises in futility and impossibility. By inclination extremist, Artaud refuses to play in the middle of the road or in the safe and normal space of mediocrity, where the bulk of human existence often occurs. Even his literary enterprises seem impossible, which is why Derrida claims that none of the present-day avant-garde theatres that claim Artaud originator can realize the full range of his ideas.[29]

In fact, in a work written as early as 1925 Artaud confesses that his "point of view is clearly anti-social" because *"nature itself is fundamentally anti-social,* it is only by a usurpation of powers that the organized body of society opposes the natural inclination of humanity." He sees human society and all forms of social-collective organization as fundamentally coercive and oppressive and dedicates himself to "a general devaluation of all values," primary among which are Reason and Rationality. To his mind, "we suffer from a rottenness, from the rottenness of Reason. / Logical Europe crushes the mind endlessly." Be that as it may, Artaud's resistance to the acculturative concepts and nucleic activities of Europe is profoundly ambiguous in the sense that he desires to be included in them. Artaud wants to belong and be included in these nucleic activities, and he makes himself conspicuous enough not to be missed. At the height of one of his fascinating tirades against the West, for instance, he stops abruptly, saying: "Enough I shall be understood in ten years by people who will be doing what you do today. Then my geysers will be known, my ice floes will be seen, the secret of my poisons will have been revealed. . . . They will understand how I lost my mind . . ." "then all will be accepted," "and I shall have no further need to speak."[30]

For Artaud, the creation of literature and representation is a solipsistic activity that serves collective interests. It is the voice of the individual raised against the pressures of society as a means of creating "toxins" within private language and injecting them into public Language. The supreme aim of the activity is to make public language and representation more comprehensive and comprehending. To Artaud, the individual, not society, is the central agent of self-and-world revolution and redemption. Thus, every choice he or she makes, even if it is made on behalf of present society, must be relevant first and last, to his own individual self. Artaud calls this supreme self of the individual the flesh. The self is essentially the flesh, but Artaud still claims to "worship not the self but the flesh, in the palpable sense of the word. . . . Nothing touches me, nothing interests me except what addresses itself directly to my flesh." This "theory of the Flesh or, more accurately, of Existence," underwrites visceral attempt to reach a more profound level of being and representation, the "subtlety of the marrow." In the sublime framework of flesh-marrow representation, opposites are the same or, at least, they can be reconciled as one and same. Moreover, all representation is total: "the Self and Other are two distinct terms which should not be confused" but they "are precisely the opposing terms that maintain the equilibrium of the Flesh." This search for the sublime "Flesh" is, in fact, a "quest for the redeemed body,"[31] a total body that is not unlike Appia's previously-discussed Communal Body.

Artaud's conception of the sublime Flesh valorizes cruelty, self-discipline, and "implacable rigour" that comes close to Appia's idea of discipline in the *Work of Living Art*. Both concepts are opposed to the putative softness or lack of rigor in Western existence. Cruelty, in Artaud's writings, is akin to the painful effort that attends life in its seasonal-periodic reawakenings. It is reminiscent of "the cries of a man engaged in remaking his life," and if this man were a plant he would sigh that "April is the cruellest month, breeding / Lilacs out of the dead land, mixing / Memory and Desire." To Artaud, Flesh means knowledge and acceptance of phenomenal-existential necessity, an affirmation of the cruel and circular symphony of life. Flesh is "apprehension, hair standing on end, flesh laid bare with the intellectual profundity of pure flesh."[32]

This view of the redeemed and redeeming flesh seems to be the leitmotif of Artaud's seminal work on theatre and representation,

The Theater and its Double. The coda to the Preface of this celebrated work declares that:

> if there is one truly hellish, truly accursed thing in our time, it is our
> artistic dallying with forms, *instead of being like victims burnt at the
> stake, signaling through the flames.*[33]

The Primitivist-Orientalist Terms in Artaud's Argument of Balinese Dance-Theatre as Total Art and Their Implications on and Terminations of that Other

> The theater, which is no thing, but makes use of everything—
> gestures, sound, words, screams, light, darkness—rediscovers
> itself at precisely the point where the mind requires a language
> to express its manifestations.
>
> —Artaud

According to Alain Cuny, "Artaud's vision of a radical theater
antedates his work with Dullin" at the Atelier in the early 1920s.
Artaud himself writes that the "Atelier" "is both a theater and a
school" "whose purpose is to *internalize* the actor's performance.
It's almost chamber theater, . . . like [André Antoine's] L'Oeuvre
or [Jacques Copeau's] Vieux Colombier." The orientalist underpinnings of this theatre are evident in Artaud's claim that the "Japa-
nese are our masters and our inspiration, together with Edgar Allan
Poe." Poe represents the horrific and sensationalistic spheres of
this theatre, but it wants to reach even further into the well of the
human psyche. For, "in addition to the purification of the stage,"
Dullin "aimed at . . . its renovation, or more accurately, its total
originality. . . . All the action takes place in the soul."[34]

During the Atelier period, Artaud continued his search for a
radical-revolutionary theatre that could comprehend all other art-
forms and, thereby, play "the role of total art." Modris Eksteins
observes in his *Rites of Spring,* that "the search for the *Gesamtkunstwerk*—for the holy grail that is the 'total art form'—was actually a universal one by the end of the nineteenth century." Thus,
Artaud's endeavors are an integral part of a general tendency begun in late nineteenth-century Western art and representation. Following his correspondence with Rivière, he had vacillated mainly
between live theatre and the cinema, but in "late 1926," Sontag
writes, his "search for a total art form centered upon theater"
alone.[35]

The first phase of Artaud's investigation of theatre in the light of total art, which went from 1926 until 1937, centered on such occidental forms of theatre as ancient Greek and Roman tragedy, particularly Senecan tragedy, or rather, melodrama. His ultimate disillusionment with the investigation and production of "masterpeices" of Western theatre compelled Artaud to leave for Mexico and Japan in 1937. The ostensible aim of this journey was to acquaint himself with alternative (that is, non-occidental or, in his words, "oriental") forms of theatre and representation. In program notes and manifestos written for the "Alfred Jarry Theatre," Artaud declares that current Western theatre lacks the "brilliance, the bite, that quality of something unique, unprecedented, [and] whole" that is present in "literature and painting." He proposes "the idea of pure theater" as the worthy equivalent of Western literature and painting.[36]

The "pure theatre" Artaud endorses seeks to "reduce to an impossible minimum . . . the visual display and to overlay [it] with the seriousness and the disturbing quality of the action." In the interest of tight discipline and control, moreover, it makes one individual, the theatre director, the sovereign individual in the theatre. Significantly, this pure theatre, which Artaud also calls the "Theater of Cruelty," is not meant to produce canonical texts or masterpieces of the occidental theatre. Still, Artaud's quest to find or found the disturbing quality of action in theatre, and his inclination toward what is shockingly immediate and transgressive (taboo) led him to acclaim Seneca the "best tragedian" and to make exceptions for Senecan tragedy. To this list he adds John Ford's *'Tis a Pity She's a Whore* and other Western "tragedies of blood," all of which he proposes to perform under the auspices of his Theatre of Cruelty. *Les Cenci,* the only play produced under the auspices of Artaud's Theatre of Cruelty, underlines Artaud's obsession with such primal transgressions and taboo themes as incest and blood crime. But, by all accounts, this production offers no evidence that Artaud was able to realize his primary goal of investing his theatre with the "seriousness and disturbing quality of action."[37]

When the Theater Alfred Jarry or the Theater of Cruelty failed, Artaud, very much in character, went to the extreme of questioning the reality, if not the possibility, of theatre as a whole. In his "Manifesto For a Theater that Failed," he declares that "we do not believe, we cannot believe that there is something in the world that can be called a theater, we see no reality to which such an appellation might be applied." His Mexican-Japan junket of 1937 was undertaken in search for a theatre would prove him wrong and restore his faith in theatre. He was looking for a form that is so total in its representations that "there will not be a single theatrical gesture that will not carry behind it all the fatality of life." Sometimes, however, Artaud undercuts the absolute and (w)holistic character of his theatrical quest with well-placed ironies and paradoxes. For instance, he confesses to a friend that "I think it's very smart to be revolutionary these days: it's the only way to be commercial!!!"[38]

Ultimately, Balinese dance-theatre came to be for Artaud total theatre or the total work of art. Sontag writes that he "discovered the Balinese theater at the Colonial Exposition in Paris in [May or July] 1931." In any case, his "Le Théâtre Balinais" was first published in *La Nouvelle Revue Française* in October 1931. This essay was later expanded with excerpts from letters of clarification he had written to the editor of this magazine, Jean Paulhan, into the chapter on Balinese theatre in his *magnum opus, The Theater and its Double*. In an unfinished letter addressed to Paulhan, Artaud underlines his "intense feeling of intellectual sympathy" for "the beneficent, the miraculous spectacle of the Balinese Theater." This theatre represents "that kind of simultaneous stimulation of all the senses, of all the faculties of the mind at the same time, which is so total that in the end one is unable to make any distinctions."

> To say the least, it constitutes an affront to our western conceptions of theater. . . . The Balinese theater reveals the secret existence of a kind of authentic theatrical language of such power that it seems to eliminate the very mental gestures that seem to have given birth to it, that it renders all translation into words impossible and useless.

Revealed in this unfinished and undelivered letter are three cardinal elements in Artaud's conception of theatre; the first is an omnipresent hostility to the "Occidental theater of psychological tendencies"; the second is his apotheosis of the theatrical mise-en-scène as the representation of manifest ideality and/or originality; and the third is his view of oriental forms as the most effective means with which to overcome the alienations of the occidental self-and-world. This third term is, of course the basis of Artaud's "Orientalism." In the Preface to The *Theater and Its Double*, Artaud notes "the curious parallel between the generalized collapse of life at the root of [the] present demoralization [of Europe] and [its] concern for a culture which has never been coincident with life." He goes on to say that "if confusion is the sign of the times, I see at the root of this confusion a rupture between things and words, between things and the ideas and signs that are their representation."[40] The scientific-psychological term for this split between related things is, of course, alienation and/or schizophrenia.

Balinese dance-theatre is in Artaud's eyes a totalistic means of overcoming both his personal psychological alienation (schizophrenia) and the collective sociological alienation of occidental civilization. He wants to attain "a sense of life renewed by theater, a sense of life in which man fearlessly makes himself master of what does not yet exist." The Balinese theatre, which he views as the highest manifestation of "pure" or "essential" theatre, will help him achieve this goal "because it moves and makes use of living instruments, continues to stir up shadows where life has never ceased to grope its way." The very force and capability of theatre lies in its multiplicity and omnivorousness: "The theatre, which is no thing, but makes use of everything—gestures, sound, words, screams, light, darkness—rediscovers itself at precisely the point where the mind requires a language to express its manifestations."[41]

Artaud views the Balinese theatre as a vessel of pure or uncontaminated originality whose its central agent (actor/performer) brutalizes forms only so as to restore them to a higher reality. This actor does not make the same gesture twice because he is "not satisfied to remain [a] mere recording organism." Instead, he tries "to create or recreate the theater" by "break[ing] through language in order to touch life." This singular effort "leads to the rejection of the usual limitations of man and man's powers, and infinitely extends the frontiers of what is called reality." This kind of theatre, Artaud believes, pushes life beyond its "surface of fact" towards "that fragile, fluctuating center which forms never reach." Hereafter, theatrical representation ceases to be an "artistic dallying with forms" and its agents become "victims burnt at the stake signaling through the flames." As Derrida rightly observes, "for Artaud the future of the theater—thus the future in general—is opened only by the anaphora which dates from the eve prior to birth. Theatricality must traverse and restore 'existence' and 'flesh' in each of their aspects."[42]

Artaud's theatre is essentially deconstructive in that it seeks, first and foremost, to destroy dominant pathological forms. The ideal or pure theatre comes into being during those moments when "all social forms disintegrate" and "order collapses." At least, this is how Artaud constructs the profound relationship between theatre and the plague in the opening chapter of the *Theater and Its Double*. The plague intrudes into teeming life, initially destroying any prevalent values and forms but ultimately restores a new or other post-traumatic order. Because it inoculates and renews, the plague can be seen as a form and phenomenon of sickness/insanity. For, often, "it appears that by means of the plague, a gigantic abscess, as much moral or social, has been collectively drained."[43]

Artaud believes that "like the plague, the theater has been created to drain abscesses collectively" and that "the theater like the plague is a crisis which is resolved by death or cure." Theatre, like the plague, causes "men to see themselves as they are, it causes the mask to fall, reveals the lie, the slackness, baseness, and hypocrisy of the world"; "it invites them to take, in the face of destiny, a superior and heroic attitude they would never have assumed without it." The plague is a rite of passage, and the moment of its eruption is when it appears that present forms of life and representation are pathological and entropic. In such a moment, when human existence seems bereft of rhyme and reason, when "dregs of the population [the living] . . . enter the open houses [of the dead or dying] and pillage riches they know will serve no purpose or profit" "the theater is born. The theater, i.e., an immediate gratuitousness provoking acts without use or profit."[44]

Artaud believes that consciousness and purpose (logic) underwrite the seeming purposelessness of both theatre and the plague, that "like the theater, the plague . . . is [both] a delirium and communcative; it is both meaninglessness and meaningfulness." Pure theatre, like the plague, "manifest[s] its presence" "in the particular sites . . . where human will, consciousness, and thought are imminent and apt to occur." The locus and focus of pure essential theatre is however impure; herein lies its paradoxical passion. "Like the plague it is the revelation, the bringing forth, the exteriorization of a depth of latent cruelty by means of which all the perverse possibilities of the mind . . . are localized. Like the plague the theater is the time of evil, the triumph of dark powers that are nourished by a power even more profound until extinction."[45]

"The time of evil" and "the triumph of dark powers" is, in the gnostic framework, the moment of the necessary descent of Spirit into the sensuous-material world. Such moments are akin to the one in which, according to the Christian Bible, "the Word became Flesh, and lived among us." This word is indeed the Spirit manifest as the son sent down to save the word by bringing himself to feel what humanity feels. Artaud's essential theatre therefore tries to circumscribe the intercourse between human and divine elements that obtains in all empowered and sublime representations of experience.[46]

The essential theatre becomes the eonic and proliferative "archetypal, primitive theater" in the chapter on "The Alchemical Theater." The "origins and *raison d'être* (or primordial necessity)" of this theatre are located "metaphysically [in] the materialization or rather exteriorization of a kind of essential drama" that is "at once manifold and unique," and contains in itself "the essential principles of all drama, already *disposed and divided.*" Such a theatre can only be described "poetically" and dialectically." To "analyze" it "philosophically is impossible because it resists "excessive logical intellectualism" and presents "states of acuteness so intense and so absolute that we sense, beyond the tremors of all music and form, the underlying menace of a chaos as decisive as it is dangerous."[47]

The pure or "essential drama" of the alchemical theatre, Artaud suggests, is "something subtler than Creation itself, something which must be represented as the result of one will alone and without conflict." Situated at "the root of all the Great Mysteries," this theatre coincides with the "second phase of Creation[,] that of difficulty and the Double, that of matter and the materialization of the idea." The original essence of this theatre, once thrust into material existence, passes "through all the filters and foundations of existing matter." The "immensity of the conflicts it provokes, . . . the prodigious number of forces it throws one against the other . . . ultimately evokes in the spirit an absolute and abstract purity." Artaud is convinced that "where simplicity and order reign, there can be no theater or drama" for, each "is born out of a kind of organized anarchy after philosophical battles"

The forcefulness and cruel discipline Artaud discovers in the mise-en-scène of Balinese dance-theatre are also celebrated in his commentary on Lucas van den Leyden's "The Daughters of Lot." While he begins by noting the incestuous (taboo) nature of the relationships depicted in that painting, Artaud's main objective is the metaphysical-celestial fire (depicted by a fiery splash of paint) that "cleave[s]" the painting "like an element still active and in motion." To his mind, this "produces an impression of intelligence and malice" that can "affect the brain directly, like a physical agent." This fire compels the "submission of the different elements of the landscape."[49]

To Artaud, all originality, is oriental; "the plague brought by the *Grand-Saint-Antoine* [to Marseilles in the spring of 1720] was the Oriental plague, the original virus." Similarly, "the only authentic plague is the plague from Egypt which rises from the cemeteries uncovered when the Nile recedes." Artaud's endorsement of the

Balinese theatre runs along similar imputations of originality and antiquity. In the mise-en-scène of this oriental form of theatre, he perceives themes that are initially "vague, abstract, [and] extremely general" but which become concretized or embodied in the body and bodily accoutrements of the Balinese actor-dancer. These then appear as "animated hieroglyphs" imbued with "a precise meaning which strikes us only intuitively but with enough violence to make useless any translation into logical discursive language."[50]

The hieroglyphized space or mise-en-scène of the Balinese theatre is also, for Artaud, the active and enactive nemesis of the once-hallowed, but now hollowed, occidental Word/Spirit. This kind of staging or materialization requires "the absolute preponderance of the director (metteur-en-scène) whose creative power eliminates words." This autocratic metteur-en-scène is an artist "who has become a kind of manager of magic, a master of sacred ceremonies" who produces themes derived "from the gods" and "sets in motion . . . the MANIFESTED."

By overemphasizing discipline and unilateral control in the Balinese theatre, if only so as to oppose it to the alleged want of discipline and order in the occidental one, however, Artaud makes the former form appear oppressive and unchanging. He celebrates the spectre of childish fear he sees etched on the faces of the Balinese dancer-actors, writing that in both the principal dancer and his

> double who is terrified by the apparitions from beyond . . . there is a description of fear valid in every latitude, an indication that in the human as well as the superhuman the Orientals are more than a match for us in matters of reality.
> The Balinese, who have a vocabulary of gesture and mime for every circumstance of life, reinstate the superior worth of theatrical conventions, demonstrate the forcefulness and greater emotional value of a certain number of perfectly learned and above all masterfully applied conventions.[51]

Artaud suggests that "one of the reasons for the physical efficacity upon the mind, for the force of the direct images of action in certain productions of the Balinese theatre, is that the theatre is based upon age-old traditions which have preserved intact the secrets of using gestures, intonations, and harmonies in relation to the senses on all possible levels." The "powerful signs" of the Balinese theatre "give us the impression that their power has not weakened during thousands of years." In other words, they are eternal and unchanging, and, as such, they lie beyond the linear-progressive Western paradigm. Sadly, Artaud locates the powerful signs of this theatre in "mechanically rolling eyes, pouting lips, and muscular spasms, all producing methodically calculated effects which forbid any recourse to spontaneous improvisation." These mechanical and puppet like effects "shock our European sense of stage freedom and spontaneous inspiration" but Artaud dares anyone to prove that the Balinese "system" "creates sterility or uniformity."[52]

Wittingly or unwittingly, Artaud answers his own dare and proves the oriental system is, in fact, sterile and primitive. He contends that in contrast to the Western theatre "which has never had the idea of [the] metaphysics of gesture," the "purely popular and not sacred theater [of Bali] gives us an extraordinary idea of the intellectual level of a people who take the struggles of a soul preyed upon the ghosts and phantoms from beyond as the basis for their civic festivals." In the representations of this theatre, "there is no transition from a gesture to a cry or a sound: all the senses interpenetrate, as if through strange channels hollowed out in the mind itself!" Its "whole collection of ritual gestures" "seems intended to encircle thought, to hound it down and lead it into an inextricable and certain system. In fact everything in this theater is calculated with an enchanting mathematical meticulousness. Nothing is left to chance or personal initiative."

> Everything is thus regulated and impersonal . . . . And the strange thing is that in this systematic depersonalization . . . everything produces a significance, everything affords the maximum effect.
>
> A kind of terror seizes us at the thought of these mechanized beings, whose joys and griefs seem not their own but at the service of age-old rites, as if they were dictated by superior intelligences. In the last analysis it is this impression of a superior and prescribed Life which strikes us most in this spectacle. . . . The hieractic quality of the costumes gives each actor a double body and a double set of limbs—and the dancer bundled into his costume seems to be nothing more than his own effigy.[53]

Artaud claims "purity," "spirituality," "priority," and "intellectuality" for the Balinese theatre but in terms dogged by insectological and animalistic metaphors. For example, "these strange games of flying hands, like insects in the green air of evening, communicate a sort of horrible obsession, an inexhaustible mental ratiocination, like a mind ceaselessly taking its bearings in the maze of its unconscious." Other sounds that come to his mind are "the sound of the rattlesnake and rustlings of dried insects against each other." "And they suggest the glade of a swarming landscape ready to hurl into chaos." Of "these dancers dressed in dazzling clothes," "there is something umbilical, larval in their movement," "they are like huge insects full of lines and segments drawn to connect them with an unknown natural perspective of which they seem nothing more than a kind of detached geometry." The "abstract rotations when they walk, and the strange criss-crossings of their feet" make them seem like creatures "at the mercy of phantasms from the Beyond." In their "profound intoxication" and "ecstasy," moreover, Artaud "discovers the dry seething, the mineral friction of plants, vestiges and ruins of trees illuminated on the faces. Bestiality and every trace of animality are reduced to their spare gesture: mutinous noises of the splitting earth, the sap of trees, animal yawns."[54]

Artaud's conception of the Balinese theatre fits to a "T" Western definitions of primitivity and Orientalism. But it must be said in fairness that he does not treat the West any better. He tends to limit his description of Western forms to their most problematic or unsalutary aspects. Idealization is a form of distortion, and Artaud idealizes both the Occident and the Orient, the former negatively and the latter positively, at least in the beginning. This naive and uncritical embrace of the Orient, Artaud's seemingly affirmative Orientalism, is, in fact, a way of pushing away the Occident and reaching for it at one and the same time. It invites his own world, the Occident, to find a way of including him and comprehending his allegedly idiosyncratic forms of expression and representation, or else . . . Artaud is the prodigal son who must be fêted and seduced back into the fold. He embraces the Orient as one would step outside the claustrophobic walls or limits of an intolerable situation for a little while, for a breath of fresh air, or to attain a different perspective. Such a one utlimately returns to the fold because it is, after all, home and its representations however excluding, are more "familiar" and/or better "known."

In the process of his imaginative or symbolic consumption of Balinese theatre and the Orient as a whole, Artaud ignores its definitive ethnological and historical conditions. For example, he dismisses either one of the principal attendants on the leading characters of one particular form of Balinese theatre (Delem/Sangut; Twalen/Wredah) as a "childish double" who moves "unaware in the midst of the spells of which he has understood nothing." But these so-called childish doubles are, in reality, the aboriginal ancestors of Bali and of Balinese theatre. To quote from Walter Spies and Beryl de Zoete:

The role of Toealen [Twalen] is really a very mysterious one. He is, it seems, almost a divinity, full of good counsel for the hero, but always with a clumsy, grotesque exterior. It has been surmised that he is the true Indonesian ancestor, subordinate to the adopted demi-gods of the great Hindu epics, but always enshrined in the popular imagination as a powerful benefactor and bringer of good luck.[55]

According to I-Made Bandem and F. Eugene de Boer, the comical attendants of Balinese theatre "have a certain license, and are favourites with the audience as they talk Balinese and disport themselves in a somewhat homely manner." Beyond this simple comical role, however, these characters are the only means by which the ancient *Kawi* text spoken by the elevated figures of Balinese dante-theatre is translated into contemporary Balinese. Without them, the present audience cannot follow or participate in the representation. Thus, they link past and present. Furthermore, the improvisations these "comical" attendant-ancestral figures make in the vernacular are often the sources of innovation. For contrary to Artaud's claims, "Balinese drama is not static or uniform."[56]

Not every form of Balinese theatre has attendant figures such as those described by Artaud, and, if Bandem and de Boer are right, the two forms of Balinese theatre presented at the Paris Exposition of 1931 Artaud attended (the *Legong* and the *Kebyar Duduk*) do not have such figures. Artaud's conceptions of Balinese theatre are, therefore, imaginative in every imaginable sense of the word. This is not to suggest, however, that they are not useful for the understanding of the fundamental relationships between theatre and the representation of human experience. Even though he is "misinformed in a number of particulars," Bandem and de Boer believe that Artaud does understand Balinese theatre on some profound level.[57]

Nevertheless, Artaud's Orientalism is questionable precisely because it constructs and consumes an other self-and-world in a cavalier fashion. "Like most western orientalists, Artaud's argument "refuses to submit to the disillusionment of accurate historical knowledge. . . . It never sought such knowledge. The other civilizations are [merely] used as stimulants to the imagination precisely because they are not accessible. They are both models and mysteries." Sontag continues that this kind of

nostalgia for a past that is often so electic as to be quite unlocatable historically. . . is a facet of the modernist sensibility which has seemed increasingly suspect in recent decades. It is an ultimate refinement of the colonialist outlook; an imaginative exploitation of non-white cultures, whose moral life it drastically oversimplifies, whose wisdom it plunders and parodies. To that criticism there is no convincing reply.[58]

Since the late nineteenth century, such orientalist-primitivist strategies have been used by enable alienated westerners to reduce and consume other cultures. The triumph of Western colonialism, and the dominance of Western hegemony in the present-day world, make such consumptions of the material and symbolic resources of other cultures profoundly unpalatable. Besides, when the primitivist-orientalist self-otherer returns into the Western fold, by choice or by force of reassimilation, the other self-and-world to which this Westerner clung appears pacified as well. The same problem exists for the Other who is compelled to articulate, in English, a resistance to Western power and hegemony. Such is the predicament of Caliban, the character in Shakespeare's *Tempest* who used the master's tongue to curse and speak his need to be free. Such was the fate of African négritudinism.

In *Orphée Noir*, a preface he was commissioned to write for an anthology of poems by his black or "Negro" compadres, for example, Jean-Paul Sartre maps Hegel's Master-Slave dialectic onto white-black politics. He concludes that the Western Master can assimilate and pacify négritudinist resistance precisely because it is formulated in western terms. Such negations appear to be no more than minor moments in the absolutist bacchanalian whirl of the Western Spirit and Logos. Needless to say, Frantz Fanon is appalled by Sartre's argument, seeing it as a betrayal of the Negro by "a friend of the colored peoples" in a work that "is a date in the intellectualization of the *experience* of being black."[59]

Fanon's protestations notwithstanding, the overwhelming evidence supports Sartre's conclusion that no profound or lasting changes can come by way of symbolic-theatrical negations of a dominant system of representation, especially if one uses its language and terms to articulate one's resistance. Artaud's orientalist resistance to Logical Europe and sub-Saharan African négritudinist rejection of Western paradigms both face eventual pacification by the West. The crucial difference between them is that Artaud's Orientalism seemed geared toward his eventual comprehension by the West. Thus, it is not at all surprising that close to the end of his life, in 1946 to be exact, he rejects the Balinese theatre and its orientalist representations on the revealing grounds that, through its recourse to repetition and curtailment of wasteful experimentation, it creates an "economy." He is unhappy that this system conserves human effort as against consuming each and every act totally, uneconomically, and unecologically in each and every manifestation. He protests that:

> The theater is a passionate overflowing / a frightful transfer of forces / from body / to body. / This transfer cannot be produced twice. / Nothing more impious than the system of the Balinese which consists, / after having produced this transfer one time, / instead of seeking another, / in resorting to a system of particular enchantments / in order to deprive astral photography of the gestures thus obtained.[60]

What seems to make all human self-and-world representations (self-making, world-making, myth-making, food-making; all kinds of making) untenable to Artaud, therefore, is that through repetitions of past actions and forms they become economical and conventional. In reaction, he reaches toward anarchic and autistic-solipsistic forms of expression, The most extreme and final form of which was glossolalia. Unable to decide whether To Represent or Not to Represent Artaud embraces nihilism. But even his ultimate stance on representation, does not so much make Artaud eschew comprehension as play and ply strategically the abysmal gap between public nonsense and private sense. In the end, unable to hold his silence and rage, Artaud descends into madness, a symbolic form of death that is only superseded and terminated by his biological death.[61]

At the end of my encounter with Artaud, I stand alone in the all-too-total void created by his symbolic-metaphorical absentings from the stage of existence of both self and other as well as their constitutive representations. I wonder about what justice there could be in dragging an other self-and-world into what is essentially an individual or occidental dance of death. Walking the question, skirting the void, looking for an answer, I spy the "Bird of the Wayside" (Akasanoma) sit at the edge of my wondering and begin to sing. I sense a heroic effort on its part to fill my emptiness and absence. I lend it my ear, and it sings:

> You, mortal wayfarer, you
> it sings
> because you're human, or so it seems
> yours it is, the primal need to belong,
> somewhere, somehow, to some world or other,
> know this
> for you're human, because you're human
> the beckon of home, the warmth of the hearth

is both your dire desire
and your eternal dread
it seems
because you're human, you're self or other
but at best, more whole, both self and other
the wisdom of being human is knowing this
be
be wise, be enough
mortal wayfarer, know this
and spreading wing upon the wind it went
tweet, tweet, tweet, twit!, twit!!, twit!!!

6

Bertolt Brecht: The Epic and Dialectical Theatres and the *Verfremdungseffekt,* Their Common Means of Revolutionizing Western Capitalist Society

Every art contributes to the greatest art of all, the art of living.
—Brecht

Bertolt Brecht's approach to theatre is based in the view that "different periods' pleasures varied naturally according to the system under which people lived in society at the time." In his early works, Brecht argues that the "traditional major . . . dramatic form," which he terms Aristotelian theatre, "isn't suitable for present-day subjects." In contrast his own "*epic theatre* is the theatrical style of our time" because it "corresponds to the sociological situation." As such, this form of theatre cannot only effect a "radical transformation of the theatre" but also undersee "the whole radical transformation of the mentality of our time."[1]

Brecht holds that "only a new purpose can lead to a new art. The new purpose is called paedagogics." The fundamental aim of his theatre is to make "scientific man" inhabit his times "scientifically"; he had often "spoken of the producer's duty 'to raise the theatre to the level of science.'" Willett points out that "'Wissenschaft' in German is a broader term than the English 'science' and that Brecht certainly regarded it as embracing the Marxist view of history as well as the natural sciences." Still, Brecht's view of representation appears narrowly mimetic; "art follows reality" in such a way that "simply to comprehend . . . new areas of subject matter imposes a new dramatic and theatrical form." The way in which Brecht often writes of this process of scientification of theatre and ideology (or culture) makes it appear predetermined; he

159

writes that "scientific man is to have his theatre like everybody
else" if only because "the theatre has already got scientific man
for its audience, even if it doesn't do anything to acknowledge the
fact." This theatrical quest for a "scientific" form of self-and-world
representation positions Brecht's work in the Western Enlightenment tradition, a position that is further stabilized by his acolytic
relationships to Bacon and Marx.[2]

Ralph Ley believes that "Brecht's debt to Bacon is considerable"
and that "the key to a proper understanding of Brecht's methodology lies in grasping the connection among the *organa* of Aristotle,
Bacon, and Brecht."

> Brecht was to call his [famous] treatise *Kleines Organon* and link
> Bacon's work to his own on the basis of the mutual opposition to the
> *Organum* of Aristotle, an indication that the playwright's quarrel with
> the Greek philosopher was engendered by more than a difference of
> opinion over poetics. It was in fact grounded in a considerable measure
> on a difference over metaphysics.

Also, Brecht's view of "Bacon . . . [as] the great pioneer of practical thinking" makes Bacon in "some sense a precursor of Marx"
who had himself proclaimed Bacon "the first theorizer of vulgar
materialism and 'the real founder of . . . all modern experimental science.'"[3]

The triangular relationship between Brecht, Marx, and Bacon
appears complete when, in 1926, Brecht declared that "when I read
Marx's *Capital* I understood my plays" and that "this man Marx
was the only spectator of my plays I'd ever come across." "During
his American exile," moreover, he "began to put Marx's Communist Manifesto into verse." Finally, in his last writings, Brecht sums
up his entire career in the theatre as an attempt "to take the principle that it was not just a matter of interpreting the world but of
changing it, and apply that to the theatre."[4]

The "principle that it was not just a matter of interpreting the
world but of changing it" is, of course, a restatement of Marx's
claim in his eleventh "Theses on Feuerbach" that "the philosophers have only *interpreted* the world, in various ways; the point,
however, is to *change* it." If Brecht finds the general direction of
his theatrical career in Marx, he owes to Bacon his ostentatious
hostility to Aristotle and Aristotelian representation. Indeed, the
Baconian desire to make "fruits and works" the "sureties and sponsors" of human knowledge coincides at some point with the Marxian quest to change the human self-and-world. "Brecht's quarrel

with Aristotle stands most clearly revealed," Ley suggests, "on the question of activism." Incidentally, Bacon condemned Aristotle for the not dissimilar reason that his "writings were 'barren of the production of works for the benefit of the life of man.'"[5]

The benefits Brecht expected his early theatre to provide were framed in the light of the pathological conditions in Weimar Germany. Claude Hill notes that the "search for a new man and a new morality rose to a feverish pitch" in the Weimar Republic. To a similar end, John Willett suggests that Brecht's *Lehrstücke* form, the precursor of his epic theatre, "should be read in the light of the political and economic crisis which developed in Germany during the second half of 1929, making revolutionary change seem not only desirable but imminent." Incidentally, Brecht's *Lehrstücke* shares with the *Neue Sachlichkeit* movement of the Weimar Republic a common emphasis on "reportage and documentary" and the quest to create a "sober, functional aesthetic" that reflects a "new realism bearing a socialistic flavour." Apparently, the socialistic flavor desired by both this movement and Brecht's early theatre were opposed to the dominant capitalistic ethos of Weimar Germany.[6]

Brecht seems to share many of the central aims of the *Neue Sachlichkeit* movement, even if his attitude to the movement itself is ambivalent. In his early essays he declares himself opposed to "the flabby lack of matter-of-factness that alone keeps the present-day bourgeois theatre on its legs." He believes that change is "bound to come," that "a *new human type* should now be evolving, at this very moment, and . . . the entire interest of the world should be concentrated on his development." The hint of determinism in these declarations aside, Brecht does not take the evolution of this "new human type" for granted. Rather, by means of plays and the essays and interviews resulting from them, he attempts to influence that important process or evolution and revolution.[7]

The basic premise of Brecht's first important play, *Mann ist Mann*, he suggests, is that "the continuity of the [human] ego is a myth. A man is an atom that perpetually breaks up and forms anew." Elisabeth Hauptmann, Brecht's secretary, notes in her diary that "Brecht developed his theory of the 'epic drama'" in the course of his ruminations on the fact that "as soon as one sees that the modern world is no longer reconcilable with the drama then the drama can no longer be reconciled with the world." Brecht made the first public endorsement of this "epic theatre" in an interview with Bernard Guillemin. In subsequent clarifications, Willett suggests, Brecht makes his epic theatre coincident "with reason

(*Verstand*) and opposed to *Einfühlung* or empathy, the process by which the audience is made to identify itself with the character on the stage and actually feel his emotions." Brecht considers youthful impetuousness and sin symbolic coefficients of revolution and change. "Sin, . . . strangeness and incomprehensibility" are for him ostentatious opposites to old and settled notions and moralities, so "already there seems to have been a dramatic element in this pursuit of strangeness. It implied the need for change."[8]

Among other deliberate provocations of the audience in his notes to the *Lehrstücke, Der Flug der Lindberghs* (1930), Brecht suggests that "the text is to be spoken and sung *mechanically;* a break must be made at the end of each line or verse; the part listened to must be *mechanically followed.*" In this affectation of "mechanism," Brecht duplicates the very mode of (self-and-world) production said by Marx to be responsible for the "alienation" of the human being under Western capitalism. By repeating or simulating this pathological mode, Brecht "second-orders" it and creates that "terror of recognition" that always precedes change. The hopeful outcome of this "alienation effect" is that both the actor (producer) and audience (consumer) of these mechanical self-and-world representations can come to recognize their pathological character and begin to work towards changing them.[9]

The "alienation effects" Brecht hopes to achieve by means of the *Lehrstücke,* the early form of his epic theatre, obtain in its hybrid character. He defines the *Lehrstücke* as a "didactic cantata, with solos, choruses and scraps of acting," thus underlining its fragmentary and mosaic character. The juxtaposition of such diverse internal elements as drama and music, speech and song, acted and screen-projected texts, among others, in the *Lehrstücke* disturbs any seamless flow of significations and identifications, leading to a series of shocks and recognitions. The new cognitions obtained thereby are expected to be the precursors and of change. Interestingly, the hybridity of what Brecht considered an empowered mode or form of theatre and representation reflects a major tendency in modern Western conceptions of theatre in the light of ideology and acculturation. As Modris Eksteins notes, all searches for a "total" or "totalizing" art-form in Europe since the late nineteenth century have tended to settle on some such syncretistic form as "music-drama" or "dance-theatre."[10]

Brecht formulates his epic theatre most fully in relation to his operatic or musical-dramatic play, *Mahagonny.* In his "Notes on *Mahagonny,*" Brecht suggests that his play undercuts and co-opts the "culinary" or aestheticist fundaments of the operatic form by investing it with a serious scientific-materialistic content. He suggests that while "the opera *Mahagonny* pays conscious tribute to the senselessness of the operatic form," it also defeats this lack of seriousness by doubling its normal dose of fun. "The intention was that a certain unreality, irrationality and lack of seriousness should be introduced at the right moment, and so strike it with a double meaning." By "introducing an element of instruction" into it, Brecht compels this form to look in a mirror, as it were, and see itself in a contrary, as well as double, light. "Fun," the chief end of opera, appears in this light, "not only as form but as subject-matter;" "enjoyment" remains "the object of inquiry even if the inquiry was intended to be the object of enjoyment."[11]

In circumnavigating one end (inquiry) by way of its opposite (enjoyment), and vice versa, Brecht courts the possibility that the tension between them will lead to "alienation effects" which can serve as the precursors to new insights and change. Sadly, however, he represses these paradoxical juxtapositions, teasing circularities, and vibrant-yet-critical conjunctions of learning and pleasure from his famous categorical-schematic opposition of the epic and the aristotelian "dramatic" theatres. He, of course, appends a footnote that cautions that his schema "does not show absolute antithesis but mere shifts of accent . . . [or emphasis between] emotional suggestion . . . [and] plain rational argument." But, because Brecht himself ignores this warning when doing so serves the unilateral claims he makes for his epic theatre, many commentators have paid little or no heed to this note of caution. In fact, one Brecht disciple, Augusto Boal, goes so far as to institute a full-blown witch hunt against Aristotelian representation (as articulated in the *Poetics*) on the grounds that it constitutes and institutes a universal "Coercive System."[12]

Brecht's epic theatre is grounded in a narrative bias and empowered with authorial omniscience, and in it, he submits, "the spectator stands outside, studies" life, and concludes that humanity "is alterable and able to alter." To Brecht, the epic theatre is the only form that "arouses [the spectator's] capacity for action; forces him to take [sic] decisions" based in the view of himself "as a process" rather than a fixed essence. The fundamental opposition between this epic theatre and the traditional Aristotelian or dramatic theatre seems to lie in Brecht's supposition that in the latter "thought determines being" while in his epic theatre "social being determines thought." But in separating "thought" and "social being" Brecht reduces a circular metaphorical relationship into a linear sociological one.[13]

Indeed, the subjugation of thought to social being in epic self-and-world representation makes it unable to account for the onset of alienation in human experience. Without this, the disalienation sought through Brecht's *V-effekt* cannot be possible. The generation of new thoughts is a precondition to overcoming alienation, but if "social being" unidirectionally determines "thought," then humanity is doomed to any first or original state of being. Every thought generated in such a state will already have been predetermined by that pathological "social being." Without the allowance for the mutual circulations and interpenetrations of thought and social being, therefore, Brecht's theatrological quest for change is a lost cause. Epic representation cannot possibly explain how capitalistic or "ruling class" thought and social being overcame the precapitalistic or "communal" ones to begin with. It appears, then that, blinded by his polemics against Aristotle, Brecht drives his theatrological revolution into a sociological cul-de-sac.

According to Grace M. Allen, Brecht's "notes headed 'Critique of Empathy'" show that he can "go along" with Aristotle where the latter "speaks generally about the pleasure to be derived from mimetic pleasure." The point at which Brecht departs from Aristotle, Allen adds, is where the latter "becomes more specific and limits the field of mimesis for tragedy." If Aristotle limits the field of mimesis for tragedy it is because he views it as mimesis par excellence. It is from the exemplary perspective of tragedy that he makes his seminal defense of mimesis (the most basic and perhaps naive form of representation), art, and theatre in the *Republic*. But, the ideological priorities underlying Aristotle's conception of tragedy as the highest form of representation are not very different from Brecht's own belief that "every art contributes to the greatest art of all, the art of living."[14]

Perhaps in deliberate opposition to Aristotle, Brecht views comedy as art and mimesis par excellence. Bentley believes that Brecht's "new-fangled notion of Epic Theater can be construed as a synonym for traditional comedy." This claim is supported by Brecht's own view that "the problems of today . . . can only be grasped by the theatre in so far as they are problems of comedy" because "comedy allows of solutions." But in taking his polemics against Aristotle too far, "Brecht mars his highly interesting suggestions with dogmatism and oversimplification." In one such notorious instance, he claims that "only the Epic form can enable the dramatist to find a comprehensive image of the world . . . as a totality of social relationships."[15]

Commentators who concentrate on Brecht's ostentatious early

contestations of Aristotle and traditional Aristotelian theatre fail
to see and remark on his autumnal overtures to a naive form of
theatre and representation (a dialectical theatre) whose basis or
ground of operation almost coincides with Aristotle's notion of
mimesis. Claude Hill, for example, believes that mimesis as a
whole "is one of the basic concepts of the Aristotelian theatre that
Brecht rejects."[16] But Hill cannot be right because, as Aristotle
conceives it, mimesis is the most basic or rudimentary form of
representing human experience. Besides, Brecht's own arguments
show that he does not so much reject mimesis, or even Aristotle's
conception of mimesis, as attempt to reformulate and orient it scientifically and context-historically. He tries to make Aristotelian
theatre more critical by repressing its alleged foundation in a naive
and empathetic identification between actor and audience.

Brecht's dogmatic opposition to Aritstotle is grounded, for the
most part, in a conscious or unconscious misconstruction of the
Aristotle's views on theatre and representation. He writes in section twelve of the *Short Organon,* for instance, that "according to
Aristotle—and we agree—narrative is the soul of drama," mistak-
ing "narrative" to mean simple "story or fable." Brecht bases his
famous schematization on the difference between his epic theatre
and Aristotelian or Dramatic theatre, in his "Notes on *Mahagonny,*" on this mistake. This view of plot reduces Aristotle's more
intricate conception of *mythos* in the *Poetics.* In this original work,
plot (*mythos*) is not the loose arrangement of events suggested
by Brecht's notion of "story or fable." Rather, it is the "proper
arrangement" of mythological actions and events into a form that
is aesthetically pleasing and ideologically significant. Such an arrangement, Aristotle submits, obeys a localized set of "probabilities and necessities" as well as describes rearrangements and
reinterpretations of the defining actions and events of a certain
self-and-world.[17]

One contrast Brecht attempts to draw between his allegedly scientific epic theatre and the mythological or pre-scientific Aristotelian (traditional-dramatic) theatre is that in his epic theatre the
ideal relationship between actor and spectator is marked by the
existence of critical distance. His theatre holds that "spectator and
actor ought not to approach one another but to move apart. Each
ought to move away from himself. Otherwise the element of terror
necessary to all recognition is lacking." Nevertheless, the "terror
of recognition" or distancing effect (*V-effekt*) Brecht views as endemic to his epic form of theatre and representation is akin to the
role of *anagnorisis* or discovery in Aristotle's description of trag-

edy. *Anagnorisis* cooperates with *peripeteia* (reversal or change) in Aristotelian representation to bring new insights and resolutions (equilibriums) to the tragic self-and-world. Recognition points toward new revelations that lead to changes or reversal (*peripeteia*) which, in turn, lead the drive toward change, or the creation of new forms and states of knowing and being. If as Brecht suggests Aristotelian tragic theatre "consumes itself affirmatively," it does so in a way not very different from that of Brecht's epic-comedic theatre.[18]

Toward the end of his career, Brecht attempts to replace his epic theatre with a "dialectical theatre" that he proclaims to be a "new aesthetic category." But Bentley contradicts that "if Epic theater represents a puritanical extreme, what Brecht then 'developed' as an alternative 'aesthetic' was nothing more remarkable then what most poeple already believe: that pleasure, in some definition or other . . . is the main end of art." Still, one cannot go as far as Bentley does to say that "there is no philosophic interest" in Brecht's dialectical theatre. The very reversal of original position, manifest in Brecht's endorsement of naivety as the sine qua non of this theatre, is important. Besides, Brecht had been moving gradually, but perhaps too surreptitiously, toward his ultimate reversal of original views long before his final espousal of the dialectial theatre. In his "Street Scene" of 1938 (whose dramaturgical corollary is the "Parable Play") and, especially, in his *Short Organon* of 1948 he had sought to renovate some of his original conceptions and to make his view of theatre and representation more "naive," comprehensive, and dialectical.[19]

Ley writes that in the *Short Organon* Brecht "calls for a new epistemology which combines the attitude of wonderment typical of a Galileo with the principal epistemological weapon of Marxism, the dialectic of history." Brecht proposes not only to "set this species of theatre in its aesthetic background" but, even more dismaying, "to take up lodging" in "the realm of the merely enjoyable." Indeed, he seems to have known all along that "naïve entertainment" was the raison d'être of all theatre and that, at any rate, critique-laden alienation effects can coexist with simple pleasure or naïve enjoyment in any form of representation. He knew that in the right circumstances even plays that were avowedly Aristotelian, such as his own *Señora Carrar's Rifles* and *Fear and Misery of the Third Reich* (ca. 1936), can have alienation effects. In other words, the epiphanic or peripatetic value of the play can be found not only in its quintessential form or character but also in its contextual-historical deployment. Walter Benjamin recognizes this much in his review of a production of Brecht's *Fear and Misery* in *Die Neue Weltbühne* of May 1938. He writes that:

> Brecht had turned aside from his experiments in 'epic theatre' out of consideration for [the] emigré groups and their audiences. These needed no specific aids to "alienate" them from the events shown: the alienation was already there, thanks to their political experience, and this made the new balance of the artistic and the political in the new scenes epic indeed.[20]

In a retrospective look at his early theatrical endeavors, Brecht observes, "I think the root of the trouble was that my plays have to be properly performed if they are to be effective, so that for the sake of (oh dear me!) a non-aristotelian dramaturgy I had to outline (calamity!) an epic theatre." Of his attempts to replace the epic theatre with the "dialectical theatre," between 1953 and his death in 1956, Brecht cautions: "If we now discard the concept of EPIC THEATRE we are not discarding that progress towards conscious experience which it still makes possible." Willett notes ominously that "*Verfremdung,* or alienation, is not mentioned" in the glossary of terms Brecht appended to his writings on the dialectical theatre. However, the conspicuous absence of *Verfremdung* in the descriptions of the dialectical theatre could mean that it has become more naturalized and/or taken for granted. The *V-effekt* is the singular means of making that "progress towards conscious experience" and, as such, it could not have become irrelevant or inoperative in his dialectical theatre. Besides, as it will also appear in a later section, both alienation and the alienation effect are inalienable features of human experience and represenation. Insofar as the project of disalienation (overcoming alienation) is the basic agenda of Brecht's theatre the *V-effekt* cannot but be an inalienable feature.[21]

According to Ley, Brecht's *V-effekt* is a "dialecticizing of events" equally manifest in simple story telling and the sophisticated "historical dialectic." Brecht's dialectical theatre is both simple and sophisticated, but its most marked feature is naivety. According to Hill, the "naive in [Brecht's] sense stands for full-blooded, contradictory, lively, more to be felt rather than rationally understood." Be that as it may, the naive in Brecht is not altogether devoid of rationality; its form of rationality, for Brecht as for Aristotle, is extensive and comprehensive without necessarily being irrational. Hill himself observes that Brecht "praised the naive as the most concrete aesthetic category" and insisted that "undifferentiated naivety is primitive." The naivety that underlies Brecht's conception of the dialectical theatre is, therefore, sophisticated; it indicates a movement toward a more open and paralogical view of theatre and representation.[22]

With every entrenchment in the face of opposition, Brecht's epic theatre moved closer and closer to dogmatic "Socialist Realism." His dialectical theatre seems intended to correct his imbalance. At least, Ley believes that Brecht's descriptions of the dialectical theatre:

> equate dialectical methodology with the concept of naivety, which for him was the direct opposite of the naturalistic form, a form canonized by the aesthetic doctrine of Socialist Realism and detrimental to the effect he wished his theater to have on audiences.

On another hand, Hill writes that "in a conversation with one of his assistants Brecht regretfully reveals that he had not mentioned the naive in his theoretical writings because he had taken [it] for granted." Of his early works, moreover, Brecht himself observes ruefully that "aiming to avoid artificial heat, [they] fall short in natural warmth" and rob the theatre of "imagination, humour and meaning."[23]

Brecht had shown his awareness of the creative-yet-critical acculturative force of naive mimetic representations of human experience in his essay "Three Cheers for Shaw," written as early as 1926, nearly thirty years before his espousal of the dialectical theatre. Shaw's "naïve view of writing" and his "terroristic" dramaturgy, Brecht writes, "proves that the right attitude to any really important phenomenon is a casual (contemptuous) one, because it is the only one which permits complete concentration and real alertness." A playful-yet-serious strategy of indirection and doubling-back and pretense is evident in this kind of (naive) representation. The acculturative interplay of playfulness and seriousness in simple or naive theatrical representations of the human self-and-world is most conspicuous, however, in Brecht's "Two Essays on Unprofessional Acting."[24] These two essays were written in the 1940s but were not published until 1976 when they were included in *Brecht on Theatre,* and one cannot help but wonder why they were repressd for so long.

In the two essays on unprofessional acting, Brecht attempts to "study the art of the theatre and its social function" in the naive or simple perspective of habitual mimesis. He is particularly interested in "the theatre'—even the suposedly unpolitical theatre'—

political influence . . . on the formation of taste." He submits that
"art is never without consequences," because "good or bad, a play
always includes an image of the world. Good or bad, the actors
show how people behave under given circumstances" and "the
spectator is encouraged to draw certain conclusions about how the
world works." Brecht notes and celebrates the ubiquity of theatre
and theatricality in the acculturation and socialization of the human being when he writes that "one easily forgets that human
education proceeds along highly theatrical lines. In quite a theatrical manner the child is taught how to behave; logical arguments
only come later. . . . It is no different with grown-ups. Their education never finishes. Only the dead are beyond being altered by
their fellow-men." He considers the theatre to be "the most human
and universal art of all."[25]

Brecht's quest to change the world by making the theatrical
representation of human experience scientific enough to suit the
scientific-technological times bespeaks his belief in the acculturative force of theatre in its nature as the most human, universal or
naive form of representation. The early desire to answer Marx's
call to change the world appears to have compelled him to conceal
his belief in naive theatre and representation behind the veils of
Marxian sophistication. Aristotle and Aristotelian representation
were merely the scapegoats in this quest to defamiliarize the familiar so as to change it. Incidentally, the grounds for this project
of defamiliarization had been cleared by the provision in Bacon's
Novum Organum that "things of familiar and frequent occurrence
do not arrest and detain the thoughts of men, but are received in
passing without enquiry into their causes."[26]

Brecht's autumnal quest for naive representation by means of
the dialectical theatre reflects a belated awareness that any project
of defamiliarization and disalienation (critique), if carried too far,
can become counterproductive. "Socialist Realism," for example,
is nothing more that socialistic critique come full circle into self-
mystification. Defamiliarizing or deconstructive critique, therefore, needs to be limited or circumscribed by naïvety, in the same
way that familiarizing or constructive naïvety needs to be checked
by critique. Naïvety, to appropriate words Rivière writes to Artaud, is "the innocence of facts," a barrier or boundary erected
against potentially interminable possibility of experimentation and
differentiation. Without the limitive or arresting operations of naivety, human existence is marked by restless desire, endless and
wasteful innovation, interminable differentiations, and rapid obso-
lescences. There is no stability, no restful acquiescence, and no

affirmation of life without the innocence of facts that wears the mantle of naivety. And without this "all is futility and chasing of the wind" (Ecclesiates 2:17).[27]

In Brecht's post–1953 writings, the concept of naivety functions as a limit to the potentially interminable alienations or self-and-world differentiations implicated in the *V-effekt*. It provides for the symbolic or ritualistic cultural obstacles against which critique is brought to rest, if not to an end. Naivety is that pause taken for the sake of life, without which human experience is all "sound and fury signifying nothing." It is the constitutive extreme in self-and-world representations at which economies are created and controls instituted on wasteful expenditure. At this pole of representation, historical happenstances are assimilated into and/or pacified by the regnant symbols and structures. Critique, on the other hand, is the site of restless changes and variations, and without coming against the resignations of naive faith, whatever is attained through critique and change cannot be stabilized on behalf of the human self-and-world.

Deconstructive criticism and integrative naivety are constitutive opposites; the momentary ascendance of one means the prostration of the other. Neither extreme is sufficient unto itself, though, in any given time and place, one may be more probable and/or necessary than the other. For instance, the emphasis on "matter of factness" and a "sober functional" attitude makes more sense in an entropic context such as Weimar Germany than does an emphasis on unquestioning or accepting naïvety. Unlimited or unchecked, however, his deconstructive attitude can reify and become counterproductive. Brecht's attempt to replace the over-rational epic theatre with a more naïve dialectical theatre, as a way of avoiding the reifications of Socialist Realism, is a case in point.

The *Verfremdungseffekt* in the Light of Brecht's Acolytic Relationship to Marx

Brecht's adoption of an affirmative perspective on alienation can be traced to the proposal, in his 1926 notes on *Baal,* of a "smokers' theatre" aimed at "dislocating our stock associations" and introducing a "jarring element" into the consumption of theatrical representations. Such a theatre is opposed to the traditional theatre which, according to Brecht, aims at "carrying people away" and encouraging the unquestioning identification of the audience with its fictional characters and real actors. Interestingly, Brechts see his smokers' theatre as existing "only for such philosophers who wished not just to explain the world but also to change it." Its basic methodology "corresponds to the reader's habit of turning back in order to check a point."[28]

Brecht arrived at the critical method he calls the *V-effekt* by way of an attempt to get "close to the old Asiatic theatre," and, significantly, the "first mention in his writings of the term *Verfrem-dungseffekt*" occurs in an essay titled "Alienation Effects in Chinese Acting." The pertinence of Chinese acting to Brecht's epic theatre lies in the fact that it is "directed to playing in such a way that the audience was hindered from simply identifying itself with the characters in the play. Acceptance or rejection of their actions and utterances were meant to take place on a conscious plane, instead of, hitherto, in the audience's subconscious." To Brecht, the principle of "complete conversion" central to the "European stage's characteristic illusions" appears uneconomical and "very exhausting." He believes that "the Western actor" operating the Stanislavsky system, in doing "all he can to bring the spectator to the closest proximity to the events and characters he has to portray . . . gets exhausted and soon begins to just copy the superficialities of the other person's speech and hearing." Such a wasteful method of acting and representation, he believes, is "unknown to the Chinese performer . . . for he rejects complete conversion." The Chinese actor "points at outward signs" and uses abstract masks, emblematic gestures, and presentational effects to import a "pathos of distance" into whatever representations "he" makes of the referent self-and-world. "Acting like this is healthier and in our view less unworthy of a thinking being; it demands a considerable knowledge of humanity and wordly wisdom, and a keen eye for what is socially important. In this case too there is of course a creative process at work; but it is a higher one, because it is raised to the conscious level."[29]

Ironically, the terms in which Brecht valorizes the Chinese mode of histrionic representation are Orientalist and primitivist. He suggests that the Chinese actor courts mystery and seems "uninterested in disclosing mystery to us" and he "allows nobody to examine" or understand how, and "nature does not allow him to understand as he produces it."

We have here the artistic counterpart of a primitive technology, a rudimentary science. The Chinese performer gets his A-effect by association with magic. "How it's done" remains hidden; knowledge is a

matter of knowing the tricks and is in the hands of men who guard it
jealously and profit from their secrets.[30]

In a contrary view, Brecht suggests that "the Chinese actor's A-
effect is a transportable piece of technique: a conception that can
be prised loose from the Chinese theatre," perhaps because it is
"scientific" or, at least, prescientific. In it "there is already an attempt to interfere with the course of nature," through "questioning" and "adopting a standpoint from which [nature] appears
mysterious, incomprehensible and beyond control." The "future
explorer" who takes up this "attitude of somebody wondering" is,
according to Brecht, "applying A-effect." If so, then Brecht's *V-
effekt* (Or A-effect as it is also called) is no more than another name
for the wondering attitude that Aristotle (of all people) suggests as
a precondition for all mimesis and/or representations of human
experience. This precognitive attitude has been termed "psychical
distance" by some Western thinkers and a "pathos of distance"
by others.[31]

In Brechtian theatre and representation the "*V-Effekt* is the artistic tool for nurturing the critical faculty which is the *sin qua non*
of revolutionizing society." It is the "key concept in the Brechtian
theater," the "one structural device that gives unity to [his] writing
and directing." In the light of Brecht's avowal of Marxian objectives, however, the affirmative conception of alienation in the
V-effekt leaves some critics and commentators perplexed. The
view of alienation in Brecht's V-effekt seems to second-order
Marx's conception of alienation (*Entfremdung*), returning it, nico-
demously, to its more ambiguous Gnostic-Hegelian precedents.
The fundmental problem in Brecht's conception of alienation, as
Bentley puts it, is that:

Hegel and Marx have made a very important principal out of Entfremdung, the normal German word for alienation or estrangement. Verfremdung is Brecht's word for the process of making alien or strange.
Now, since it is well known that alienation especially in the writing of
Karl Marx, is an appalling phenomenon—the estrangement of the
worker from the ownership and meaning of what he works at—it will
be asked: how can the Marxist Brecht actually call for alienation?[32]

The answer lies in the fact observed by Bentley himself that
"already in Hegel alienation is a positive as well as a negative
thing." Still, "there is no unanimity among critics as to whether
the *Verfremdungseffekt* . . . should be seen in the philosophical-

historical context of the Hegelian-Marxist concept of *Entfrem-dung*." Some critics dismiss any congruence between Brecht and Marx's usage of alienation on the grounds that Brecht based his notion of *Verfremdung* not on Marx's *Entfremdung* but on the Russian concept *Ostrannenie*. Hill, for example, finds it extremely significant that "Brecht used [*Verfremdung*] for the first time around 1936 after he had come across the Russian equivalent (the word *ostrannenie*) in the writings of the formalistic critic Viktor Shlovksy." Willett also believes that "it can hardly be a coincidence that ["Viktor Shklovskiji's phrase 'Priem Ostrannenija,' or 'device for making strange'"] should have entered Brecht's vocabulary after his Moscow visit." Nonetheless, Willett points out that Brecht's *Verfremdung* is "virtually a neologism, for Grimm's dictionary gives only two obscure early examples for the use of 'ver-fremden' as a transitive verb."[33]

Inconsistent translations of both Brecht's *Verfremdung* and Marx's *Entfremdung* have also militated against making a consistent analysis of the relationships between them. There is no consensus as to whether "alienation" or "estrangement" are the best English translations for either of these German terms. However, the genealogy of the Latin term *Alienatio* suggests Marx's and Brecht's usages to be merely two of the many possible manifestations of alienation. Indeed, it is increasingly the case in present-day commentaries that alienation is viewed as "the necessary preface for experience," to quote Brian O'Doherty. M. H Abrams also explains that "we in our time are . . . the heirs of a very old and expanding tradition . . . that it is the lot of man to be fragmented and cut off, but haunted in his exile and solitariness by the presentiment of a lost condition of wholeness and community." Themes connected with "the alienated hero, in an inhuman universe and a disintegrated social order," Abrams adds "have become obsessive in philosophers, poets, novelists, and dramatists of the last two or three decades."[34]

In the comprehensive frame work of Gnostic or Neoplatonic thought, Peter C. Ludz argues, "alienation is not only something negative, but also a determining element of the human condition."[35] The gnostic view of alienation reappears in Hegel's *Phenomenology of Mind* where "alienation is viewed as a force that stimulates historical development." According to Ludz, "Hegel conceptualizes alienation even more concretely in a positive way, to the extent that the 'self' has the possibility of becoming an object, or of 'externalising itself' or losing itself in the object, and then of dialectically taking this being-different back into itself, and reconciling this within itself." Significantly:

> With its positive connotations the concept [of alienation] . . . is pertinent particularly to creative man, to the artist and the critic. Alienation, positively conceived, provides an instrument which seems appropriate to grasp specific aspects of the man-world relationship in the context of the arts or the world of creativity. If applied otherwise, it loses its grip.[36]

The view of art and the artist as the bearers of the torch of self-and-world disalienation and change has been shown to underlie the works of Appia and Artaud. The same view seems to underwrite Brecht's conception of the *V-effekt* as an artistic or aesthetic means of change. Interestingly, this view of art as a paramount means of disalienation obtains in the arguments of Karl Marx himself. In fact, Stefan Morawski, believes that "the major problems of art are unsolvable without reference to the question of artistic alienation, which was raised by Marx." Marx believed that "the whole late history of culture entails the removal of art from life," its turning "away from production *sensu stricto,* and the estrangement of the aesthetic attitude" as a whole. "The sum of this is alienation, the loss of any chance for art to achieve a general and harmonizing effect. . . ." Yet, at the same time, "the alienation processes, if deleterious to artistic creation, have secured for art a relative autonomy, . . . art has, through the interplay, prepared itself for the superseding of alienation." Indeed, the artist has always been attuned to nature and "his product has always had a general social significance . . . which has tended to militate against a narrow outlook limited by official ideology."[37]

Marx views alienation as a result of parochial and distortive representation of relations in the human self-and-world by the ruling class. Thus, until this ruling-class ideology is replaced by the ideology of the working class, art cannot completely overcome the falsifications and distortions perpetrated by official ideology. In other worlds, "alienation cannot be completely superseded except with communism, in the Marxian view," because it is only in the state of communism that "all men would be artists to some degree." Marx's "prediction" of the coming into being of "aesthetic man" in his communist state, Morawski suggests, "undoubtedly has utopian antecedents . . . in Rousseau." Still, it is not "just the aberration in a genius's thought." On the contrary, "it expresses an empirically founded, acute perception of an intolerable antinomy between art and society—along with a genial hunch as to the undoing of that antinomy."[38]

My own congenial hunch is that Brecht's conception of the *V-effekt* as a theatrical-aesthetic means of disalienation does not only echo Marx's "genial hunch" but also the more general hunch of many modern European writers and movements. Brecht's *V-effekt*, "which in its simplest level entails a gaining of new insights into the world around us by glimpsing it in a different and previously unfamiliar light," is a form of "meta-alienation" or "double play" on alienation. In Herbert Blau's view, alienation is "a sensitivity to the means of producing illusions, in life, in theater." The point is that "if you don't keep the comma between them (life, theater) as impeccably as the edge of the stage you are producing illusion. You may be producing it anyway, but with no sense of the issues at stake." Blau believes that in his conception of the *V-effekt*, Brecht "was philosophically engaged with this double play of illusion, the relation of theater to theatricalized reality, the idols of the cave and the tribe, and not only the marketplace." And true enough, to quote Hill, "the connection [Bacon, for one, had made] between life—theater—idols—Aristotle was not lost on Brecht."[39]

It is worth noting that while Brecht sought to create new works "suitable for present-day subjects" Marx looked back to "Shakespeare and the classics." "In spite of his enthusiasm for the nineteenth century novel and particularly for Balzac," Morawski suggests, "Marx returned again and again to Shakespeare and the classics. Like Hegel, Marx saw in the art of antiquity a humankind still harmoniously linked to nature, yet not so alienated that the social binds have been dissolved." This nostalgic view of art contradicts the "system of dependency" Marx himself had established between the economic "base" and the noneconomic spheres of human activity. "For, when certain aesthetic standards are shown to outlast fundamental historical changes in the economic structure of society," even though "art had not been expressly exempted" from the subordinate superstructure, they "put into question" the overall coherence of Marx's discursive system. In contrast to Marx, Brecht believed that "Shakespeare's great plays, the basis of our drama, are no longer effective" and that "what killed them was not capitalism's consequences but capitalism itself." As such, "there is little point mentioning post-Shakespearean drama, as it is invariably much feebler, and in Germany has been debauched by Latin influences."[40]

Brecht meant his theatrical and critical works to be answers to Marx's call to change the world, but the way he goes about this

project ultimately overwrites and overrides not only his own ideological intentions but also those of his mentor Marx. Generally
speaking, Brecht's art and theatre often outstrip his theories, leading one to suspect that the effectiveness of art lies in its resistance
of simple ideological formulas and agendas.

7

The Ghana National Theatre Movement: Obviating the Problem(s) of Language(s) in the Theatre of Ghanaian-African Self-and-World Decolonization

> The existency of diverse languages in active use among regions of the same country could lead to schisms unless an ulterior identity is revealed.
>
> —W. E. Abraham

The prime objective of the Ghana National Theatre Movement (NTM) was to create an African National Theatre that will oversee the creation of a decolonized "African Personality" and foster continental African unity. The postcolonial African National Theatre was to foster a countercolonial consciousness with which to overcome the prostration of the newly decolonized self-and-world in the discourse of the colonizer. This stage of decolonization was termed secondary decolonization, and viewed by strategists of African decolonization as the most crucial stage of self-and-world decolonization. They believed that without this stage of decolonization the decolonized subject and world merely become a "neo-colonial" one; that is, a poorly paid producer of raw materials for the industries of the industrial countries.

The primary stage of decolonization is conceived as essentially the stage of political independence. Economic freedom is usually a part and parcel of the independence sought by the architects of decolonization, but the colonizer seldom includes this in the concessions it is compelled to make. On the other hand, some architects of independence often suppose, erroneously, that the attainment of political independence will necessarily result in cultural-psychological and economic emancipation. In the words of Kwame Nkrumah, the chief actor in Ghanaian political independence: "Seek ye first the political kingdom, and all others shall be added unto you." After primary decolonization or political independence, however, the economic, cultural-pedagogical, and even political paradigms of the colonizer are usually retained in essence, if not in their entirety, by the newly independent nations. As a result, the newly decolonized territories become more subtly recolonized or neocolonial worlds. The only difference between colonialism and neocolonialism is the cosmetic-titular changes made at the apex of political power.[1]

Economic emancipation is often an impossible dream after primary decolonization or political independence, but the signs of economic dependency are tangible and material enough to be easily identified. The signs of psychological or ideological dependency, that is, the dependence of the decolonized subject on the self-and-world representations of the dearly departed colonial master, on the other hand, are not as easy to detect. In the neocolonial situation, the mind-set or mentality of the postcolonial subject remains tuned and attuned to the seductive forms and representations of the ever-palpable, ever-dominant colonizer. The newly decolonized subject continues to articulate its self-and-world in colonial terms. The common phrase used to describe this aping or uncritical mimesis is *colonial mentality*.

The stage of secondary decolonization, needless to say, was a cultural-ideological as well as magical-symbolic (ritualistic) one. More often than not a total or totalizing form of theatre was the means proposed to oversee this project. The overriding concern of such postcolonial nationalist cultural institutions as the NTM of Ghana was to spearhead a cultural-ontological revolution that could eradicate the colonial mentality from the newly decolonized self-and-world. Such movements attempt to recuperate a largely nostalgic and/or imagined precolonial national-racial self (personality) and world (forms of association; society). This nostalgic precolonial self-and-world is both the chief means and the fact of the overcoming of the colonial mentality and/or the enfeeblement of the colonized by the colonizer.

The importance of cultural-psychological or ideological decolonization to strategists of Ghanaian-African independence is evident in W. E. Abraham's observation that:

The politicians and statesmen of Africa have . . . recognised the relevance of African cultures to the process of reconstruction. In the preoccupation with the African Personality they appear to hold that the guiding principles of the future of Africa will be those authenticated in the African experience and cultures. Progress, its objectives, and some of its avenues are thought of in terms of a picture of the African Personality.[2]

Similarly, Janheinz Jahn submits in his book *Muntu,* subtitled "An Outline of the New African Culture," that "the question of the future of Africa becomes the question of the existence of the future of African culture." He calls for an "African Renaissance," "a genuine Renaissance, which does not remain a merely formal renewal and imitation of the past, but permits something new to emerge. This something new is already at hand; we call it neo-African culture." In *Muntu* Jahn endeavors to "present a systematic exposition of [a] neo-African culture" in terms of its "two [African and European] components." He treats the "traditional African component" of this culture in "greater details" because he believed that the "European component is generally known . . . [and] recognizable to the reader without difficulty." In his arguments, therefore, the "unity" of neo-African culture "is slightly stressed."[3]

To his credit, Jahn acknowledges that the "neo-African culture" is "a myth, instead of an objective picture of history. But this is the case with every history."

The Africa presented by the ethnologist is a legend in which we used to believe. The African tradition as it appears in the light of the neo-African culture may also be a legend—but it is a legend in which African intelligence believes. And it is their perfect right to declare authentic, correct and true those components of their past they believe to be so. In the same way a Christian, asked about the nature of Christianity, will point to the gospel teaching "Love my neighbour" and not to the Inquisition.[4]

The quest for an ulterior precolonial national personality and culture was not peculiar to Ghana and the National Theatre Movement; rather, it appears to be a crucial part of worldwide decolonization. The declarations at the Conference of Non-Aligned at Bandung (1953) bear this out, as does Clifford Geertz's documentation of the search for an "Indonesian Personality" in Indonesia under Bung Sukharno. In a communiqué issued in 1972, the FRELIMO, the movement fighting for the independence of Mozambique, stressed the need to develop both a "Mozambican personality." It also called for the creation of a new culture . . . based on traditional forms with a new content dictated by our new reality [because] culture plays an important role in the reinforcement of national unity. . . . The militants from other regions there bring their way of living, their dances, their songs, and from this a new culture, national in its form and revolutionary in content, is born.

Similarly, after a brief visit to the Gold Coast (Ghana) in the 1950s, Richard Wright writes and laments that:

African culture has not developed the personalities of the people to the degree that they are stout, hard, sharply-defined; there is too much cloudiness in the African's mentality, a kind of sodden vagueness that makes for lack of confidence, an absence of focus that renders that mentality incapable of grasping the workaday world. And until confidence is established at the center of African personality, until there is an inner reorganization of that personality, there can be no question of marching from the tribal order to the twentieth century.[5]

For Wright, the reorganization of the "African personality" and culture means their modernization and/or Westernization, thus it is not at all strange that he blames the African for the ills that beset his or her self-and-world in the aftermath of Western colonialism. Wright laments that the African personality and mentality is not "stout, hard, sharply-defined" or Western enough, but most strategists of African decolonization are wont to agree with Abraham that "the three-dimensional individual, completely subsistent, and a distinct atom, was non-existent" in the paradigmatic African culture. Thus, to them, and presumably to the paradigmatic African, Wright's lamentations are profoundly irrelevant. Still, Wright remains in good company when he calls for the radical reorientation of the postcolonial sub-Saharan African self-and-world. In fact, after a similarly Wrightian junket through the new states of sub-Saharan Africa in 1960, Frantz Fanon writes that "the deeper I enter into the cultures and the political circles the surer I am that the great danger that threatens Africa is the absence of an ideology." Incidentally, he viewed "African unity" as a good starting point for the creation of such a unifying ideology.[6]

Even though it was primarily a Ghanaian theatrical-cultural movement, the aims of the Ghana National Theatre Movement (NTM) were broadly continental-Africanist. Its dual objective was to create a postcolonial "African Personality" and foster "African Unity" through theatricalizations of the postcolonial African experience. Kwame Nkrumah had declared on the eve of Ghana's independence that "the independence of Ghana is meaningless unless it was linked with the total liberation of Africa." And barely a year after Ghanaian political independence, in 1958, the National Theatre Movement was launched to help with the more total, or psycho-cultural, liberation of Africa. The NTM lasted only as long as Nkrumah's regime, which was overthrown in 1966. However, the great bulk of the articles and debates on the problems and possibilities of the "African theatre" were published in Ghanaian literary magazines (such as *Okyeame, The Ghana Cultural Review,* and *The Legon Observer*) well after 1966.

The main subject of the Ghana NTM debates was the envisaged role of the African national theatre in the creation of a postcolonial and countercolonial African national personality and consciousness. This African theatre was conceived predominantly as a recombination or syncresis of deliberately deethnicized indigenous dances. This syncretic dancerly African theatre (which embraces and internalizes other African arts, such as music and drumming, ritual enactments, crafts, and textiles) was to be the singular means of comprehending and representing the multiethnic, multisubjective, and multilinguistic postcolonial Ghanaian-African self-and-world.

The choice of dance as the quintessential and/or exemplary form of African theatre was based in a cross-factional belief in the "fundamentality of the dance idiom in Africa." Two main ideological factions existed in the NTM; the first can be described as exclusively dancerly in that it fought against the use of verbal language in the African theatre. It believed that pantomimic or nonverbal African dance (but helped by music, singing—but ah, there's the rub!), drumming, and visual display should be the sole form of representation in the African theatre. This faction formed the majority in the NTM, and among the artists and writers who belonged to it were A. M. Opoku and Saka Acquaye. A minority of people in the Ghana NTM opposed to the exclusively dancerly faction, insisting that the verbal-spoken and/or literary traditions of drama needed to be reconciled with pantomimic ethnic dance to create a more total or totalizing African theatre. Kojo Senanu is perhaps the most vocal or articulate member of this faction; at least, his essay contains the sole extant argument of that position.[7]

Both factions within the Ghana NTM agreed that the prime, if not sole, objective of African theatre was to create a postcolonial African personality that will be the agent of African unity. As Senanu phrases it, the prime objective of the "African Theatre" is "the very basic one of creating an indigenous and virile popular theatre." Senanu adds that:

Nobody who has given any thought to the matter can doubt that in the dance we already have the most direct, and yet the most complex, form of dramatic and theatrical communication, which is both prior to, and transcends the verbal drama[!] . . .

. . . [D]ance, movement, and the use of space, generally, [is] a much more direct and complex form of communicating thoughts, emotions, and attitudes—those things which constitute the subtext of any written script.[8]

A. M. Opoku, then a teacher of dance at the School of Dance and Music of the Institute of African Studies, Legon, goes even further to suggest that "to us, Life with its rhythms and cycles is Dance, and Dance is Life." Dance is "the most complete of the arts," and, as such, the ideal means for training the neo-African body "so that it could express love, hatred, comedy, tragedy . . . to the accompaniment of music and drums." Opoku believes that "body movement varies from place to place and every movement [is] true to the Region from which it originated." But:

Movement changes with change in the living or working conditions of a people, and it has a way of showing the change in the dance of a new generation. All such changes[,] however, draw inspiration from the past to interpret the inspirations of a new generation in terms that they will understand.

Sharing dances and dancing together, Opoku seems to imply, is a means of fostering unity: "Our dancers and musicians, drawn from a variety of tribal backgrounds, have demonstrated beyond doubt that through sharing our dance experiences we are made effectively aware of our National Unity."[9]

The NTM view of dance as the exemplary form of African self-and-world representation is shared by some British and European ethnographers. Even a rationalist-functionalist such as E. E. Evans-Pritchard writes of Azande witch doctors that "when asked a question they will always dance rather than ponder it to find an answer." Similarly, Geoffrey Gorer suggests that:

From the esthetic point of view the dance is undoubtedly the chief African art; all other arts, music, singing, sculpture, textiles, and lesser handicrafts have been diverted to serve and enhance the dance. From a religious point of view it is hardly less important; the West Africans worship their gods, control the dangerous forces of nature, and call down divine power into themselves by dancing.

Gorer goes on to say that "for the West Africans the dance is the chief medium which gives meaning to their lives and united [*sic*] them with the forces which people their universe." The dance in West Africa also performs "important social functions" in that a:

> group of warriorrs and initiates assert their unity by dancing together. Crime is controlled by the witch-finding trance-dance which discovers criminals, and the chief moment when the more primitive groups gather together is when they are all watching some of their number dance for the whole community.[10]

The lone dissenter to the predominant NTM view of unspoken or pantomimic dance as the exemplary form of African theatre, and, indeed, against the conception of theatre as a means of socialization, politicization, and acculturation, was J. C. de Graft. In his report, "Drama Workshop, 1963," de Graft insists that the primary objective of African art and theatre is not the creation of a new human being and culture but the "artistic mastery of means." He laments that:

> during the discussion of the idea of the National Theatre [,] . . . the human element seemed to loom up larger and larger until it seemed to dwarf comletely such considerations as buildings and equipment. The human element *and* the ARTISTIC PRODUCT. A Theatre is good only as a place where people go to participate in something. . . . If we are building a theatre, then we must *also* make sure that we can present in that theatre shows of artistic merit. . . . So it would seem that at the centre of our theatre building schemes [*sic*] must be MAN: man the . . . [total artist-performer] and man the auditor. Our supreme task is to get MAN into our theatre.[11]

In de Graft's view, the African theatre must, above all else, address the "need for more and better opportunities for 'Theatre People' in Ghana to learn more about the theatre and its problems, to develop their capabilities, . . . [and] to gain a mastery of their art."[12] Right as de Graft is, especially in hindsight, he is only partly so. In a newly decolonized developing country such as Ghana the question of representation and acculturation can never be avoided or overlooked; art-for-the-sake-of-art, and, in general, any activity that does not address itself to immediate (physical-material) and mediate (psychic-spiritual) needs of humanity appears insupportable. In such a critical time and context, disinterested or non-purposeful endeavors appear to be a fearful waste of time, talent, and money. Sad, perhaps, but true.

De Graft also barks up the wrong tree when he blames the frustrations of the "young people [who] genuinely want to make the theatre their career" on governmental indifference. The NTM was a satellite, a cultural arm, of the ruling Convention People's Party (CPP) which had also established and financially supported two "Worker's Brigade Drama groups" as well as the "Ghana National Dance Ensemble." It is true that these artistic-cultural institutions were "folkloric museums" or showcases for a nostalgic "authentic African culture." It is also undeniable that the drama groups were patronage systems that provided jobs for the "lumpen-proletariat" or glorified "Verandah Boys" who were the power base of Nkrumah's CPP. But the fact still remains that the CPP did what it thought was necessary to develop the arts and theatre in post-independence Ghana. The problem lay in the Africanist or neo-Africanist definition of theatre as something that de-emphasized such material elements as a theatre building and aesthetic considerations such as mastery of means. On this level, mainly, de Graft is right.[13]

On the whole, de Graft's basic quarrel with the state of affairs in the art-theatre scene in Ghana after independence makes him "wear his urbanity on his sleeve" and to elevate Western forms over African ones. He also belittles the endeavors of his Afrocentric or neo-Africanist compatriots. Jawa Apronti quotes de Graft as saying that "he has not written 'African poetry' since he was 'neither a tribe living in some long inaccessible African jungle, nor a committee of pan-Africanist ethnographers.'" In a similar light, de Graft praises J. W. Abruquah's novel *The Catechist* for having

No pretensions to African avant-garde fiction-writing; none of the rather over-played conflicts between 'traditional' and present-day Africa; [it is] not larded with folk wisdom congealed in proverbs; [makes] no attempt to show off or put over 'our beloved Africa'; [shows] no striving towards a hybrid of the English language that will pass for African—a language which alas! is becoming such a tiresome feature of so many West African fiction[s] in English.[14]

All this suggests that de Graft is not a disinterested or impartial observer when it comes to determining the role of art and theatre in the postcolonial Ghanaian-African world. In fact, notwithstanding him, a great many Africans and sympathetic non-Africans considered the role of African art, to borrow words from J. H. Nketia, as "traditional-functionalist-utilitarian." Saka Acquaye, for instance, allows that "art for art's sake has its place" for the ones with the flair for [that kind of] writing." But, "to [his] mind, most of our art forms have always been utilitarian." Some believe that the "functional-utilitarian" characteristic is unique to African art, but the greater bulk of evidence suggests this to be applicable to simple or undomesticated (premodern) societies as a whole. These are societies in which ritual-religious forms (the precursors of art forms) have not been directed away from "serious" worship and toward "playful" art. In any case, the NTM view of art and theatre is not unique or idiosyncratic; on the contrary, it is reminiscent of "intellectual trends towards primitivism in many fields of [European] thought around the turn of the century."[15]

The NTM attempt to recuperate a nostalgic-atavistic precolonial self-and-world (personality and culture) explains its primitivist-atavist view of art and theatre. This inclination coincides with the self-orientalizations or self-otherings of such neo-Africanist Westerners as Leo Frobenius and Janheinz Jahn. Frobenius's forays into Africa at the beginning of the twentieth century, Jahn writes, were motivated by "only the one aspiration 'to find among the naive peoples the happiness which was languishing in Europe' (a romantic escape from reality), and to discover the remains of an alien past." Jahn's own attempt to differentiate between the essential natures and forms of African and Western dance comes to rest "in the sense, in the meaning of the dance," and in the belief that African "dance is paradigmatic, illustrative and self-evident. By contrast "the English style is pure form, it no longer expresses anything, it is pure beauty."[16]

Because they often view the nature of African theatre and art as self-evident and unchanging, the NTM exegetes do not explain the specifics of how the "African theatre" will undersee the psycho-ideological decolonization of the Ghanaian-African self-and-world. The fortunate exception is Felix Morriseau-Leroy, a transplanted Haitian, who dedicates his essay "African National Theatre: For Whom?" to "the delicate work of converting the traditional fete into a form of theatre valid for the new societies" of sub-Saharan Africa. The vital question he poses at the outset of this symbolic conversion and empowerment is: "For whom do you wish to make the theatre? . . . For the tourists? Or for the African people?" He submits in answer that:

> The response to this questions [sic] presupposes an ideological stand and the most regrettable is that of "art for art's sake". Hypocritical or unconscious, this stand is favourable to the enemies of Africa. On the contrary, by taking the part of Africa with all the implications of self-

denial and reward, people concerned with the theatre will embark upon an experience of extraordinary dynamism.

Enthusiasm seizes each member of the team and transforms him into a poet of the African revolution; then comes the intellectual and sentimental adhesion to popular wisdom and ecstasy ... [discoverable] by methods of knowledge other than [the] Western. ...

It is necessary to let oneself be possessed by rhythm and to abandon oneself to the infallibility of the dance; ... to identify oneself with the crowd in a collective trance. ... It is in this state of grace that the poet exercises the liberty of his creation which is without limit.[17]

Like Jahn, who believes that "neo-African culture reveals itself to us as a spiritual phenomenon," Morriseau-Leroy submits that:

African drama is born of the burst of the gods in each man. The intelligence of the spectator is increased, as it were, in the sharing of collective possession: the barrier of languages is broken; the audience is *subjugated,* and the ancient songs are mixed with the new.

Its mystical character notwithstanding, the African theatre has a social-realist agenda: "one of its most foremost roles is to give the people a civic education"; it "addresses itself to party members, co-operative unions, youth organisations and the army" and appropriates "the formula 'diversity in unity' . . . to encourage political union on national and inter-African levels." Most of all, it eschews "debauched commercialism" and "consecrates [itself] more to adapting modern techniques to the essential objectives of the national movement than to discussing the merits and demerits of a proscenium or a backdrop."[18]

Morriseau-Leroy wants to create "a national theatre for the people, a national theatre conceived by the intellectual leaders who have the vision of the complete liberation of the people of Africa from the [sic] criminal cultural suppression. A national theatre with the [sic] only artists capable of making themselves understood by the people. And everything is possible." In pursuit of this objective, he applauds the "many great artists who express themselves [in] their language and in the language of the spectators for whom the national theatre is being conceived." This is to say that he supports such artists as Acquaye who write and produce "indigenous language plays" against those who write in English and have "British accents."[19]

To Saka Acquaye the neo-African self-and-world is an undifferentiated totality because if you were in (West) Africa and you looked at a group of excited people in conversation at a distance beyond your hearing. You would no doubt observe that there is a similar trait in the gestures and mannerisms found common to all these people from different areas. Their way of expression with their [*sic*] hands, bodies and faces, can be found to have incarnated vital physical expressions, which have developed along with their culture to make them identical in a large family. To me, this is the core of our personality which holds out the broad answer to the problem [of language in the development of the African Theatre].[20]

It is of no small significance that Acquaye's eavesdropper is placed "beyond . . . hearing" and presented only with "incarnated vital *physical* expressions." What this observer sees is a dumb show, a theatre without words or spoken language! The lure of pantomimic dance has for Acquaye, Opoku, and other dancerly exegetes of the NTM obtains in its alleged obviation of the problem of lanugage(s). In opposition, a minority faction of Western-educated people in the NTM, Kojo Senanu among them, argued that the African theatre must reconcile verbal-literary with nonverbal or bodily-dancerly idioms. They seemed to believe that the postcolonial Ghanaian-African self-and-world is of necessity both African and Western and that to be at all viable its representations must include and reconcile these constitutive extremes.

In the other-excluding ambience of the NTM, however, the suggestion that the neo-African theatre should contain a Western element seemed ideologically indefensible. The more politically and ideologically correct attitude was for one to be resigned to the thought that "the problems of language or languages in the African theatre" were intractable. The linguistic problems of the African theatre, Jones-Quartey believes, ultimately eroded any common ground shared by the two main factions in the NTM. Senanu, for instance, could agree with Acquaye that "miming, in the form of dance—body *movement* (Senanu)—is obviously one-half of the equation for successful theatre in Africa." But this agreement comes apart in the light of "the other half of the equation, the *verbal* part of drama [because it] raises again the problem of language."[22]

The "problem of language(s)" is, thus, the most ubiquitous theme and singular anxiety in the NTM debates. The near-consensus on the "fundamentality of the dance" in African theatre remarks a profound awareness of the intractable problems that come with the adoption of either the colonial language (English) or any of the proliferative indigenous languages in Ghana as the means of theatro-cultural self-and-world expression. As Acquaye expresses

it, most of the NTM debaters believed that "the stubborn problem
of the spoken word is what will stop the Ghanaian theatre from
making smooth progress." Juxtaposing Acquaye and Senanu's con-
trasted arguments of the African theatre leads Jones-Quartey to
the conclusion that Acquaye had:

> anticipated Senanu's analysis and criticism by two years in as much as
> he had argued that the "sophisticated actor . . . will depend on words
> as his chief medium of communication, with the result that, limited to
> the use of only one language, which is only understood by only one
> segment of the people, he is ineffective and his message is lost on the
> majority of the audience.[23]

Unfortunately Jones-Quartey's comparisons are marred by the
fact that he reduces Acquaye's analysis of the problem of lan-
guage(s) in the African theatre to the singular question of "sophistication in the actor." What Acquaye had said was that "in Africa
now less sophisiticated plays presented by a less sophisticated cast
are more likely to go down better than highly sophisticated plays
that depend on the spoken word for their effect." Jones-Quartey
goes even further to accuse Acquaye of bad faith toward the "less
sophisticated actor" in whom he localizes a problem facing Acquaye himself in his capacity as a creator of operatic ballets. He
writes that:

> faced with an internal problem which was intractable to him personally,
> Mr. Acquaye passed it on to entirely the wrong party. Surely, *words,*
> as the "chief medium of communication" in a play—as distinct from a
> story played out in dance form, e.g. ballet—are not the responsibility
> of "the sophisticated actor" but of the author of the play?

Jones-Quartey's own citations of Acquaye prove his accusations
unjust. Besides, Acquaye's malapropistic use of "sophisticated"
(when he obviously means "educated") cannot justify his demonization. By substituting "educated" for "sophisticated" every time
it is used in Acquaye's argument, and by placing this argument "in
its particularistic context in Africa," Jones-Quartey "immediately"
raises "a new set of polemical problems." Ironically, these problems disclose the personal-polemical nature of Jones-Quartey's attack on Acquaye.[24]
   According to Jones-Quartey, Acquaye's endorsement of pantomimic theatre is based in three pregnant hypotheses:

(a) That "the life of the African is generally communal, [that] he moves and lives in groups, and even if he is to act alone he does so in the shadow of his entire people";
(b) that "it takes the Ghanaian about twenty of his impressionable years to get to understand Western culture, in an effort to secure a position for his material needs"; and
(c) that "it is not easy to find any Ghanaian who can express himself well in English who has not [at the same time] lost something of his personality."

His undoubted ability to "express himself well in English" makes Jones-Quartey appear in the light of Acquaye's third hypothesis to be a Ghanaian who has "lost something of his personality." This places in question his role in the theatre of secondary African decolonization. If so, then his attack on Acquaye is an attack on someone who excludes him and other members of the Western-educated elite from active and unproblematic participation in the vital representations of the Ghanaian-African national theatre. It is, thus, difficult to accept Jones-Quartey's claim that he wrote his article in "identification with and sympathy for [Acquaye's] general concern."[25] The contrary motivation seems more plausible.

Acquaye's three hypotheses show him to be conversant with the basic tenets of neo-Africanist and pan-Africanist thought. His first hypothesis reiterates the pan-Africanist conception of the African past as "communal" or communalist, in decided contrast to a Western individualistic present. The second hypothesis quantifies the real cost of Western education to the Ghanaian-African in terms of alienation from the ideal-nostalgic self-and-world. The third, and perhaps most important, hypothesis suggests that the use of a colonial language is a blight on the psychic personality or consciousness of the colonized subject. As Frantz Fanon puts it in *Black Skin, White Masks,* "to speak a language is to take on a world, a culture."[26]

The neo-Africanist/Fanonian view of language can be drawn out of Huw Morris-Jones's commentary on Collingwood's argument of language as a "social institution, part of a social culture, or as Wittgenstein puts it, of a 'form of life.'"

Learning a language therefore is part of the process of the socialization of personality. Learning to speak is a part of our learning to live with other persons, to think and feel in ways characteristic of our society. . . . Natural languages embody the thoughts and feelings characteristic of the societies whose languages they are. Different natural languages reflect different ways of life.

Morris-Jones goes on to note arguments "against this concept of language" on the grounds:

> that it is highly conservative, and that the stress on the authority of paradigmatic usages is to inhibit change, to circumscribe the range of linguistic expression to what has already been said, to limit one to the clichés and stereotyped verbalisms which are the stock moves in the language game.[27]

But, if it is indeed true that "natural languages . . . inhibit change" then they are perfectly suited to the NTM's desire to recuperate a nostalgic precolonial African past and self. The quest for a dancerly form of representation in the NTM renaissance, Opoku and Jahn's arguments show, is a search for the allegedly unchanging aspects of the Ghanaian-African self-and-world. African dance in the NTM perspective meant a body of representatons that are so immediately connected to the will and affects of the ideal Body that they leave no space in which the written or unwritten, spoken or unspoken, Western Word or Logos can once again take root and anchor the recolonization of the Ghanaian-African self-and-world.

However, no matter how intractable the problem of language or languages in the theatre or postcolonial African self-and-world representation, a mystically-and-mystifyingly-conceived dance cannot be a desirable form of representation. Dance is not explicit enough, and mystical-mystified dance is even less so. Jahn and Acquaye might believe African dance to be clear and unchanging in its meanings, but in the reality of a multiethnic postcolonial Ghana dance cannot provide for a clear and unambiguous description of material relations. Any dependence on dancerly representations in such a context will be tantamount to the mystification of power and/or a terpsichorean abdication of responsibility.[28]

In a complex modern nation with many ethnic-national subjects, the possibility of arbitrariness and mystifications of power are very great. As such, it is undesirable to allow oneself to be "possessed by rhythm," "to abandon [oneself] to the infallibility of the dance," and/or to "identify . . . with the crowd in a collective trance." Linguistically mute, or, at best, imprecise dance cannot be the sole means of representing the terms and relations in such a world. Spoken and written language might not obviate all confusion and arbitrariness of power, but it is better suited for articulating and symbolizing human experience in a complex world. Clarity and/or verbal-literary explicitness is imperative in the present-day world, and to overlook this is to court political and cultural disaster.

In apparent recognition of the necessity of verbal and written language(s) in the representation of postcolonial or decolonizing Africa, J. H. Nketia suggests that "modern African states . . . [should] follow a multilingual policy which allows for the use of dominant African languages (each in its respective area) side by side with a world language." Scott Kennedy applies Nketia's proposal to the African theatre and suggests the creation of a "bilingual acting company with a built-in research and training programme" that shuttles between a natural-indigenous and "world language." Pragmatic as Nketia and Kennedy's proposals might be, they overlook the daunting logistical problems involved in encouraging linguistic duplications. Need it be said, then, that the problems of language(s) are intractable in new states of the world? In fact, Geertz holds this problem accountable for the proliferation of "formal ideologies" in the new nations of the world.[29]

One other means proposed by some strategists for overcoming the problem of language(s) in Ghanaian-African self-and-world decolonization is the creation of an African personality. W. E. Abraham, for instance, suggests that "the existence of diverse language among regions of the same country could lead to schisms unless an ulterior identity is revealed." But the need to create an ulterior African identity or personality in the process of African decolonization was first recognized by Edward Wilmot Blyden (1832–1912). This antecedence makes the cultural-ideological panacea called the "African Personality" almost as bad as the disease it was meant to cure.

Blyden was "a native of the Danish island of St. Thomas" who "settled in West Africa [Sierra Leone] in 1851" and soon became known as "the highest intellectual representative and greatest defender of the African race" and "the greatest exponent of Pan-African concepts."[30] The primary objective in Blyden's writings, Robin Hallett suggests, "was to re-establish African dignity or rather . . . the dignity of the black race," for both were one and the same to him. To Blyden, the creation or recuperation of an "African Personality" was part and parcel of African/Black emancipation, which is why V. Bakpetu Thompson suggests that "Pan-Africanism and the concept of 'African Personality' are interchangeable." P. Olisanwuche Esedebe traces the origin of the "phrase 'African Personality'" to "a lecture" Blyden "read before the Young Men's Literary Association of Sierra Leone" and "further elaborated . . . in a series of articles written for the Sierra Leone *Weekly News*." Blyden argued that "African religion, African morality and society were natural and proper expressions of

African Personality, and to try to "improve" them would produce only bastardization, corruption, and degradation."[31]

In one revealing moment Esedebe terms Blyden's objective a "cult of African personality," but, generally, he believes that the essays Blyden wrote on the "African Personality":

> represent a passionate analysis of the social, economic and political arrangements evolved by the un-Europeanised African and under which he had lived from generation to generation. . . . This communistic or socialistic order was . . . born of centuries of experience and the outcome of philosophical and faultless logic, its idea among all the ethnic groups was enshrined in proverbs.[32]

According to Hallett, Blyden "defined the particular characteristics of the 'African Personality'" in terms of "the intense spirit of community, [and] the deep sense of religion." He "urged his fellow Africans to preserve the fundamentals of their own society and culture against the insidious influence of European innovations." As V. Y. Mudimbe sees it, the "fundamental theme of Blyden's writings is that Africans, from a historical point of view, constitute a universe apart and have their own history and traditions." Mudimbe believes that Blyden's work is a byproduct of "the romantic philosophies of otherness which flourished during the nineteenth century and which largely supported European nationalism." His "roots are in the sociology of races and more precisely in the controversial principle of differences between races" according to which "African peoples were considered a frozen state in the evolution of humankind."[33]

Mudimbe further underlines the questionable nature of the idea of the African Personality when he writes that "believing in the distinctiveness of races, Blyden equated 'purity' of race with 'purity' of personality or blood. This accounts for his 'racist' position about mulattoes. . . [and h]is thesis requiring the rejection of mulattoes from the 'race.'" Perhaps, this quest for racial separatism and purity explains Blyden's belief that the Africans "sold" in the trans-Atlantic slave trade were members of a service class whose depatriation was beneficial to Africa. But it does not account for the endorsement of Black-on-Africa colonialism implicit in his suggestion that "only blacks could colonize and reform Africa." Mudimbe explains that "by blacks," Blyden "meant 'civilized Americans and West Indians of African descent'" whom he "considered . . . possible saviors" and urged to "[re]colonize and reform Africa." In spite of all this, "Blyden saw the African future in terms of racial cooperation and integration between Black Americans and Africans."[34]

In appropriating the romantic-racialist terms of African person-alism and neo-African culturalism the Ghana National Theatre Movement acquired their problems. The intractable character of these problems is the first, deep, reason why the Ghana NTM project failed. In real terms, the Ghana NTM failed when Kwame Nkrumah's CPP-led First Republic was overthrown in February 1966, and with it went its ideological state apparati, prominent among them the NTM. The debaters on African theatre went on flogging their dead horse in Ghanaian newspapers and magazines well into the 1970s, but the movement was, well, dead.

The NTM failed also because its ideologues refused to consider the disagreeable, if not traumatic, implications of their quest to fragment and de-ethnicize lived and living ethnic representations so as to recombine them into an arbitrary and as-yet-unlived national-personal culture. To hoist it with its own purist-authenticist petards, the NTM recombinative project implied the contamination and mongrelization of ethnic integrities and purities. Thus, it is not surprising that within a year of the overthrow of Nkrumah and the CPP, the "Adidzoo Dance Company [was] formed, to present and preserve traditional dances in their existing forms." Anthony Graham-White writes with particular regard to the national folkloric group of the Ivory Coast that "the first im-pulse of many governments was to impress their European mentors with a display of indigenous culture."[35] The same can be said of other national folkoric groups in sub-Saharan Africa. The para-doxical conclusion one reaches from this is that the resistance of these folkloric movements by traditional-ethnic sectors is the more revolutionary project. That is, in as much as the folkloric endeavors are more obsessed with impressing their "European-mentors" with displays of "authentic African culture" than with honestly repre-senting themselves to and for themselves, ethnic resistances to them are positive.

Any obsession with an other is unhealthy and undesirable, and especially so if it is born out of fear, anxiety, or lack of self-confidence. Such an obsession misdirects the efforts of the self toward compulsive competition with this palpable other. In becom-ing much too much other-regarding the other-obsessed 'I' tends to negate its own self-and-world. It finds and founds its self-worth in the achievements of this other, even where it disparages these achievements ostentatiously. Even more troubling, an other-regarding self might sacrifice itself just to prove worthy to its feared-yet-desired other. In the midst of his romantic Africanist self-affirmations for instance, Blyden wagers that "Africa may yet prove to be the spiritual conservatory of the world," the last resort for the "civilized nations . . . to recover the simple elements of faith."[36] Yet, ultimately, under the guise of purifying its self-and-world of the contaminations of the other, the nationalist-personalist self often does bodily harm to this other. The murder of Jews in twentieth-century German national-personalism (nazism) is the extreme example here, but Blyden's quest to exclude mulattoes or mixed-blood Africans from the African race is just as troubling.

In the desperate attempt to forge national unity at all costs, the NTM overlooked the valuable lessons of the precolonial and colonial history of Ghana, specifically, the rather oppressive effects of precolonial Asante imperialism on other ethnic groups. Asante imperialism compelled some ethnic groups, principally the Fantis and the Akwamus, to cooperate with the British in an effort to overthrow the Asante Empire.[37] Of course, these ethnic groups had their own expansionist intentions, but their cooperation with the British earned them was another form of imperialism, and a non-African one to boot. The fact that it came from outside the rural areas might as well have made the NTM seem to be yet another Trojan horse gift to these ethnic groups.

The great anxiety with which most of the ethnic groups in the Gold Coast (now Ghana) viewed the imminence of independence is manifest in the rise of many secessionist movements in the decade before independence (1947 to 1957). Some of these movements were of course motivated by ethnocentric greed and self-aggrandizement, but a great many other fears were justifiable. In its blasé and avuncular attitude to national unity, the NTM overlooked these problems. On the other hand, caution and care were hardly virtues in the quest to "march" Ghana "from the tribal order into the twentieth century." The problem with a nation coming of age in a time of rapid changes, such as the twentieth century, is that deliberation and slow development appear ineffective beside aggressive or theatricalized politics. Thus, the fat was long in the fire before the NTM even arrived on the scene of secondary decolonization.[38]

Finally, African nationalism, which took the form of a rejection of British imperialism by the national bourgeoisie, was not firm enough grounds on which to base the foundations of a nation. As conceived by Ernest Renan in *Qu'est-ce'qu'une Nation* (1882), the existence of a nation depends on two necessary conditions. First, there must be a "common history" defined as "a memory of common sufferings which seem more important than the conflicts within that history." Secondly, there must be "a will to live together."[39] Colonialism had not been particularly harsh in the Gold Coast because of the British system of indirect rule, and as such, there was no strong "memory of common sufferings" to hold together the ethnicities within postcolonial Ghana. If anything, the oppressiveness of precolonial Asante imperialism made the "conflicts within [precolonial Ghanaian] history" more telling than the "memory of common sufferings" under British colonialism. One possible absurd outcome of this state of affairs was that in the early 1980s some Western-educated members of the Ghanaian elite came to see independence as a mistake and founded a political party whose prime mandate was to bring back the dearly departed British master! Elaborate joke or bitter commentary, this was a sign that something was rotten in the state of Ghana.

Renan also suggests that in the last resort "the existence of a nation is . . . a daily plebiscite." The promulgation of a repressive law such as the Preventive Detention Act (PDA) hardly makes national-political life "a daily plebiscite." Neither does the fact that Kwame Nkrumah's Young Pioneers (reminiscent of the Hitler Youth) encouraged its members to spy and report on others, and even on one another. In the witch-hunt atmosphere of the Ghana First Republic difference spelled sin and treason, and nationhood (as unity-in-difference) was a lost cause. Besides the great majority of Ghanaians lived in the rural, more ethnic areas, and to them the NTM project might as well be the irrelevant intellectual exercise of alienated, educated, and urbanized Ghanaians. At worst, it represented yet another form of imperialism, spearheaded this time by an indigenous elite whose Africanness was questionable at best. For it is not altogether impossible to suppose that the rural Ghanaian masses shared Saka Acquaye's belief that "it is not easy to find a Ghanaian who can express himself well in English who has not lost something of his personality."

Notes

Introduction

1. V. Y. Mudimbe, *The Invention of Africa* (Bloomington and Indianapolis: Indiana University Press, 1988), 196. F. W. G. Hegel, *Hegel on Tragedy,* ed. Anne and Henry Paolucci (New York: Doubleday and Co., 1962), 137.

2. Friedrich Nietzsche, *The Will to Power,* ed. Walter Kaufmann, trans. Kaufmann and R. J. Hollingdale (New York: Vintage Books, 1968), 451. Later cited as Nietzsche (1968a).

3. Jürgen Habermas, *The Theory of Communicative Action,* Vol. 1, trans. Thomas McCarthy (Boston: Beacon Press, 1984) 43–74. Later cited as Habermas. The second quotation from Habermas is cited in Elizabeth and Tom Burns, *The Sociology of Literature and Drama* (London: Penguin Books, 1973) 14–15. Later cited as Burns and Burns.

4. Jack Goody, *The Domestication of the Savage Mind* (Cambridge and New York: Cambridge University Press, 1977), 50.

Chapter 1. Toward a Comprehensive Framework on Ideology

1. John Godfrey Saxe, "The Blindmen and the Elephant," in *The Collected Poems* (Boston: Houghton, Osgood and Co., 1878), 260.

2. Karl Mannheim, *Ideology and Utopia,* trans. Louis Wirth and Edward Shils (San Diego: Harcourt Brace Jovanovich, 1936). 61. Later cited as Mannheim.

3. Mannheim, 88 n. 24, 89.

4. Ibid., 89–90.

5. Habermas, 43–74. Nietzsche (1968a), 174.

6. Mannheim, 87, 89–90. Karl Jaspers, quoted in Janheinz Jahn, *Muntu: An Outline of the New African Culture,* trans. Majorie Grene (New York: Grove Press, 1961), 12. Later cited as Jahn (1961).

7. Friedrich Nietzsche, *On the Genealogy of Morals,* trans. Walter Kaufmann and R. J. Hollingdale (New York: Vintage Books, 1969), 119 (italics in text). Later cited as Nietzsche (1967a).

8. Nietzsche (1967a), 119.

9. Mannheim, 61, 62. Hans Barth, *Truth and Ideology,* trans. Frederick Lilge (Berkeley, and Los Angeles: University of California Pres, 1976), 18–19. Later cited as Barth. See also Stuart Hall, "The Hinterland of Science: Ideology and the 'Sociology of Knowledge,'" in the Centre for Contemporary Cultural Studies, *On Ideology* (London: Hutchinson and Co., 1977), 9–10. Later cited as CCCS. But compare Martin Seliger, *Ideology and Politics* (London: George Allen and Unwin, 1976), 19. Later cited as Seliger.

10. Francis Bacon, *The New Organon and Related Writings,* ed. Fulton H.

Anderson (New York: The Liberal Arts Press, 1960), ix, 16, 71. Later cited as Bacon.

11. Bacon, xvi, 68, xxviii.

12. Ibid., xxvi, 76.

13. Benjamin Farrington, *The Philosophy of Francis Bacon* (Liverpool: Liverpool University Press, 1964) 30, 84–87. Later cited as Farrington.

14. Nicholas Lobkowicz, *Theory and Practice* (Notre Dame, Ind.: University of Notre Dame Press, 1974), 31–32. Later cited as Lobkowicz.

15. Ibid., 17, 26–27.

16. Bacon, xii, xvi.

17. Ibid., xvi–xvii.

18. Ibid., viii. See 48–49.

19. Ibid., ix.

20. Ibid., xxx.

21. Ibid., 22–23, 47–49.

22. Ibid., 49, 56.

23. Ibid., 49, 58, 59.

24. Ibid., 44–45.

25. Ibid., 74–75.

26. Ibid., 23, 26.

27. Ibid., xxviii–xxix.

28. Mannheim, 72.

29. Marx-Engels, 143–45. Ralph Ley, "Francis Bacon, Galileo, and the Brechtian Theater," in *Essays on Brecht,* ed. Siegfried Mews and Herbert Knust (Chapel Hill: University of North Carolina Press, 1974), 174. Later cited as Ley.

30. Marx-Engels, 66, 84 (italics in text).

31. Ibid., 172 (italics in text).

32. Ibid., 172–73. Burns and Burns 14–15.

33. Marx-Engels, 174.

34. Antonio Gramsci, *Prison Notebooks,* trans. and ed. Geoffrey Nowell and Quintin Hoare (New York: International Publishers, 1974), 404. Later cited as Gramsci.

35. Barth, 99, 110–111. Marx-Engels, 174.

36. Gramsci, 323–327, 328.

37. Ibid., 330–31; 331–32.

38. Ibid., 326–27, 327 n.

39. CCCS, 5–6.

40. Geertz, 218 (my italics).

41. Joseph Campbell, *Primitive Mythology* (New York: Penguin Books, 1976), 38, 40. Later cited as Campbell.

42. Geertz, 210–11, 213 n. 30, 218.

43. Paul Ricoeur, *Lectures on Ideology and Utopia,* ed. George H. Taylor (New York: Columbia University Press, 1986), xvi–xvii, 8–10. Later cited as Ricoeur. See Claude Lévi-Strauss, *Introduction to the Works of Marcel Mauss,* trans. Felicity Baker (London: Routledge and Kegan Paul, 1987), 26, for a discussion of symbolic surplus values in social and cultural representations.

44. Ricoeur, xix–xx.

45. Compare the following discussion to the account of Tecumseh to Tenskwatawa in Bryan Wilson, *The Noble Savages: the Primitive Origins of Charisma* (Berkeley: University of Calif Press, 1975), chaps. 1–2.

46. R. S. Rattray, *Ashanti Law and Constitution* (New York: Negro Universities Press, 1969), 73, 283. Later cited as Rattray (1969a).
47. Rattray (1969a), 270, 273, 275 n. 1.
48. Ibid., 280.
49. Ibid., 283.
50. Robert S. Rattray, *Religion and Art in Ashanti* (Oxford: The Clarendon Press, 1927), 130. Later cited as Rattray (1927). Rattray, *Ashanti* (1923; reprint, New York: Negro Universities Press, 1969), 287, 292–93.
51. Rattray (1969a), 276.
52. Seliger, 14, 15–17. Cf. 119–20.
53. Mannheim, 40–41, Part IV.
54. See Dominick LaCapra's critique of Geertz's take on Ideology in chap. 2 of *Soundings in Critical Theory* (Ithaca: Cornell University Press, 1989). See also chap. 5.
55. Friedrich Nietzsche, *The Antichrist,* in *The Portable Nietzsche,* ed. Walter Kaufmann (New York: Viking Press, 1968), 644. Later cited as Nietzsche (1968a).

Chapter 2. The Ancient Feud between Philosophy and Poetry

1. Mihai Spariosu, *Literature, Mimesis and Play* (Tübingen: Gunter Narr Verlag, 1982), 20. Later cited as Spariosu. *Great Dialogues of Plato,* ed. Philip G. Rouse and Eric H. Warmington, trans. W. W. D Rouse (New York: New American Library, 1956), 408. Later cited as Plato. Gerald Else, *Aristotle's Poetics: The Argument.* Cambridge: Harvard University Press, 1957), 640. Later cited as Else (1957).
2. Plato, 192–95, 398, 402–4.
3. Ibid., 415, 418, 419.
4. Ibid., 195, 196.
5. Ibid., 193, 393.
6. Ibid., 398–402.
7. Ibid., 403, 195.
8. Ibid., 398.
9. Ibid., 398 n. 1, 404–6.
10. Ibid., 405–6.
11. Ibid., 405–6.
12. Aristophanes, *The Frogs,* trans. David Barrett (New York: Penguin Books, 1964), 100. Later cited as Aristophanes.
13. Jonas A. Barish, *The Antitheatrical Prejudice* (Berkeley: University of California Press, 1981), 408. Later cited as Barish. Plato, 192–96, 407.
14. Else (1957), 640. Aristophanes, 193–94.
15. Else (1957), 636 (italics in text).
16. Plato, 404–5. Aristotle, *The Art of Poetry,* in *Aristotle,* ed. Philip Wheelwright (New York: The Odyssey Press, 1935), 324–25. Later cited as Aristotle.
17. Jacques Derrida, *Writing and Difference,* trans. Alan Bass (Chicago: The University of Chicago Press, 1978), 234. Aristotle, 293–94.
18. Contrast my position to Joseph Owens's, "Is Philosophy in Aristotle An Ideology," in *Ideology, Philosophy and Politics,* ed. Anthony Parel (Waterloo, Ontario: Wilfrid Laurier University Press, 1983), 163–78. Plato, 408.
19. Aristotle (Wheelwright's Introduction), xxix–xxx.
20. Ibid., xxx–xxxii.

21. Ibid., xxxii–xxxiii.

22. Ibid., 72, 72 n., 100.

23. Ibid., xxxix–xii.

24. Spariosu, 20. Nietzsche (1968a), 451.

25. Ibid., xxxiv–xxxv. Cf. R. Meager, "The Sublime and the Obscene," in *Aesthetics in the Modern World,* ed. Harold Osborne (London: Thames & Hudson, 1968), 152–54.

26. Lobkowicz, 9–14. Aristotle, xxvi.

27. Aristotle, xxvii, xxvii n. 24. Cf. Plato, 100.

28. Aristotle, xl–xli.

29. Else (1957), 331. Plato, 408. Spariosu, 19.

30. Aristotle, 73, 320. Plato, 399.

31. Else (1957), 620, 630. Marcel Detienne, *The Creation of Mythology,* trans. Margaret Cook (Chicago: The University of Chicago Press, 1986), 59. Later cited as Detienne. Nietzsche (1968a), 435.

32. Hegel, 137.

33. Plato, 403. Else (1957), 305.

34. Aristotle, 296–98.

35. Ibid., 298, 302. Else (1957), 242–43, 320 (italics in text).

36. Gilbert Murray, Preface to Ingram Bywater's *Aristotle, On the Art of Poetry* (London: OUP, 1920), 13. Later cited as Murray. James Boon, Preface to English Edition of *Between Belief and Transgression,* ed. Michel Izard and Pierre Smith (Chicago: The University of Chicago Press, 1982), vi.

37. Murray, 13. Aristotle, 308.

38. Aristotle, 306, 303. Else (1957), 375 (italics in text), 330–31.

39. Don Delillo, *Libra* (New York: Viking Penguin, 1988), 46.

40. Friedrich Nietzsche, *The Birth of Tragedy and the Case of Wagner,* trans. Walter Kaufmann (New York: Vintage Press, 1967), 60. Later cited as Nietzsche (1967b). Cf. Richard Schact, "Nietzsche on Art in the *Birth of Tragedy,*" in *Aesthetics: A Critical Anthology,* ed. George Dickie & Richard J. Sclafani (New York: St. Martin's Press, 1977), 273.

41. Michel Haar, "Nietzsche and Metaphysical Language," in *The New Nietzsche,* ed. David B. Allison, (Cambridge: The MIT Press, 1985), 32. Nietzsche (1967b), 59. Cf. H. D. F. Kitto, *The Greeks* (Baltimore: Penguin Books, 1960), 176–77, 196–200.

42. Else (1957) 423, 441.

43. Ibid., 224, 358, 380. Aristotle, 308.

44. See George Steiner, *The Death of Tragedy* (New York: Hill and Wang, 1961); contra Henry Alonzo Myers, *Tragedy: A View of Life* (Ithaca: Cornell University Press, 1965; and Richmond Y. Hathorn, *Tragedy, Myth, and Mystery* (Bloomington and London: Indiana University Press, 1966).

45. *Sophocles: The Three Theban Plays,* trans. Robert Fagles (New York: Penguin Books, 1982), 133–37, 182. Later cited as Sophocles. See Sandor Goodhart, "Ληστὰς ῎Εφασχε: Oedipus and Laius' Many Murderers," *Diacritics* 8, no.1 (Spring 1978): 55–71. LaCapra, 27–28.

46. René Girard, *Violence and the Sacred,* trans. Patrick Gregory (Baltimore and London: The Johns Hopkins University Press, 1977), 292–97. Later cited as Girard.

47. See Peter Stallybrass and Allon White, *The Politics and Poetics of Transgression* (Ithaca: Cornell University Press, 1986).

48. Else (1957), 431–32.

49. Aristotle, 307. P. K. Guha, *Tragic Relief* (London: Oxford University Press, 1942), 1, 42. Else (1957), 411–12, 441, 447–50.

Chapter 3. The Ubiquity of Theatre and Theatricality in Representations of Human Experience

1. André Helbo, J. Dines Johanson, Patrice Pavis, and Anne Ubersfeld, *Approaching Theatre* (Bloomington and Indianapolis: Indiana University Press, 1991), vii. Later cited as Helbo et al.

2. See J. L. Austin, *How To Do Things with Words,* ed. J. O. Urmson and Marina Sbisa (Cambridge: Harvard University Press, 1975).

3. Plato, 404–5.

4. Aristotle, 298–99, 324–25. Marvin Carlson, in Helbo et al., viii.

5. Barish, 400.

6. Plato, 408. See Jean-Jacques Rousseau, *Politics and the Arts, Letter to M. D'Alembert on the Theatre,* trans. Allan Bloom (Ithaca: Corrnell University Press, 1974). Later cited as Rousseau. Nietzsche 1967b. *Nietzsche Contra Wagner,* in Nietzsche 1968b.

7. Nietzsche (1968a), 272. William Shakespeare, *Hamlet,* Signet Classic Edition, ed. Sylvan Barnet (New York: Penguin Books, 1987), II:, 66.

8. Nietzsche (1967b), 3, 13, 19–20.

9. Nietzsche (1967b), 19. See Modris Eksteins, *The Rites of Spring: The Great War and the Birth of the Modern Age* (Boston: Houghton Mifflin Co., 1989), 25. Later cited as Eksteins.

10. Nietzsche (1967b), 43, 52, 109–10 (italics in text).

11. Ibid., 130.

12. Ibid., 135.

13. Nietzsche (1968b), 664–65. See also Nietzsche (1967b), 174–80.

14. Book III of the *Laws* (701a), cited in Barish 405. Nietzsche (1967b), 178–79.

15. Rousseau, 17.

16. Ibid., 20, 65, 150 n. 12.

17. Ibid., 20, 21.

18. Elizabeth Burns, *Theatricality: A Study of Convention in the Theatre and Social Life* (London: Longmann, 1972), chaps. 5–7.

19. See Marvin Carlson, *Theories of the Theatre* (Ithaca and London: Cornell University Press, 1984), 505–15. Bruce Wilshire, *Role Playing and Identity: The Limits of Theatre as Metaphor* (Bloomington: Indiana University Press, 1982), 6–7. Later cited as Wilshire.

20. See Carlson, 505–15. A very suggestive account of the philosophy of appearances or bodily projections obtains in Michel Foucault's "Theatrum Philosophicum," in *Language, Counter-Memory, and Practice,* trans. Donald Bouchard and Sherry Simon (Ithaca and London: Cornell University Press, 1977).

21. Wilshire, 6.

22. Ibid., xiii–xiv.

23. Ibid., xiv, ix.

24. Ibid., 31, 33. Cf. Lobkowicz, 17–32.

25. Wilshire, ix, 20.

26. Johannes Birringer, *Theatre, Theory, Postmodernism* (Bloomington and Indianapolis: Indiana University Press, 1991).

28. See Jane Ellen Harrison, *Ancient Art and Ritual* (London: Williams Norgate Ltd., 1918). Later cited as Harrison.

29. *The Natyasastra. Ascribed to Bharata-Muni.* Vol. 1, trans. and ed. Manohohan Ghosh (Calcutta: Manisha Granthalaya Private Ltd., 1967), 3. Later cited as Bharata-Muni.

30. Bharata-Muni, 3, 119. Cf. Aristotle, 308.

31. Bharata-Muni, 14, 15.

32. Aristotle, 296–99. Bharata-Muni, xxvii.

33. E. E. Evans-Pritchard, *Witchcraft, Oracles and Magic,* abridged with notes by Eva Giles (Oxford and London: Oxford University Press, 1976), 79. Later cited as Evans-Pritchard. Geoffrey Gorer, "Function of Dance Forms in Primitive African Communities," in *The Function of Dance in Human Society,* ed. Franz Boas (New York: The Boas School, 1944), 34. Later cited as Gorer.

34. K. A. B. Jones-Quartey, "The Problems of Languages in the Development of African Theatre," in *Okyeame* 4, no. 1 (December 1968): 96, 97. Later cited as Jones-Quartey.

Chapter 4. Adolphe Appia

1. William L. Shirer, *The Rise and Fall of the Third Reich* (Greenwich, Conn.: Fawcett Publications, 1968), 133–42. See chap. 7 of this book.

2. See Moses Hess, *Rome and Jerusalem,* trans. Meyer Waxman (New York: Bloch Publishing Co., 1918); Orlando Patterson, *Ethnic Chauvinism. The Reactionary Impulse* (New York: Stein and Day, 1977); Eugeen E. Roosens, *Creating Ethnicity: The Process of Ethnogenesis* (London: Sage Publications, 1989); Anthony D. Smith, *The Ethnic Revival* (Cambridge: Cambridge University Press, 1981); and John F. Stack, *The Primordial Challenge. Ethnicity in the Contemporary World* (Westport, Conn.: Greenwood Press, 1986).

3. See Nietzsche (1967a), 36–46, 229–31.

4. Eric Bentley, ed., *The Theory of the Modern Stage* (New York: Penguin Books, 1968), 27–50. Lee Simonson, *The Stage is Set* (New York: Harcourt and Brace Co., 1932), 354, 373. Later cited as Simonson.

5. Richard Beacham, *Adolphe Appia* (Cambridge and New York: Cambridge University Press, 1987), 162. Later cited as Beacham.

6. Simonson, 352, 359. See Adolphe Appia, *Music and the Art of the Theatre,* trans. Richard W. Corrigan and Mary Dirks Douglas (Coral Gables, Fla.: University of Miami Press, 1962), 104–97. Later cited as Appia (1962).

7. H. Darkes Albright, "Adolphe Appia Fifty Years After: I," *The Journal of Speech,* 35 (October 1949): 187. Later cited as Albright. Cf. Beacham, 14–18, 188. Walther R. Volbach, *Adolphe Appia, Prophet of the Modern Theatre,* (Middletown, Conn.: Wesleyan University Press, 1968), 3–13, 31–40, 203–4. Later cited as Volbach. Simonson, 318–41.

8. Cited in Volbach, 15. Appia (1962), 127. Beacham, 14, 16.

9. Beacham, 2, Appia (1962), 4.

10. Beacham 2, 5. Appia (1962), 4. *Staging Wagnerian Drama,* trans. Peter Loeffler (Basel, Stuttgart, and Boston: Birkhäuser Verlag, 1982). Later cited as Appia (1982).

11. Volbach, 31–40.

12. Volbach, 45. Simonson, 351, 354. Cf. Appia (1962), 147–52.

13. Albright, 188. Appia (1962), 9, 28, 103, 116, 133.

14. Appia (1962), 6, 140. For a sampling of Richard Wagner's own views, see *Wagner's Aesthetics,* sel. and ed. Carl Dalhaus (Bayreuth: Editions Musica Bayreuth, 1972) and "What is German," in *Richard Wagner: Stories and Essays,* sel. and ed. Charles Osborne (New York: The Library Press, 1973), 40–55.

15. Appia (1962) 17–20, 101. Cf. "So the Word became Flesh; he made his home among us." John 1:14.

16. Appia (1962) motto page, 13–14, 57, 102, Adolphe Appia, *The Work of Living Art,* trans. H. Darkes Albright (Coral Gables, Fla.: University of Miami Press, 1960), 19. Later cited as Appia (1960).

17. Susanne K. Langer, *Philosophy in a New Key. A Study in the Symbolism of Reason, Rite, and Art* (New York: Penguin Books, Inc., 1948), 169–99. Later cited as Langer. J. A. Reid, "Art, Truth and Reality," in *Aesthetics in the Modern World,* ed. Harold Osborne (London: Thames and Hudson, 1968), 79. Later cited as Osborne.

18. Volbach, 42. Appia (1962), 115, 136.

19. Appia (1982), 39, 56, 57.

20. Michael Hays, *The Public and Performance* (Ann Arbor, Mich.: UMI Research Press, 1981), 116.

21. Appia (1982), 53.

22. Appia (1962) 4–5.

23. Donald C. Mullin, *The Development of the Playhouse* (Berkeley: University of California Press, 1970), 148. Appia (1962), 53; cf. 91–98.

24. Appia (1962), 72–78.

25. Ibid., 75, 66. The circular conception of expression is evidence of Appia's investment in late nineteenth- and early twentieth-century European discourse. Cf. Philip Rawson, "An Exalted Theory of Ornament: a Study in Indian Aesthetics," in Osborne, 228–29.

26. See Volbach, 49–50 and 63–67.

27. Appia (1962), 98–101.

28. Ibid., 104, 147–48, 149–50.

29. Ibid., 150–51 italics in text. Cf. Eksteins, 49, 76–89.

30. Eksteins, 78. Nietzsche (1968a), 346.

31. Volbach, 111–12. Cf. Eksteins, 51.

32. Volbach, 77, 83. Cf. Beacham, 42–47, 56, 78–80, 135–64.

33. Appia (1962), 4. Quoted in Beacham, 48. Eksteins, 37, 50–54.

34. Beacham, 53–54. Cf. Volbach, 85–87.

35. Beacham, 57–62.

36. Beacham, 68–73. See Volbach, 89–93.

37. Beacham, 70–78.

38. Beacham, 78–79; Eksteins, 51.

39. Beacham, 79–81.

40. "Curriculum Vita," in *Adolphe Appia: Essays, Scenarios, Designs,* trans. Walther R. Volbach, edited with notes and commentary by Richard C. Beacham, (Ann Arbor, Mich. and London: UMI Research Press, 1989), 78. Beacham, 61, 79–80. Appia (1960), xvi, 5.

41. Appia (1960), 18, 21.

42. Ibid., 9, 55, 75.

43. Ibid., 12, 23.

44. Ibid., 47, 48, 51, 53.

45. Ibid., 54–55.

46. Ibid., 55–56, 59.

47. Ibid., 60, 61, 62.

48. Ibid., 64–65. Cf. Rousseau, 124–36.

49. Stefan Morawski, *Inquiries into the Fundamentals of Aesthetics* (Cambridge, and London: The MIT Press, 1974), 329. Later cited as Morawski. Cf. Nietzsche (1968a), 318, 451–52.

50. Morawski, 328. Appia (1960), 66–67 (italics in text).

51. Ibid., 69–71.

52. Ibid., 71. Cf. Eksteins, xiv 9–135.

53. Appia (1960), 75, 77.

54. Ibid., 78.

Chapter 5. Antonin Artaud

1. Susan Sontag, ed., *Antonin Artaud: Selected Writings* (New York: Farrar, Straus, and Giroux, 1976), 17, 616. Later cited as Artaud (1976). Copeau's obituary notice is reprinted in Volbach, 206–8. Cf. Beacham, 114ff.

2. Derrida, 234, 243–46. Artaud (1976), xliv, xxxviii. Simonson, 359. Beacham, 164. Antonin Artaud, *The Theater and its Double,* trans. Mary Caroline Richards (New York: Grove Press, Inc., 1958), 154. Later cited as Artaud (1958).

3. Artaud (1976), 160–61.

4. See Gerald F. Else, *The Origins and Early Form of Greek Tragedy* (Cambridge: Harvard University Press, 1965), 4, 10; Edward Said, *Orientalism* (New York: Vintage Books, 1979), 67–105.

5. See Volbach, 93–95. Appia (1960), 64. Cf. Rousseau, 124–36; Plato, 408.

6. Artaud (1976), 145–46.

7. Ibid., 161–62, 357. Cf. the critique of social panaceas in Fyodor Dostoyevsky, *Notes from Underground,* trans. Andrew MacAndrew (New York and Scarborough, Ontario: New American Library, 1960), 105–20.

8. Artaud (1976), 590. Derrida, 180–81, 232.

9. Artaud (1976), 31–49. Ironically, most of the essays in Artaud's magnum opus, *The Theater and its Double,* were first published in *La Nouvelle Revue Française* by Jean Paulhan, Rivière's immediate successor.

10. Ibid., 31.

11. Artaud (1976), 31–32; cf. 44.

12. Ibid., 31, 38, 42. Rivière critiques the "Surrealists" on 40–41. Cf. Sontag, in Artaud (1976), li–liii.

13. Ibid., 43. Cf. 32–33.

14. Ibid., 44.

15. Ibid., 34–36, 42.

16. Ibid., 32, 36, 46.

17. Huw Morris-Jones, "The Language of Feelings," in Osborne, 101.

18. Frantz Fanon, *Black Skin, White Masks,* trans. Charles L. Markmann (New York: Grove Press, Inc. 1967), 218. Later cited as Fanon (1967). G. W. F. Hegel, *The Phenomenology of Mind,* trans. J. B. Baillie (London: George Allen and Unwin Ltd., 1977), 228–40. Sontag discusses the gnostic terms of Artaud's thought in Artaud (1976), xlv–liii.

19. Artaud (1976), 43–44.

20. Artaud (1976), 35, 39.

21. Ibid., 40. For a description of Rivière, see Eksteins, 52, 174.

22. Artaud (1976), 39, 40.

23. Ibid., 99–101.
24. See Ibid., 48.
25. Ibid., 49.
26. Ibid., xxii, 39, 41, 42.
27. Ibid., liii; 59, 85.
28. Ibid., lii, 83, 85, 86.
29. See Derrida, 243–48.
30. Artaud (1976), 86–87, 99, 104–5.
31. Artaud (1976), 93, 110. Cf. "Language to Infinity" and "Threatrum Philo-sophicum," in Foucault, 53–67, 165–96.
32. Artaud (1976), 109–11. T. S. Eliot, *Selected Poems* (San Diego, New York, and London: Harcourt, Brace, and Jovanovich, 1932), 51.
33. Artaud (1958), 13.
34. Artaud (1976), 16, 17, 601.
35. Eksteins, 25. Artaud (1976), 616.
36. Artaud (1976), 149–52, 155.
37. Ibid., 159–60. See *Oeuvres Complètes V* (Paris: Éditions Gallimard, 1967), 45–60. Later cited as Artaud V; and *Oeuvres Complètes IV* (Paris: Éditions Gallimard, 1967), 183–271. Later cited as Artaud IV.
38. Artaud (1976), 160–61, 204. See Artaud V, 45–60.
39. Artaud (1976), 208–9, 616.
40. Artaud (1958), 7, 44.
41. Ibid., 12, 13.
42. Ibid., 12, 13; Derrida, 232.
43. Artaud (1958), 27.
44. Ibid., 31.
45. Ibid., 21, 24, 30.
46. See John 1:4.
47. Ibid., 50–51.
48. Ibid., 51–52.
49. Ibid., 33–36.
50. Artaud (1958), 17, 18, 54.
51. Ibid., 53–54, 54–55, 60.
52. Ibid., 47, 55.
53. Artaud (1958), 56–58.
54. Ibid., 63–66.
55. Artaud (1958), 67. Walter Spies and B. de Zoete, *Dance and Drama in Bali* (1938; reprint, Kuala Lumpur: Oxford University Press, 1973, 156. Later cited as Spies and de Zoete.
56. I Madé Bandem and Frederik E. deBoer, *Kaja and Kelod: Balinese Dance in Transition,* (Kuala Lumpur Oxford, New York, Melbourne: Oxford University Press, 1981), 39, 64; 84. Later cited as Bandem and de Boer. Spies and de Zoete, 140 n. 1. Bandem and de Boer discuss the sources and forms of innovation in Balinese theatre in chaps. 9–10. Cf. Miguel Covarrubias, *Island of Bali* (New York: A. A. Knopf, Inc., 1938).
57. Bandem and de Boer, 44–45, 84n; 89.
58. Artaud (1976), xl.
59. See Jean-Paul Sartre, *Orphée Noir,* preface to *Anthologie de la nouvelle poésie nègre et malgache,* quoted in Fanon (1967), 134 (italics in text). Cf. "The Negro and Hegel," in Fanon (1967), 216–22.

60. Derrida, 250.
61. Artaud (1976), li–liii. 537–51, 652–58.

Chapter 6. Bertolt Brecht

1. *Brecht on Theatre,* ed. John Willett (London: Methuen, 1976), 21, 23, 25, 29, 277. Later cited as Brecht.
2. Ibid., 29, 29n. 30. See Ralph Ley, "Francis Bacon, *Galileo,* and the Brechtian Theater," in *Essays on Brecht,* ed. Siegfried Mews and Herbert Knust (Chapel Hill: The University of North Carolina Press, 1974), 174–83. Later cited as Ley (1).
3. Ley (1), 174, 183. Ralph Ley, *Brecht as Thinker* (Ann Arbor, Mich.: UMI & Applied Literature Press, 1979), 5.
4. Brecht, 23–24, 24n, 248. See John Willett, *The Theatre of Bertolt Brecht* (1959; reprint, London: Methuen, 1967), 193.
5. Marx-Engels, 145. Ley, 183; Farrington, 30.
6. Claude Hill, *Bertolt Brecht* (Boston: Twayne Publishers, 1975), 40. Later cited as Hill. Brecht, 33 n., 17 n.
7. Brecht, 17, n. 18. Cf. David Pike, "Brecht and 'Inoperative Thinking,'" in *Critical Essays on Bertolt Brecht,* ed. Siegfried Mews (Boston: G. K. Hall and Co., 1989), 253–75. Later cited as Mews.
8. Brecht, 15, 17 n. 16 n. 19, 20 n.
9. Ibid., 31.
10. Ibid., 33 n. Eksteins, xvi, 25, 36–37, 76–77.
11. Brecht, 35–37.
12. Ibid., 37. Augusto Boal, *Theatre of the Oppressed,* trans. Charles and M-O Leal-McBride (New York: Theatre Communication Group, 1985), chap. 1.
13. Brecht, 37.
14. Mews and Knust, 116. Brecht, 277.
15. Eric Bentley, *The Brecht Commentaries 1943–1980,* (London, New York, Eyre, Methuen; Grove Press, Inc., 1981), 45, 77. Later cited as Bentley.
16. Hill, 145.
17. Brecht, 183. Cf. Ley (1), 160–63.
18. Brecht, 26.
19. Bentley, 133; Brecht, 121–29, 179–205, 276–82.
20. Ley (1), 179. Brecht, 180. Benjamin is quoted in the Introduction of *Bertolt Brecht: Collected Plays,* vol. 4, pt. 3, ed. John Willett and Ralph Manheim (London: Methuen, 1983), xiii.
21. Brecht, 246, 248, 276.
22. Ley (1), 176. Hill, 196.
23. Ley (1), 176. Hill, 146. Brecht, 248.
24. Brecht, 10–11, 151–52.
25. Ibid, 149–52, 152. Cf. Campbell 38–44; Bentley, 102.
26. Cited in Ley (1), 188.
27. Artaud (1976), 40. See Nietzsche (1968b), 644.
28. Brecht, 8, 71, 72.
29. Brecht, 91–95, 99 n.
30. Ibid., 95–96.
31. Brecht, 96. See Langer, 180–81.
32. Ley (1), 179. Hill, 146–47. Bentley, 255–56.

33. Bentley, 256. Mews, 6. Hill, 146. Brecht, 99 n.
34. Brian O'Doherty is cited in Herbert Blau, "Receding into Illusion: Alienation, the Audience, Technique, Anatomy," in the *New German Critique* 47 (1989): 117. Later cited as Blau. M. H. Abrams, *Natural Supernaturalism: Tradition and Revolution in Romantic Literature* (London: W. W. Norton and Co., 1971), 313. Later cited as Abrams.
35. Ludz, 22, 24. Cf. Abrams, 145, 182–83, 231–34, 313–15.
36. Ludz, 24, 32.
37. Morawski, 327–28. Cf. Marx-Engels, 70–103, 252–93, 133n, 221n, 320–26.
38. Ibid., 228–29. Cf. Ley (1979), 419–62.
39. Mews, 6. Blau, 92–93. Hill, 152.
40. Morawski, 327. Barth, 98–99. Brecht, 20–21. Cf. Marx-Engels, 109–20, 245–46. In blaming the alleged enfeeblement and debauching of German drama on Latin influences Brecht curiously echoes Appia's holding the "oppressive effects of French Genius" in particular and "Latinic" culture in general accountable for the alleged deconstruction of a vital-nostalgic "German culture" (*MAT*, 150). Bad faith has a funny way of repeating itself in unlikely places.

Chapter 7. The Ghana National Theatre Movement

1. See Kwame Nkrumah, *Neo-colonialism: the Last Stage of Imperialism* (New York: International Publishers., 1966). Walter Rodney, *How Europe Underdeveloped Africa* (Washington, D.C.: Howard University Press, 1972). Frantz Fanon, *The Wretched of the Earth,* trans. by Constance Farrington (New York: Grove Press, 1968), 148–248.
2. W. E. Abraham, *The Mind of Africa* (Chicago: The Chicago University Press, 1962), 38. Later cited as Abraham. Cf. Kofi Antubam, *Ghana's Heritage of Culture* (Leipzig: Koehler and Amelang, 1963), 19–24. Later cited as Antubam.
3. Jahnheinz Jahn, *Muntu: An Outline of the New African Culture,* trans. Marjorie Grene (New York: Grove Press, 1961), 12, 16–17. Later cited as Jahn (1961). Cf. Antubam, 24.
4. Jahn (1961), 17. Cf. Mudimbe, 196.
5. The FRELIMO declaration is quoted in "Revolutionary Education," in *The African Liberation Reader,* ed. Aquino de Braganca and Immanuel Wallerstein, (London and Westport, Conn.: Zed Press and Lawrence Hill, 1982), 195–96. Later cited as de Braganica and Wallerstein. Geertz, 226–27. Richard Wright, *Black Power: a Record of Reactions in a Land of Pathos* (Westport, Conn.: Greenwood Press, 1974), 343. Later cited as Wright.
6. Abraham, 97. Frantz Fanon, *Towards the African Revolution,* trans. Haakon Chevalier (New York: Grove Press, Inc., 1967), 186, 187.
7. See Jones-Quartey, 95–102. Cf. K. E. Senanu, "Some Thoughts on Creating the Popular Theare—I and II," in *The Legion Observer* (September 29–October 12): 25–26 and (October 13–26): 22–23.
8. Cited in Jones-Quartey, 96, 97.
9. A. M. Opoku, "Thoughts From the School of Music and Drama," *Okyeame* 2, No. 1 (1964): 51–54. Later cited as Opoku.
10. Evans-Pritchard, 79. Gorer, 34.
11. J. C. De Graft, "Drama Workshop. 1963, *Okyeame* 2, no. 1 (1964): 48, 49–50. Later cited as de Graft. Cf. J. C. de Graft, "Roots in African Drama and Theatre" in *African Literature Today No. 8: Drama in Africa,* ed. E. Durosimi Jones (London: Heinemann, 1976), 1–25.

12. De Graft, 49.
13. Ibid., 49. See Kwabena N. Bame, "Contemporary Comic Plays in Ghana" (Master's thesis, University of Western Ontario, 1969).
14. *Okyeame* 5 (November 1972): 117. *Okyeame* 3, (December 1966): 63.
15. J. H. Nketia, "The Artist in Contemporary Africa: The Challenge of Tradition," *Okyeame* 2 No. 1 (1964): 57–62. "Kofi Antubam: The Symbolic Artist," *Okyeame* 2, no. 1 (1964): 69–73. Saka Acquaye, "The Problem of Language in the Development of the African Theatre," *Okyeame* 4, no. 2 (June 1969): 71. Later cited as Acquaye. Cf. Abraham, 44–115. Gerald F. Else, *The Origins and Early Form of Greek Tragedy* (Cambridge: Harvard University Press, 1965), 4, 10. See Jane Ellen Harrison, *Ancient Art and Ritual* (London: Williams and Norgate Ltd., 1918), v, 9–28. Janheinz Jahn, *Leo Frobenius: Demonic Child,* trans. Reinhard Sander (Austin, Tex.: AASRC Occasional Publications, 1974), 6–17. Later cited as Jahn (1974).
16. Jahn (1974), 13. Jahn (1961), 85. Cf. Acquaye, 70–76.
17. Felix Morriseau-Leroy, "African National Theatre: For Whom?" *Okyeame* Vol. 4 No. 1 (December 1968): 91. Later cited as Morriseau-Leroy. Incidentally, the national *Fest, Fête,* or "Festival" was the ideal form of theatre for Rousseau, Wagner, and Appia.
18. Morriseau-Leroy, 92–93. The "proscenium or a backdrop" bit seems to be a polemic barb aimed at the likes of J. C. de Graft.
19. Ibid., 94.
20. Acquaye, 70.
22. Jones-Quartey, 97.
23. Jones-Quartey, 98.
24. Jones-Quartey, 98–99.
25. Ibid., 100.
26. Fanon (1967a), 38.
27. Huw Morris-Jones, "The Language of Feelings," in Osborne, 101, 102.
28. See Jahn (1961), 85, Opoku 70.
29. Nketia is cited in Scott Kennedy, "Language and Communication Problems in the Ghanaian Theatre," *Okyeame* 4 (1968): 105. Cf. R. F. Amonoo, "Problems of Ghanaian Lingue Franche," in *Language in Africa,* ed. John Spencer (Cambridge and New York: Cambridge University Press, 1963) and Vladimir Klima et al., *Black Africa: Language and Literature* (Prague: Academia Publishing House, 1976), 30–37. See Geertz, chaps. 9–10.
30. Abraham, 153. P. Olisanwuche Esedebe, *Pan-Africanism: The Idea and Movement 1776–1963* (Washington, D.C.: Howard University Press, 1982), 29–30. Later cited as Esedebe.
31. Mudimbe, 98. Robin Hallett, *Africa since 1875* (Ann Arbor: The University of Michigan Press, 1974) 399. Later refs. to Hallett. Esedebe 3, 36, 58, 61. See also Robert W. July, *The Origins of Modern African Thought* (London: Faber and Faber, 1968), 104, 450, 480.
32. Esedebe, 61. Cf. Antubam, 18–19.
33. Hallett, 349. Mudimbe, 107, 132.
34. Mudimbe, 105–6, 119.
35. Anthony Graham-White, *The Drama of Black Africa* (New York and London,: Samuel French Inc., 1972), 90, 171.
36. Cited in Hallett, 349.
37. See W. E. F. Ward, *A History of Ghana* (London: George Unwin and

Allen Ltd, 1958), 114–61. David Apter, *Ghana in Transition* (Princeton: Princeton University Press, 1972), 3–20. Later cited as Apter.

38. See Apter, 156–361; Dennis Austin, *Politics in Ghana* (London: Oxford University Press, 1964), 49–102, 250–315.

39. Ernest Renan is cited in Eugene Kamenka, *Nationalism: The Nature and Evolution of an Idea* (New York: St. Martin's Press, 1976), 12.

Bibliography

Abraham, W. E. *The Mind of Africa*. Chicago: The Chicago University Press, 1962.

Abrams, M. H. *Natural Supernaturalism: Tradition and Revolution in Romantic Literature*. London: W. W. Norton & Co., 1971.

Acquaye, Saka. "The Problem of Language in the Development of the African Theatre." *Okyeame* 4 (June 1969): 70–76.

Albright, H. Darkes. "Adolphe Appia Fifty Years After: I." *The Journal of Speech* 35 (October 1949): 180–89.

Allison, David B., ed. *The New Nietzsche*. Cambridge: The MIT Press, 1985.

Amonoo, R. F.. "Problems of Ghanaian Lingue Franche." In *Language in Africa*, edited by John Spencer. Cambridge and New York: Cambridge University Press, 1963.

Anderson, Fulton H.. *The Philosophy of Francis Bacon*. Chicago: The University of Chicago Press, 1948.

Antubam, Kofi. *Ghana's Heritage of Culture*. Leipzig: Koehler and Amelang, 1963.

Appia, Adolphe. *Adolphe Appia: Essays, Scenarios, and Designs*. Translated by Walther R. Volbach. Edited and with notes and commentary by Richard C. Beacham. Ann Arbor, Mich. and London: UMI Research Press, 1989.

———. *Music and the Art of the Theatre*. Translated by Robert W. Corrigan and Mary D. Dirks. Coral Gables: University of Miami Press, 1962.

———. *Staging Wagnerian Drama*. Translated by Peter Loeffler. Basel: Birkhäuser Verlag, 1982.

———. *The Work of Living Art*. Translated by H. D. Albright. Coral Gables, Fla.: University of Miami Press, 1960.

Aristotle. *Aristotle, On the Art of Poetry*. Translated by Ingram Bywater. Oxford and London: Oxford University Press, 1920.

———. *Aristotle Poetics*. Translated by Gerald F. Else. Ann Arbor: University of Michigan Press, 1967.

———. "The Art of Poetry." In *Aristotle*, translated by Philip Wheelwright. New York: The Odyssey Press, 1935.

Artaud, Antonin. *Antonin Artaud: Selected Writings*. Edited by Susan Sontag. New York: Farrar, Straus, and Giroux, 1976.

———. *Oeuvres Complètes* Vols. 4–5. Paris: Éditions Gallimard, 1964.

———. *The Theater and its Double*. Translated by Mary Caroline Richards. New York: Grove Press, Inc., 1958.

Austin, Dennis. *Politics in Ghana*. London: Oxford University Press, 1964.

Austin, J. L. *How To Do Things with Words*. Edited by J. O. Urmson and Marina Sbisa. Cambridge: Harvard University Press, 1975.

Bacon, Francis. *The New Organon and Related Writings.* Edited by Fulton H. Anderson. New York: The Liberal Arts Press, 1960.

Bame, Kwabena N. "Drama and Theatre in Traditional African Societies." *The Conch* 6 (1964): 80–98.

———. *"Contemporary Comic Plays in Ghana."* Master's thesis, University of Western Ontario, 1969.

Bandem, I-Made, and F. E. deBoer. *Kaja and Kelod: Balinese Dance in Transition.* Oxford: Oxford University Press, 1981.

Barish, Jonas A. *The Antitheatrical Prejudice.* Berkeley: University of California Press, 1981.

Barth, Hans. *Truth and Ideology.* Translated by Frederick Lilge. Berkeley, Los Angeles, and London: University of California Press, 1976.

Barthes, Roland. *Mythologies.* Translated by Annette Lavers. New York: Hill and Wang, 1972.

Beacham, Richard. *Adolphe Appia.* Cambridge and New York: Cambridge University Press, 1987.

Bentley, Eric. *The Brecht Commentaries 1943–1980.* New York: Grove Press, Inc., 1981.

Bharata-Muni. *The Natyasastra. Ascribed to Bharata-Muni.* Vol. 1 translated and edited Manohohan Ghosh. Calcutta: Manisha Granthalaya Private Ltd., 1967.

Blau, Herbert. "Receding into Illusion: Alienation, the Audience, Technique, Anatomy." *New German Critique* 47 (1989): 93–117.

Boal, Augusto. *Theatre of the Oppressed.* Translated by Charles McBride and Marie Odilia-McBride. New York: Theatre Communications Group, 1985.

Brecht, Bertolt. *Brecht on Theatre.* Edited by John Willett. London: Methuen, 1976.

———. *Mother Courage and Her Children: A Chronicle of the Thirty Years' War.* Translated by Eric Bentley. New York: Grove Press, 1966.

———. *Two Plays by Bertolt Brecht.* Translated and revised by Eric Bentley. New York and Scarborough, Ontario: New American Library, 1983.

Burns, Elizabeth, *Theatricality: A Study of Convention in Theatre and Social Life.* London: Longmans, 1973.

Burns, Elizabeth, and Tom Burns. *The Sociology of Literature and Drama.* London: Penguin Books, 1973.

Campbell, Joseph. *Primitive Mythology: The Masks of God.* New York: Penguin Books, 1959.

Carlson, Marvin. *Theories of the Theatre.* Ithaca and London: Cornell University Press, 1984.

Centre for Contemporary Cultural Studies. *On Ideology.* London: Hutchison and Co., 1977.

Covarrubias, Miguel. *Island of Bali.* New York: A. A. Knopf, Inc., 1938.

Cunard, Nancy. *Negro.* New York: Negro Universities Press, 1969.

De Braganica, Aquino and Immanuel Wallerstein eds. *The African Liberation Reader.* London and Westport, Conn.: Zed Press and Lawrence Hill, 1982.

De Graft, Joe C. "Drama Workshop, 1963." *Okyeame* 1 (1969): 48–50.

———. "Roots in African Drama and Theatre." *African Literature Today 8: Drama in Africa.* Edited by Eldred D. Jones. London: Heinemann, 1974.

Delillo, Don. *Libra*. New York: Viking Penguin Press, 1988.

Derrida, Jacques. *Writing and Difference*. Translated by Alan Bass. Chicago: The University of Chicago Press, 1978.

Detienne, Marcel. *The Creation of Mythology*. Translated by Margaret Cook. Chicago: The University of Chicago Press, 1986.

Dickie, George, and Richard J. Sclafani, eds. *Aesthetics: A Critical Anthology*. New York: St. Martin's Press, 1977.

Dostoyevsky, Fyodor. *Notes From Underground*. Translated by Andrew Mac-Andrew. New York and Scarborough, Ontario: New American Library, 1960.

Douglas, Mary. *Purity and Danger: An Analysis of the Concepts of Pollution and Taboo*. London and New York: Ark Paperbacks, 1984.

Eksteins, Modris. *The Rites of Spring: The Great War and the Birth of the Modern Age*. Boston: Houghton Mifflin Co., 1989.

Eliot, T. S. *Selected Poems*. San Diego: Harcourt Brace Jovanovich, 1932.

Else, Gerald F. *Aristotle's Poetics: The Argument*. Cambridge: Harvard University Press, 1957.

———. *The Origins and Early Form of Greek Tragedy*. Cambridge: Harvard University Press, 1965.

Esedebe, P. Olisanwuche. *Pan-Africanism: The Idea and Movement 1776–1963*. Washington, D.C.: Howard University Press, 1982.

Evans-Pritchard, E. E. *Witchcraft, Oracles and Magic*. Abridged and annotated by Eva Giles. Oxford and London: Oxford University Press, 1976.

Fagles, Robert. *Sophocles: The Three Theban Plays*. New York: Penguin Books, 1982.

Fanon, Frantz. *Black Skin, White Masks*. Translated by Charles L. Markmann. New York: Grove Press, Inc., 1967.

———. *Towards the African Revolution*. Translated by Haakon Chevalier. New York: Grove Press, Inc., 1967.

———. *The Wretched of the Earth*. Translated by Constance Farrington. New York: Grove Press, Inc., 1968.

Farrington, Benjamin. *The Philosophy of Francis Bacon*. Liverpool: Liverpool University Press, 1964.

Frankfort, Henri, et al. *Before Philosophy*. Aylesbury and London: Penguin Books, 1949.

Foucault, Michel. *Language, Counter-Memory, and Practice*. Translated by Donald Bouchard and Sherry Simon. Ithaca and London: Cornell University Press, 1977.

Geertz, Clifford. *The Interpretation of Cultures*. New York: Basic Books, Inc., 1973.

Gellrich, Michele. *Tragedy and Theory: The Problem of Conflict Since Aristotle*. Princeton: Princeton University Press, 1988.

Geyer, R. Felix, and David Schweitzer. *Theories of Alienation*. Leiden: Martinus Nijhoff, 1976.

———. *Alienation: Problems of Meaning, Theory and Method*. London: Routledge and Kegan Paul, 1981.

Girard, René. *Violence and the Sacred*. Translated by Patrick Gregory. Baltimore and London: The Johns Hopkins University Press, 1977.

Goodhart, Sandor. "Ληστὰς ᵛΕφασχε: Oedipus' and Laius' Many Murderers." *Diacritics* 8, no. 1 (Spring 1978): 55–71.

Goody, Jack. *The Domestication of the Savage Mind.* Cambridge and New York: Cambridge University Press, 1977.

Gorer, Geoffrey. "Functions of Dance Forms in Primitive African Communities." In *The Function of Dance in Human Society,* edited by Franz Boas. New York: The Boas School, 1944.

Graham-White, Anthony, *The Drama of Black Africa.* New York: Samuel French Inc., 1972.

Gramsci, Antonio. *Prison Notebooks.* Translated by Geoffrey N. Smith and Quintin Hoare. New York: International Publishers, 1976.

Guha, P. K. *Tragic Relief.* London: Oxford University Press, 1942.

Guthrie, W. K. C. *The Greek Philosophers.* New York: Harper and Row, 1975.

Habermas, Jürgen. *Knowledge and Human Interests.* Translated by Jeremy Shapiro. Boston: Beacon Press, 1971.

———. *The Theory of Communicative Action 1.* Translated by Thomas McCarthy. Boston: Beacon Press, 1984.

Hallett, Robin. *Africa since 1875.* Ann Arbor: The University of Michigan Press, 1974.

Harrison, Jane Ellen. *Ancient Art and Ritual.* London: Williams Norgate Ltd., 1918.

Hathorn, Richmond Y. *Tragedy, Myth and Mystery.* Bloomington and London: Indiana University Press, 1966.

Hays, Michael. *The Public and Performance.* Ann Arbor, Mich.: UMI Research Press, 1981.

Hegel, Friedrich W. G. *Hegel on Tragedy.* Edited by Anne Paolucci and Henry Paolucci. New York: Doubleday and Co., Inc., 1962.

———. *Texts and Commentary.* Translated by Walter Kaufmann. Notre Dame, Ind.: University of Notre Dame Press, 1977.

Helbo, André, et al. *Approaching Theatre.* Bloomington and Indianapolis: Indiana University Press, 1991.

Hill, Claude. *Bertolt Brecht.* Boston: Twayne Publishers, 1975.

Hodgkin, Thomas. *Nationalism in Colonial Africa.* London: Frederick Muller, 1956.

Izard, Michel, and Pierre Smith, eds. *Between Belief and Transgression.* Translated by John Leavitt. Chicago and London: The University of Chicago Press, 1982.

Jackson-Lears, T. J. "The Concept of Cultural Hegemony." *American Historical Review* 90 (1985): 567–93.

Jahn, Janheinz. *Leo Frobenius: Demonic Child.* Translated by Richard Sander. Austin, Tex.: AASRC Occasional Publications, 1974.

———. *Muntu: An Outline of the New African Culture.* Translated by Marjorie Grene. New York: Grove Press, 1961.

———. *Through African Doors: Experiences and Encounters in West Africa.* Translated by Oliver Coburn. London: Faber and Faber Ltd., 1962.

Jones, John. *On Aristotle and Greek Tragedy.* Stanford, Calif.: Stanford University Press, 1982.

Jones-Quarty, K. A. B. "The Problems of Languages in the Development of the African Theatre." *Okyeame* 4 (December 1968): 95–102.

July, Robert. *The Origins of Modern African Thought.* London: Faber and Faber, 1968.

Kamenka, Eugene. *Nationalism: The Nature and Evolution of an Idea.* New York: St. Martin's Press, 1976.

Kennedy, Scott. "Language and Communication in the Ghanaian Theatre." *Okyeame* 4 (December 1968): 103–9.

Kitto, H. D. F. *The Greeks.* Baltimore: Penguin Books, 1960.

Klima, Vladimir, et al. *Black Africa: Literature and Language.* Prague: Academia Publishing House, 1976.

LaCapra, Dominick. *Soundings in Critical Theory.* Ithaca: Cornell University Press, 1989.

Lacoue-Labarthe, Phillippe. "Mimesis and Truth." *Diacritics* (March 1978): 10–23.

Langer, Susanne K. *Philosophy in a New Key: A Study in the Symbolism of Reason, Rite, and Art.* New York: Penguin Books, Inc., 1948.

Lévi, Sylvain. *The Theatre of India.* Vol. 1. Translated by Narayan Mukherji. Calcutta: Lake Garden's Press, 1978.

Lévi-Strauss, Claude. *Introduction to the Works of Marcel Mauss.* Translated by Felicity Baker. London: Routledge and Kegan Paul, 1987.

Ley, Ralph. *Brecht as Thinker: Studies in Literary Marxism and Existentialism.* Ann Arbor, Mich.: UMI/Applied Literature Press, 1979.

Lobkowicz, Nicholas. *Theory and Practice.* Notre Dame, Ind.: University of Notre Dame Press, 1974.

Mannheim, Karl. *Ideology and Utopia.* Translated by Louis Wirth and Edward Shils. San Diego: Harcourt Brace Jovanovich, 1936.

———. *Diagnosis of Our Time.* New York: Oxford University Press, 1944.

Mews, Siegfried, and Herbert Knust, eds. *Essays on Brecht.* Chapel Hill: The University of North Carolina Press, 1974.

Mews, Siegfried, ed. *Critical Essays On Bertolt Brecht.* Boston: G. K. Hall and Co., 1989.

Morawski, Stefan. *Inquiries into the Fundamentals of Aesthetics.* Cambridge and London: The MIT Press, 1974.

Morley, Michael. *Brecht: A Study.* London: Heinemann, 1977.

Morriseau-Leroy, Félix. "African National Theatre: For Whom?" *Okyeame* (December 1968): 91–94.

Mudimbe, V. Y. *The Invention of Africa.* Bloomington and Indianapolis: Indiana University Press, 1988.

Mullin, Donald C. *The Development of the Playhouse.* Berkeley and Los Angeles: University of California Press, 1970.

Myers, Alonzo. *Tragedy: A View of Life.* Ithaca and New York: Cornell University Press, 1965.

Nietzsche, Friedrich. *The Birth of Tragedy and the Case of Wagner.* Translated by Walter Kaufmann. New York: Vintage Books, 1967b.

———. *Beyond Good and Evil.* Translated by Walter Kaufmann. New York: Vintage Books, 1966.

———. *On the Genealogy of Morals and Ecce Homo.* Translated by Walter Kaufmann and H. J. Hollingdale. New York: Vintage Books, 1967a.

———. *The Portable Nietzsche.* Edited, translated, and annotated by Walter Kaufmann. New York: The Viking Press, 1968b.

———. *The Will to Power.* Edited by Walter Kaufmann and translated by Walter Kaufmann and R. J. Hollingdale. New York: Vintage Books, 1968a.

Nketia, J. H. "The Artist in Contemporary Africa: The Challenge of Tradition." *Okyeame* 2 (1964): 57–62.

———. "Kofi Antubam: The Symbolic Artist." *Okyeame* 2 (1964): 69–73.

Nkrumah, Kwame. *Africa Must Unite.* New York: International Publishers, 1963.

———. *Consciencism.* London: Heinemann, 1964.

———. *Neo-colonialism: The Last Stage of Imperialism.* New York: International Publishers, 1966.

———. *Revolutionary Path.* New York: International Publishers, 1973.

Ong, Walter R. *Orality and Literacy.* London and New York: Methuen, 1982.

Opoku, Asare M. "Thoughts From the School of Music and Drama." *Okyeame* 2 (1964): 51–54.

Osborne, Harold, ed. *Aesthetics in the Modern World.* London: Thames and Hudson, 1968.

Parel, Anthony, ed. *Ideology, Philosophy and Politics.* Waterloo, Ontario: Wilfrid Laurier University Press, 1983.

Pavis, Patrice. *Languages of the Stage.* New York: PAJ Publications, 1982.

Plato. *Great Dialogues of Plato.* Edited by Philip G. Rouse and Eric H. Warmington and translated by W. H. D Rouse. New York: New American Library, 1956.

Pole, David. *Aesthetics, Form and Emotion.* Edited by George Roberts. New York: St. Martin's Press, 1983.

Rattray, R. S. *Ashanti.* New York: Negro Universities Press, 1969.

———. *Ashanti Law and Constitution.* New York: International Publishers, 1969.

———. *Religion and Art in Ashanti.* Oxford: Clarendon Press, 1927.

Reiss, Timothy, J. *Tragedy and Truth.* New Haven: Yale University Press, 1980.

Ricoeur, Paul. *Lectures on Ideology and Utopia.* Edited by George H. Taylor. New York: Columbia University Press, 1986.

Rodney, Walter. *How Europe Underdeveloped Africa.* Washington, D.C.: Howard University Press, 1972.

Rousseau, Jean-Jacques. *Politics and the Arts: Letter to M. D' Alembert on the Theatre.* Translated by Allan Bloom. Ithaca: Cornell University Press, 1974.

Sahlins, Marshall. *Culture and Practical Reason.* Chicago: The University of Chicago Press, 1976.

Said, Edward W. *Orientalism.* New York: Vintage Books, 1979.

Saxe, John Godfrey. *The Collected Poems.* Boston: Houghton and Mifflin, 1896.

Schultz, Alfred. *Collected Papers 1.* Edited by Maurice Natanson. The Hague: Martinus Nijhoff, 1962.

Seliger, Martin. *Ideology and Politics.* London: George Allen and Unwin Ltd., 1976.

Senanu, Kojo. "Thoughts on Creating the Popular Theatre." The Legon Observer (September 29–October 12, 1967): 25–26 and (October 13–26, 1967): 22–23.

Shirer, William L.. *The Rise and Fall of the Third Reich*. Greenwich, Conn.: Fawcett Publications, 1968.

Simonson, Lee. *The Stage is Set*. New York: Harcourt and Brace Co., 1932.

Sontag, Susan, ed. *Antonin Artaud: Selected Writings*. New York: Farrar, Straus, and Giroux, 1976.

Soyinka, Wole. *Myth, Literature and the African World*. London: Cambridge University Press, 1976.

Spariosu, Mihai. *Literature, Mimesis and Play*. Tübingen: Gunter Narr Verlag, 1982.

Spies, Walter, and Beryl de Zoete. *Dance and Drama in Bali*. Kuala Lumpur and London: Oxford University Press, 1973.

Stallybrass, Peter, and Allon White. *The Politics and Poetics of Transgression*. Ithaca: Cornell University Press, 1986.

Steiner, George. *The Death of Tragedy*. New York: Hill and Wang, 1961.

Tucker, Robert C., ed. *The Marx-Engels Reader*. New York and London: W. W. Norton and Co., 1978.

Volbach, Walther R. *Adolphe Appia, Prophet of the Modern Theatre*. Middletown, Conn.: Wesleyan University Press, 1968.

Wagner, Richard. *Wagner's Aesthetics*. Selected and edited by Carl Darlhaus. Bayreuth: Edition Musica Bayreuth, 1972.

—————. *Richard Wagner: Stories and Essays*. Selected and edited by Charles Osborne. New York: The New Library Press, 1973.

Ward, W. E. F. *A History of Ghana*. London: George Unwin and Allen Ltd., 1958.

Wheelwright, Philip. *Aristotle*. New York: The Odyssey Press, 1935.

Will, Hubert, ed. *Brecht As They Knew Him*. Translated by John Peet. New York: International Publishers, 1974.

Willett, John. *The Theatre of Bertolt Brecht*. London: Methuen, 1967.

Willett, John, and Ralph Manheim. *Bertolt Brecht: Collected Plays 4 Part 3*. London: Methuen, 1983.

Wilshire, Bruce. *Role Playing and Identity: The Limits of Theatre as Metaphor*. Bloomington: Indiana University Press, 1982.

Wilson, Bryan, R. *The Noble Savages: The Primitive Origins of Charisma*. Berkeley: University of California Press, 1975.

Wright, Richard. *Black Power: A Record of Reactions in a Land of Pathos*. Westport, Conn.: Greenwood Press, 1974.

Index

217

Beacham, Richard, 10, 133
Being: and becoming, 70; intellectual, 137; knowing as, 138; and non-being, 72; poison of, 138; Real, 69; social, 163–64; thought and, 163–64; and truth, 69
Being and becoming, 70
Benjamin Walter, 166
Bentley, Eric, 94, 166, 172
Bharata Muni, 100–101
Birringer, Johannes, 16
Blau, Herbert, 175
Blyden, Edward Wilmot, 191–93, 194
Boal, Augusto, 163
Body: body-to-body, transfer of forces, 157; Communal, 127–30; creator of values, as, 128–29; culture and pedagogy (*Leibeskultur*), 122, 127, 129; ideal, 190; metaphors, 16–19; music-theatre and the, 112, 116–17, 122, 124–27, 157; stolen, 136; theatre and the, 157; transcending the, 143; will and affects, proximity to, 190
Bonifas, H. C., 124
Book of Mormon, 60
Brecht, Bertolt: acting, essays on unprofessional, 168–69; actor, in the epic theatre of, 165; alienation and disalienation, 23; alienation effects, 23, 162, 165, 166–67; Aristotelian theatre, opposition of, 163, 164; art and mimesis, view of, 16, 159; Bacon, relationship to, 160–61, 175; Chinese acting, valorization of, 171; comedy, apotheosis of, 164; dialectical theatre, 166–68; epic theatre, 159, 161–66, 167; Latin culture, demonization of, 206 n.40; *Lehrstücke*, 162; Marx, relationship to, 160, 172–76; naive view of theatre, 166, 168–70; *Neue Sachlichkeit* Movement, relationship to, 161, 170; Orientalism, 171–72; science and the theatre, 159–60; Shakespeare's plays, assessment of present effectiveness of, 175; social change, service of, 160; Socialist Realism, 168, 170; *V-effekt*, 165, 167, 170–75
Breton, André, 140
Burns, Elizabeth, 92

Caliban, 156
Campbell, Joseph, 49
Capitalistic ethos, 161
Carlson, Marvin, 84
Carnivalesque, 18
Carnivals of truth, 17–19
Catharsis (*katharsis*), 75, 77, 79, 92
Cathedral of the future, 130–31
Centre for Contemporary Cultural Studies, 47–48
Chamberlain, Houston S., 120
Chance, 141, 142
Chance mechanisms as cultural limits, 141
Change: dance movement and material, 182; aesthetic, 174; revolutionary social, 160–63, 166, 169, 170; theory of being and, 69. *See also* Revolution
Charisma, 51
Christian Bible and ideology, 60, 179
Circularity, 33
City of God, 22, 23, 60. *See also* Utopia(s)
Class: defenders, of, 44; revolution, 45; rule, 45; single, 44–45; social, 43–46; suicide, 44; war, 44–46; working, 44–46
Claudel, Paul, 123
Colonial Exposition of Paris (1931), 148, 155
Colonial mentality, 178; neo-, 177; post-, 178, 180; pre-, 178
Colonialism: black-on-black, 192; British Indirect Rule, 195; neo-, 178
Colonized/colonizer, 178
Color (of human interests), 12–13. *See also* Light
Comedy, 164
Communal: past, African, 189; Body, 129–30; work, 128
Communalism, 89, 128
Communism, 21, 23, 43, 56, 58
Convention People's Party (CPP), 184, 193
Copeau, Jacques, 132, 146
Craig, C. Gordon, 110–11, 132
Critique, 10, 13–14, 18, 20, 29; ideology and, 29–30; naivety, opposed to, 169–70

ernist, 98–99; pure, 147, 149; radical, 147; ritual and, 99; Sanskrit, 100–101; scientification of, 159; staging, 15, 67; and theory, 15–16; as total art, 114, 126–27, 130–31, 135, 143, 146, 162; totalizing, 149, 162; and truth, 84, 86
Theatre director, absolute preponderance of, 133, 147, 152
Theatrical, 86, 88–90, 103, 165, 169
Theatricality, 18, 86–93, 138, 149
Theatrocracy, 67, 90
Theatron (place of seeing), 15–16, 95. *See also* perception; Seeing
Theoria, 15, 95
Theory: of being and change, 69; flesh, theory of the, 145–46; idols of, 34–35, 39–40, 41; of lights, 118–19; meta-, 16; practice, relationship between, 37; theatre and, 15, 16, 95
Theory of idols (Bacon's), 34–35, 39–40, 41
Thinking: as origin of human endeavor, 70, 135; class, 44; private language as non-thinking, 139
Thompson, V. Bakpetu, 191
Thought: destruction of, 141; outside of, 140; normal, so-called, 141; profound uncertainty of, 137; rejection of, 143; social being and, 163–64. *See also* Thinking
Total work of art, 88, 101, 124–25, 133–34, 135, 136; as holy grail, 146; hybrid or mosaic form of the, 162; poetry as, 135; theatre as, 114, 126–27, 130–31, 135, 143, 146, 162. See also *Gesamtjunstwerk*
Tradition: African, 179; ancient Greek acting (histrionic), 67, 68; of Hellas, 67; morality and, 59; Western enlightenment, 160
Tragedy: Aristotle's definition of, 74–79, 84–86; Brecht against, 164; comedy and, 164; Nietzsche's reading of, 88–89; scapegoat violence and, 80–82; Socrates/Plato's view of, 66–67; as unauthorized transgression, 82
Tragic: Aristotle's conception of the, 73–74, 82; pleasure, 83; representa-

tion, 80–83; stage, the fourth century B.C., 67–68; violence *(pathos)*, 79–82
Tragic pleasure, 83
Truth: accessible and communicable nature of, 141; Gnostic or bodily view of, 16–23; canonical, 19–20; carnivals of, 17–19; crossroads of, 22; dead or dying body, 18–19; death of, 18; ideology (false consciousness) and, 30; mimetic, 65; mythopoetic, 17–19; naïve, 108; parochial, 30; perspectivist, 22; postalphabetical, 21; pre-literate (oral), 20–21; primary orality and, 20–22; Real Being and, 69; socratic/platonic, 69; textual, 19–20; textual criticism and, 20; universal (timeless), 22; unitarist, 21–23, 63, 65, 69
Tucker, Robert, 43
Tutu, Osai, 51
Tzara, Tristan, 140

Ulterior identity, 177, 191. *See also* African Personality; Personality
Understanding: Bacon's view of human, 38–41; mythical, 12, 32; Occidental, 12, 32
Unitarism, 64–66. *See also* Universalism; Will to single morality
Universalism, 12, 32–33, 45. *See also* Unitarism; Will to single morality
Utopia(s), 21–22, 60, 64, 128. *See also* City of God; Marx's communist state; Well-ordered city
Utopian: forms, 56; tendency in ideology, 56–57

V-effekt (Verfremdungseffekt), 23, 164, 165, 167, 171–75. *See also* Alienation Effects
Verandah Boys, 184
Verbal drama, 187
Verfremdung, 167. See also *Entfremdung; V-effekt*
Victimism/Victimization, 81–82, 146, 149
Violence: histrionic-theatrical, 152; ontological, 105; scapegoat, 80–82; tragic *(pathos)*, 79–82
Volbach, Walther R., 111, 121
Voodoo Death, 18, 139